Ann Ferguson

The Victorian Multiplot Novel

THE
VICTORIAN
MULTIPLOT NOVEL

Studies in Dialogical Form

Peter K. Garrett

Yale University Press
New Haven & London
1980

Published with assistance from the foundation
established in memory of William McKean Brown.

Designed by James J. Johnson
and set in Baskerville type.
Printed in the United States of America by
Vail-Ballou Press, Inc., Binghamton, N.Y.

Published in Great Britain, Europe, Africa, and
Asia (except Japan) by Yale University Press,
Ltd., London. Distributed in Australia and
New Zealand by Book & Film Services, Artarmon,
N.S.W., Australia; and in Japan by Harper & Row,
Publishers, Tokyo Office.

Library of Congress Cataloging in Publication Data

Garrett, Peter K
    The Victorian multiplot novel.

    Includes index.
    1. English fiction—19th century—History and criticism.   2. Fiction
—Technique.   I. Title.
PR878.T35G3   823'.03   79-18658
ISBN 0-300-02403-7

For my mother and father

Contents

Acknowledgments

These studies, which trace a dialogue between structural principles in several Victorian multiplot novels, have themselves been developed through a long dialogue with many others. Part of that dialogue is represented by comments and notes that relate my approach and interpretations to others, but these can hardly give a full account of debts and differences, and I am also aware that my strongest differences often entail the debt of clarifying opposition. Another part, equally important but even less adequately represented, has been conducted with the many students, colleagues, and friends at Princeton, the University of Illinois, and elsewhere, whose interest, skepticism, encouragement, or forbearance have helped me to work out these readings. I am especially grateful to those who read parts or stages of the manuscript and offered criticism or suggestions: Charles Altman, Jonathan Arac, Stanley Corngold, Stanley Gray, James Kincaid, Daniel Majdiak, Hillis Miller, Cary Nelson, Robert Patten, Robert Schneider, and Richard Wheeler. Most important of all has been the continuing discussion of these novels with my wife, Nina Garrett, who read them with me (or before me) and patiently helped me discover what I wanted to say about them.

I am grateful to the American Council of Learned Societies for a fellowship which gave me badly needed time for reading and writing.

I would also like to thank Therese Bourbon and Marlyn Ehlers for their help in preparing the manuscript.

Portions of the Introduction and the chapter on Thackeray appeared in an article in *Nineteenth-Century Fiction*, © 1977 by The Regents of the University of California. Reprinted from *Nineteenth-Century Fiction*, Vol. 32, No. 1, pp. 1-17, by permission of The Regents.

References made in the text to all novels cited are to chapter and, where necessary, book numbers.

Introduction

"What do such large loose baggy monsters, with their queer elements of the accidental and the arbitrary, artistically *mean*?"[1] James's question was specifically directed at *The Newcomes*, *The Three Musketeers*, and *War and Peace*, but it has acquired the force of a general challenge to the integrity of the typically large and multifarious nineteenth-century novel. It is an especially pointed question for students of the mid-Victorian novel, whose predominant form is the multiple narrative, usually large and often apparently loose. Most of the novels now generally regarded as the greatest works of Victorian fiction, such as *Vanity Fair*, *Bleak House*, *Little Dorrit*, *Our Mutual Friend*, *Middlemarch*, and *The Way We Live Now*, employ this form, and though much has been written about their individual meanings, their common form has received far less attention. Their current recognition would seem to imply that their form no longer poses any problems, that we, unlike James, know how to read them, but I believe that most modern interpretations tend to conceal rather than resolve the problematic nature of Victorian multiple narrative, and that there is still much to be learned by seriously entertaining James's exasperated rhetorical question.

These studies of multiple narrative in Dickens, Thackeray, George Eliot, and Trollope can be considered as a response to that question—to that, first of all, rather than to others which might be posed, such as *why* the multiplot novel was so important in the period from the late 1840s to the late 1870s. To answer that question we would have to begin by considering the historical conditions that induced novelists to use multiple narrative, including factors as general as the Victorian novel's cultural role of producing a representation of society and as specific as the commercial success of serial publication and the

1. Henry James, "Preface to *The Tragic Muse*," in *The Art of the Novel*, ed. R.P. Blackmur (New York: Scribners, 1934), p. 84.

1

demands of publishers and circulating libraries for three-volume works. The search for historical explanations leads away from the novels themselves to their context, from the major works to the typical, and from form to content. To ask what the great Victorian multiplot novels *artistically* mean requires us instead to work toward an understanding of their significance—including their historical significance—through an investigation of their form, to consider them and the ways we might read them as realizations of possibilities and confrontations with problems inherent in multiple narrative.

Those possibilities and problems can be named quite briefly, though to explore their implications is a much longer task. The most important possibility and primary function of multiple narrative is clearly inclusiveness: the large and densely populated worlds of most Victorian multiplot novels, the expansive effects produced by differences of situation and mode between their narrative lines, and the generalizing effects produced by similarities are all ways of achieving inclusiveness through multiplication. But every multiplication of narrative lines is at the same time a division, a breach as well as an expansion, and every multiple narrative thus raises an immediate and fundamental problem of coherence. To multiply plots is to divide the fictional world, to disrupt the continuity of each line in order to shift from one to another, to disperse the reader's attention. We cannot even name or conceive of the form without implicitly raising this problem. The only terms available for describing it—double or multiple—define it in opposition to the singular and seem to imply that it exceeds or falls short of a normative unity.

The assumption of such a norm clearly lies behind James's criticism of multiple narrative, his persistent demand in both theory and practice for a single focus of composition. He professes "a mortal horror of two stories, two pictures in one," and accordingly seeks an "indispensable centre . . . for expressing a main intention."[2] A singular norm may not be logically

2. *The Art of the Novel,* pp. 83–84. James goes on to admit: "It was a fact, apparently, that one *had* on occasion seen two pictures in one; were there not for instance certain sublime Tintorettos at Venice, a measureless Crucifixion in especial, which showed without loss of authority half a dozen actions separately taking place? Yes, that might be, but there had surely been nevertheless a mighty pictorial fusion, so that the virtue of composition had somehow thereby come all

inevitable, but it is enforced by the dominant traditions of poetics, embodied in preconceptions about narrative and dramatic unity which have prevailed since Aristotle: "It is necessary . . . for the well-constructed plot to have a single rather than a double construction."[3] Faced with this tradition, favorable accounts of multiple narrative tend to be either explicitly or implicitly defensive, and their tactics tend to follow predictable, long-established patterns. Many modern interpretations of Victorian multiplot novels still range between the two poles of the double-barreled argument with which Dryden defended the Elizabethan use of subplots against the more stringent unity of French neoclassicism, on the one hand celebrating the greater inclusiveness, "the variety and copiousness of the English," and on the other maintaining that "the under-plot, which is only different, not contrary to the great design, may naturally be conducted along with it."[4]

Dryden's conception of a larger unity is based on a cosmological analogy, the model of the Ptolemaic universe with its all-embracing primum mobile. Like Milton in *Paradise Lost*, he reverts to the older, geocentric astronomy, which offered the reassurance of a closed, hierarchical system organized around a fixed center. The analogy reveals the assumptions which underlie the traditional defense of multiple plot and persist in much later critics, even though they no longer invoke notions of cosmic design. To construe the composition of a multiplot novel or play as one or more subplots held in firm subordination to a main plot remains the most common way of establishing its unity, a way that clearly concedes the necessity of a single center. This model may be appropriate for some works, but more often for drama than fiction, since the more concentrated form of drama tends to produce tighter integration, and perhaps more often for the Elizabethans than the Victorians, since principles of hier-

---

mysteriously to its own." The pictorial analogy, common in discussions of multiple narrative, here offers no solution to the mystery of composition, the virtue which the novelist can preserve only through the power of the single center.

3. *Poetics*, trans. Leon Golden (Englewood Cliffs, N.J.: Prentice-Hall, 1968), chap. 13, p. 22. Cf. chap. 8, p. 16: "Necessarily, then, just as in other forms of imitation, one imitation is one thing, so also, a plot, since it is an imitation of an action, must be an imitation of an action that is one and whole."

4. *Of Dramatic Poesy and Other Critical Essays,* ed. George Watson (London: Dent, 1962), 1:59.

archy play a more prominent role in Renaissance than in nineteenth-century art.[5] In Victorian multiple narratives, however, there is often no clear or consistent principle of subordination, and even those novels which at first seem closest to the traditional model of main and subplot often turn out to subvert it as different plots advance or recede in importance.

Modern interpretations of Victorian multiple narratives usually attempt to reestablish a centered form and stable hierarchy by thematic abstraction and analogy. A recent full-length study of Dickens, for example, discovers patterns of concentric circles with a single, thematic center in each of the major novels;[6] another critic describes the organization of *Middlemarch* as a set of analogies centered on Dorothea's "quest" for a principle of unity;[7] yet another finds a solution to "the problem of structure in Trollope" in thematic analyses which consider his loosely connected plot lines as components of "a vast mural . . . crammed with figures and united spatially," offering as demonstration a reading of *The Last Chronicle of Barset* which (re)places Mr. Crawley firmly "at the center of the novel."[8]

The use of pictorial or spatial metaphors is common in discussions of multiple narrative, especially in this kind of thematic interpretation. They represent the effort to spatialize narrative, to rearrange its elements into atemporal categories such as patterns of similarity and difference. Every narrative permits or invites this sort of reading to some extent, usually to a greater extent as narrative order departs from linear chronology, and the inevitable discontinuity of multiple narratives, with their

5. In comparing the double plot of *Anna Karenina* with that of *King Lear*, Georg Lukács observes that "complementing parallels and contrasts are much more closely related in drama than in the novel." See *The Historical Novel*, trans. Hannah and Stanley Mitchell (Boston: Beacon Press, 1963), p. 142. I think it likely that a study of Elizabethan drama freed from traditional preconceptions about centered form would find as much tension and complexity in its multiple plotting as I find in the Victorians', but the dominant interpretive approach to these plays has also been to "demonstrate" their unity. For a review and systematic consolidation of this tendency, see Richard Levin, *The Multiple Plot in English Renaissance Drama* (Chicago: University of Chicago Press, 1971).

6. H.M. Daleski, *Dickens and the Art of Analogy* (London: Faber and Faber, 1970).

7. David R. Carroll, "Unity through Analogy: An Interpretation of *Middlemarch*," *Victorian Studies* 2 (1959): 305–16.

8. Jerome Thale, "The Problem of Structure in Trollope," *Nineteenth-Century Fiction* 15 (1960): 149.

repeated breaks and transitions, reduces the importance of
sequence and increases that of typological or analogical relationships. The essential characteristic of such relationships,
however, is that in themselves they have no necessary order. The
more we spatialize a narrative, the more possibilities for rear-
rangement emerge, the freer the play between all its elements
becomes. The logic of this process leads directly away from
traditional conceptions of unity; the patterns which exponents of
spatialized thematic unity describe are created by their restrictive
choice of terms and emphases, by an act of interpretation that
attempts to constrain and repress the very possibilities on which
it also depends.[9] The inherent plasticity and reversibility of
analogies are most clearly shown by distinctly eccentric interpretations, such as a reading of *Little Dorrit* which posits the
minor character Mr. F's Aunt as the novel's thematic center and
arranges most of the other figures around her.[10] This gives the
whole game away: if Mr. F's Aunt can be considered as the center
of the novel, why not any other figure, any other element?

Such apparently absurd questions, such vertiginous possibilities cannot be simply dismissed. They are, in fact, raised again
and again in the Victorian multiplot novels themselves, which
often show much more awareness of the problematic nature of
centered form than do most of their interpreters. Consider as only
one example George Eliot's well-known "parable" of the pier-
glass:

> Your pier-glass or extensive surface of polished steel made to be
> rubbed by a housemaid, will be minutely and multitudinously
> scratched in all directions; but place now against it a lighted candle
> as a centre of illumination, and lo! the scratches will seem to
> arrange themselves in a fine series of concentric circles around that
> little sun. It is demonstrable that the scratches are going every-
> where impartially, and it is only your candle which produces the

9. Thus one commonly encounters different thematic constructions of the
same text. Thale, for example, reads *The Last Chronicle* in terms of the theme of
"honesty," with Crawley as the preeminent example. For Robert M. Polhemus,
however, "the large and unifying theme" of the novel is "secularization," and
Crawley accordingly becomes "an ironic center," displaced because his virtues
are considered outmoded. See *The Changing World of Anthony Trollope* (Berkeley and
Los Angeles: University of California Press, 1968), pp. 129–31.

10. Alan Wilde, "Mr. F's Aunt and the Analogical Structure of *Little Dorrit,*"
Nineteenth-Century Fiction 19 (1964): 33–44.

flattering illusion of a concentric arrangement, its light falling with an exclusive optical selection. These things are a parable. [*Middlemarch*, 27]

George Eliot's narrator applies the image to moral perception: "The scratches are events, and the candle is the egoism of any person," but it is equally relevant to other modes of interpretation. It suggests, in appropriately spatial terms, that in a complex multiplot novel like *Middlemarch* or *Little Dorrit* the large number and implications of possible analogies, of overlapping similarities and differences between characters and situations, make any interpretive choice of a single center an act of arbitrary projection. Yet it remains uncertain how well the pier-glass mirrors the world or the text of which it is a part. Do the events or implications of this or any novel extend "everywhere impartially" in pure randomness? As an analogy for the workings of analogy, the passage appears to leave us suspended between a false order and chaos.[11] Like several comparable moments which we shall encounter in other multiplot novels, it raises without answering the question of how to read them.

Leaving open the question of how much, if anything, is objectively "demonstrable" about a novel's structure, George Eliot's parable can help us to recognize the "flattering" or reassuring illusions of order produced by interpretations which attempt to demonstrate the unity of multiple narratives by monocentric reconstruction. Theirs is a fundamentally conservative enterprise, an effort to rescue multiplot novels from their own multiplicity by limiting the play of analogical implications and circumscribing their centrifugal force. As Barbara Hardy has observed, "We insist that the large loose baggy monster has unity, has symbolic concentration, has patterns of imagery and a thematic construction of character, and in the result the baggy monster is processed by our New Criticism into something strikingly like the original Jamesian streamlined beast." In her opposition to this reductive tendency, however, she simply shifts toward the opposite pole of Dryden's double argument, the

11. For a discussion of some of the contradictory implications of this and related passages, see J. Hillis Miller, "Optic and Semiotic in *Middlemarch*," in *The Worlds of Victorian Fiction,* ed. Jerome H. Buckley (Cambridge, Mass.: Harvard University Press, 1975), pp. 125–45.

affirmation of "variety and copiousness," maintaining that "largeness and looseness has a special advantage, allowing the novelist to report truthfully and fully the quality of the individual moment, the loose end, the doubt and contradiction and mutability."[12] This mimetic justification may be a useful defensive tactic and has the further merit of avoiding drastic reconstruction, but like the imposition of thematic unity, it serves as a means of recuperation which limits the interplay of possible meanings by stabilizing them in correspondence with the "truth" they "report."[13] Both interpretive strategies are defenses in a double sense: while defending the validity of multiple narrative, they also defend the reader from its most troubling effects. Both fail to free us from the Aristotelian tradition: whether valued, deplored, or denied, the "looseness" of multiple narrative is still determined by a monocentric norm.[14]

To escape from these defensive positions it would seem necessary to establish a conception of multiple narrative not as a derivative, a multiplication and division of single narrative, but as an independent form with its own principles and tradition. The basis for such a conception might be taken from the study of medieval narrative, where comparable problems arise. Charles Altman has recently argued that the assumption "that all narrative texts correspond to one basic type, the single-focus form," has prevented modern criticism from dealing effectively with the "epic binarism" of texts such as the *Song of Roland*.[15] He

12. *The Appropriate Form* (London: Athlone Press, 1964), pp. 7–8.

13. On the concept and varieties of recuperation, see Jonathan Culler, *Structuralist Poetics: Structuralism, Linguistics and the Study of Literature* (Ithaca: Cornell University Press, 1975), pp. 131–60.

14. The sense that the usual ways in which modern criticism deals with the problem of multiple narrative form a limited, interrelated set from which it is difficult to escape is confirmed by observing how Victorian critics anticipate each possibility. Richard Stang's survey provides examples of those who deplore looseness (sometimes invoking the French as models of economy and unity), those who defend its variety or verisimilitude, and those who find a solution in the idea of thematic unity. See *The Theory of the Novel in England, 1850–1870* (London: Routledge, 1959), pp. 111–35.

15. "Medieval Narrative vs. Modern Assumptions: Revising Inadequate Typology," *Diacritics* 4 (Summer 1974): 16. This assumption, which, as we have seen, characterizes the traditions of Aristotle and James, is, as Altman points out, also present in the work of modern formalist and structuralist theorists such as Vladimir Propp and Tzvetan Todorov.

proposes an alternate type, the dual-focus form, structured by alternation and conflict between two groups rather than the development of a protagonist, by spatial division, repetition, and substitution rather than temporal progression.[16] This model of dual or, by extension, multiple-focus narrative seems more appropriate for analyzing Victorian multiplot novels. Instead of attempting to locate their center in a protagonist, a main plot, or a thematic focus, we could locate it in a set of consistent combinatorial rules.

Yet when we apply this model we find only a partial fit. It is clearly applicable to the devices of parallelism and contrast that play a part in all multiplot novels, but even in those that develop the most elaborate counterpoint between narrative lines, temporal progression can be as important as repetition, the development of protagonists as important as alternation. Each of the double narrative lines of *Vanity Fair* or *Daniel Deronda*, as well as the multiple lines of *Our Mutual Friend, Middlemarch,* or *The Way We Live Now*, can be regarded both as the component of a larger pattern and as an independent focus of interest. Readings of these novels that rely exclusively on a multiple-focus model will make them seem as loose and baggy or produce as much distortion as single-focus readings. Both models are applicable, but neither is sufficient. By entertaining both, however, we come closer to recognizing the constitutive indeterminacy of Victorian multiple narrative. The form of these novels is neither single- nor multiple-focus but incorporates both, and it is the interaction and tension between these structural principles which produces some of their most important and distinctive effects. No single model can accommodate texts in which different, incompatible principles of coherence are in play. In order to avoid either considering their irregularities merely as "looseness" or reducing them to a false unity, we must recognize that their form is not "monological" but "dialogical," organized by a double logic, a dialogue of structural principles.

These terms are taken from Mikhail Bakhtin, who proposes the concept of the "dialogical" or "polyphonic" novel to describe the

16. One might also adduce Angus Fletcher's conception of the two fundamental forms of symbolic action, "progress" and "battle," in *Allegory: The Theory of a Symbolic Mode* (Ithaca: Cornell University Press, 1964), pp. 151–61.

8

"plurality of independent and unmerged voices and consciousnesses" in Dostoevsky's fiction.[17] Bakhtin develops many applications and associations for these terms, but in all of them the crucial point is the recognition of radical, unresolvable differences, of oppositions that cannot be reduced to stable, abstract antinomies or subjected to dialectical mediation. In Bakhtin's account, these oppositions are always based on relations between concrete, individual consciousnesses, but I believe they can also be found in unresolved tensions between structural principles which, like different forms of consciousness, offer divergent perspectives on the world. Victorian multiple narratives develop such tensions in several ways. The most obvious of these result from discrepancies of mode and implication between separate narrative lines: stories that follow the benign logic of romantic comedy may be intersected by others that press insistently toward bitter failure and loss; satire and melodrama, visionary romance and domestic realism may be brought into uneasy confrontations and made to question, challenge, and reinterpret each other's visions. Dialogical tensions can be found in narrative perspectives as well as in lines of development.[18] They may arise between the unmerged voices of character and narrator or even within the narrative voice itself, in disruptions of monological discourse ranging from subtle shifts and contradictions to such radical divisions as the double narrative of *Bleak House*.

It can be seen from these examples that there is no necessary connection between such dialogical oppositions and multiple narrative, which may be governed by a consistent scheme of values (contrasting double plots are a common didactic device for illustrating such schemes), just as a single-focus narrative may employ incongruous modes or maintain an unresolved opposition between the consciousnesses of protagonist and narrator. In the major Victorian multiplot novels, however, the multiplication and division of both narrative perspectives and developments produce unresolvable tensions because they articulate an under-

17. *Problems of Dostoevsky's Poetics,* trans. R.W. Rotsel (Ann Arbor: Ardis, 1973), p. 4.

18. My discussion of narrative form in terms of perspective (the function of mediation between story and audience) and development (the sequential organization) is based on Monroe C. Beardsley, *Aesthetics: Problems in the Philosophy of Criticism* (New York: Harcourt, Brace, 1958), pp. 247–53.

lying dialogue between irreducibly different structural principles, between the centripetal impulse that organizes narrative around the development of a protagonist and the impulse that elaborates an inclusive pattern of simultaneous relationships. Our approach to these novels will sometimes emphasize plot, sometimes point of view, rhetoric, or theme; but through all these aspects we will repeatedly be brought back to the fundamental tensions that prevent them from resolving into any single stable order or meaning.

The full implications of dialogical form can be discovered only by tracing its workings in different novels and novelists, by seeing how its double logic can produce effects that range from the symbolic density of Dickens to the discursive openness of Trollope. But before we consider even a preliminary example it will be useful to place the concept in a larger theoretical framework in order to define the position from which those readings will be undertaken. We can begin to do this by observing the implications that have been developed from Bakhtin's terms by later theorists. One line of development pursued in Russian literary studies has led to Boris Uspensky's structural analysis of narrative point of view.[19] Here dialogical relationships are assimilated into a systematic theory that locates possible points of view on ideological, phraseological, spatial-temporal, and psychological levels. Uspensky notes the possibilities of "nonconcurrence" between any of these levels and recognizes the increased compositional complexity and interest these tensions can produce, but in his account they do not exert much disruptive force and usually appear only as local discrepancies contained within a larger unity. By confining his analysis to a limited set of formal features, he can use the concept of dialogical or polyphonic narrative without reconsidering traditional assumptions about aesthetic coherence.

Those assumptions are aggressively challenged, however, by Julia Kristeva's interpretation and extension of Bakhtin's ideas, which she claims as anticipations of some of the most radical

19. *A Poetics of Composition: The Structure of the Artistic Text and Typology of a Compositional Form*, trans. Valentin Zavarin and Susan Wittig (Berkeley and Los Angeles: University of California Press, 1973).

tendencies of contemporary poststructuralist thought.[20] Thus the
concept of dialogue, in which the speaker's language is marked
by the influence of the other to whom it is addressed, is linked
both to Lacan's psychic doubling, in which the self is constituted
by and as the other, and to the *Tel Quel* theory of intertextuality,
which regards every text as a mcsaic of citations, a dialogue of
and with other texts. In this account of the dialogical, the unities
of subject, discourse, and meaning are radically divided and
dispersed into a plural structure that cannot be grasped as a
totality, a matrix of undefinable, undecidable relations. For
Kristeva, dialogical division opens the way to the most extreme
modern experimentation: "It destroys the monologic of representational literary discourse and sets the general scene for a
kaleidoscopic and pluralist way of writing in which we see
nothing, for it is the writing which sees us."[21]

The avant-garde "general scene" Kristeva evokes hardly seems
to be an appropriate setting for Victorian multiple narrative,
which relies heavily on the conventions of representation through
which we "see" characters, events, and fictional worlds. Yet as
those novels articulate their dialogues of structural principles
they develop their own "pluralist way of writing" which calls
those conventions into question and cannot be accommodated by
traditional conceptions of form and meaning. Although
Kristeva's radical interpretation of Bakhtin's terms may not be
directly applicable to Victorian fiction, it can at least help to free
us from those inadequate conceptions and point the way toward
more appropriate ones. In place of the defensive strategies that
attempt to limit the play of meaning by imposing a center, such
a conception of dialogical form can open our reading to the
multiplicity and instability of decentered structure.

Here we make contact with the thought of Jacques Derrida, the
poststructuralist theorist whose arguments seem most relevant to

20. See especially "Le Texte clos," and "Le Mot, le dialogue, et le roman," in
Semiotikè: Recherches pour un sémanalyse (Paris: Seuil, 1969), pp. 113–73. Kristeva
has also written an introduction to the French translation of Bakhtin, *La Poetique
de Dostoïevski*, trans. Isabelle Kolitcheff (Paris: Seuil, 1970), pp 5–27, which has
been translated as "The Ruin of a Poetics," in *Russian Formalism: A Collection of
Articles and Texts in Translation*, ed. Stephen Bann and John E. Bowlt (New York:
Barnes and Noble, 1973), pp. 102–19.
21. "The Ruin of a Poetics," p. 115.

our problem because they challenge the basic concept of centered structure, expose its inherent contradictions, and in place of its stability, coherence, and totality introduce the possibilities of *"freeplay*... a field of infinite substitutions in the closure of a finite ensemble."[22] Again, the notion of such a radical multiplication of meanings seems too extreme to apply to Victorian fiction; it seems more relevant to *Finnegans Wake* than *Middlemarch*,[23] applicable only to writing produced after that historical "rupture" manifested in the "destructive discourses" of Nietzsche, Freud, and Heidegger which Derrida interprets and extends.[24] But Derrida does not simply describe and endorse freer modes of writing and interpretation. The possibilities of decentering and free play he reveals coexist in any structure or text with the possibilities of unity and determinate meaning which they subvert. This inclusiveness presents a different, more troubling difficulty: to invoke Derrida's arguments for theoretical support is to risk the assimilation of our subject into much larger philosophical problems of order and meaning where it would lose its distinctive features and interest. The problem is not so much that his terms are inappropriate as that they are too general, since they would presumably be equally applicable to any text grounded in the Western tradition whose metaphysical presuppositions he deconstructs. For a criticism based on his arguments, modeled on his interpretive practice, "any running discourse, any story or narrative will be dialogical not monological," because it

22. "Structure, Sign, and Play in the Discourse of the Human Sciences," in *The Languages of Criticism and the Sciences of Man,* ed. Richard Macksey and Eugenio Donato (Baltimore: Johns Hopkins University Press, 1970), p. 260. Derrida continues, explaining why a decentered system or language "excludes totalization": "This field permits these infinite substitutions only because it is finite, that is to say, because instead of being an inexhaustible field, as in the classical hypothesis, instead of being too large, there is something missing from it: a center which arrests and founds the freeplay of substitutions."
23. The relevance of such terms to Joyce is demonstrated in Margot Norris, *The Decentered Universe of Finnegans Wake: A Structuralist Analysis* (Baltimore: Johns Hopkins University Press, 1977).
24. "Structure, Sign, and Play," p. 250. Derrida employs the modernist fiction of a historical "rupture" "with caution and as if in quotation marks" (p. 247), leaving open the possibility that it has, as he would say, "always already" taken place, yet occurs more clearly in some discourses than others. Cf. his comment in *Positions* (Paris: Minuit, 1972), p. 35: "Je ne crois pas à la rupture décisive, à l'unicité d'une 'coupure épistémologique,' comme on le dit souvent aujourd'hui."

can always be shown to contain contrary implications that cannot be attributed to a single "voice" or source.[25]

To keep our conception of dialogical form focused on the specific qualities of Victorian multiple narrative, we shall have to make our way between the monological rock and the deconstructive whirlpool, between, that is, the two most strongly opposed positions in current critical theory. On the one hand, there are several critics working in the tradition of Chicago neo-Aristotelian theory who have developed rigorous, extended arguments that would seem to exclude the very possibility of a double logic. Sheldon Sacks, for example, sets up a classification of types of prose fiction in which each is defined by its unique purpose and principle of organization. Satire, apologue, and represented action (or novel) each has its own "grammar" which is fundamentally incompatible with those of the other types. "One cannot create an action which is also a satire," Sacks insists, "any more than he can write an active sentence which is also a passive sentence in English."[26] Sacks would presumably find it equally impossible to create a multiple-focus narrative which is also a single-focus narrative.

Ralph Rader augments this monological generic theory with an argument that the reading process always aims at the perception of coherent form and univocal meaning, that our understanding of literature derives "from a comprehensive inferential grasp of an author's overall creative intention in a work, which allows us to eliminate in the act of reading any potential incoherencies and ambiguities which cannot be resolved within our appreciation of the coherence of the whole."[27] Any troubling distractions or apparent contradictions that cannot be completely eliminated, he adds in a later essay, can be understood "simply as the *unintended and unavoidable negative*

25. J. Hillis Miller, "Ariachne's Broken Woof," *Georgia Review* 31 (1977): 59. Miller uses "dialogical" interchangeably with "alogical" and "monological" with "logocentric," Derrida's term for the underlying bias of Western metaphysics.

26. *Fiction and the Shape of Belief* (Berkeley and Los Angeles: University of California Press, 1966), p. 46.

27. "The Concept of Genre and Eighteenth-Century Studies," in *New Approaches to Eighteenth-Century Literature*, ed. Philip Harth (New York: Columbia University Press, 1974), p. 86.

consequences of the artist's positive constructive intention."[28]
Just as Sacks's account of literary creation attempts to rule out
the possibility of multiple compositional principles, Rader's
account of reception denies that "inconsistencies and incoherencies" can ever be "positively significant." Indeed, he warns us,
"any method of interpretation which assumes that contradiction
between elements of meaning is itself meaningful can only end by
proving that all discourse is meaningless."[29]

These arguments clearly depend on postulating a center, an
origin in the author whose intention determines meaning and
guarantees coherence,[30] and they are clearly vulnerable to decentering counterarguments. The authorial center Rader posits
displays the same "coherence in contradiction" that Derrida
reveals in the general concept: it is both *"within* the structure and
outside it"[31]—within it as the generic principle of "an
inherently significant representational structure," and outside it
since "in literary works the language is intelligible only in
relation to the author's presumed intention."[32] In its double
location this center itself displays the instability and uncertainty
it is supposed to control.[33] Rader's theory of reading shows with
equal clarity that to proceed on this monological assumption
requires a constant effort of repression to "eliminate . . . any
potential incoherencies and ambiguities" (much as readings of
multiplot novels based on monocentric assumptions tend to

28. "Fact, Theory, and Literary Explanation," *Critical Inquiry* 1 (1974): 253.
29. Ibid., p. 270.
30. A similar argument is developed in Wayne C. Booth, *A Rhetoric of Irony*
(Chicago: University of Chicago Press, 1974), where "stable irony" is established
by "reconstruction" of an author's intention.
31. "Structure, Sign, and Play," p. 248.
32. Rader, "The Concept of Genre," p. 89.
33. Deconstructive readings offer a different kind of challenge to the power of
"the author's presumed intention" to control meaning. Thus, in response to the
claim by Wayne Booth and M.H. Abrams that "every effort at original or 'free'
interpretation is plainly and simply parasitical" on "the obvious and univocal
reading," J. Hillis Miller dismantles the opposition of "parasite" and "host,"
showing how the multiple associations and constituents of these terms make the
antithesis reverse and collapse, how each term is split by internal differences, and
thus how his opponents are unable to determine the meaning of the language
they use. See Wayne C. Booth, "M.H. Abrams: Historian as Critic, Critic as
Pluralist," *Critical Inquiry* 2 (1976): 441; M.H. Abrams, "Rationality and
Imagination in Cultural History: A Reply to Wayne Booth," *Critical Inquiry* 2
(1976): 457; J. Hillis Miller, "The Critic as Host," *Critical Inquiry* 3 (1977):
439–47.

repress their multiplicity).[34] To deny the need for a single dominant structuring principle, however, does not necessarily lead to absorption in infinite free play. For the proponents of univocality the only alternative to systematic repression is the licentiousness of "meaningless" indeterminacy; but the concept of dialogical form, of meaning produced by tensions between structuring principles, permits us to refuse that dichotomy and undertake readings that explore a middle ground.

One line of argument for such an intermediate position has recently been advanced by James R. Kincaid, whose strategy is to grant that monological theories do describe the necessary conditions of coherence and the normal procedures of reading but to deny that these norms apply to "works of any interest to us."[35] Instead of a single pattern, literary texts present "a structure of mutually competing coherences"; instead of allowing us to eliminate inconsistencies, "the text finds ways to counteract that tendency in us by insisting alternatively and maddeningly that contradictory details are both insignificant and crucial."[36] The position Kincaid stakes out "in the no-man's-land of a partly stabilized and determinate incoherence" is still a form of genre theory, but one that insists on the coexistence of several incompatible generic systems within each text. Thus he indicates the way *Wuthering Heights* can be construed according to each of Northrop Frye's four narrative patterns, and the Alice books according to each of Sacks's three types. In both cases, all the possibilities envisaged by a scheme of classification are present in a single work but cannot be integrated: none is dominant, it is impossible to entertain all at once, and "there is no pattern, on whatever level of abstraction, that can contain them all."[37]

Kincaid's theory of generic incoherence has much in common with my conception of dialogical form. Both recognize the

34. The single-focus model plays a crucial role in the seminal essay by R.S. Crane from which the theories of Sacks and Rader are developed. See "The Concept of Plot and the Plot of *Tom Jones*," in *Critics and Criticism,* ed. R.S. Crane (Chicago: University of Chicago Press, 1952), pp. 616–47.

35. "Coherent Readers, Incoherent Texts," *Critical Inquiry* 3 (1977): 785.

36. Ibid., pp. 783, 789.

37. Ibid., p. 796. My reading of *Wuthering Heights* below as a dialogical narrative is largely compatible with Kincaid's, though it focuses more on formal features than generic patterns.

importance of basic conventional organizing patterns yet challenge traditional assumptions about unity by attempting to demonstrate the presence of multiple and irreconcilable patterns. But Kincaid's version of limited indeterminacy is less useful for differentiating between texts or groups of texts and producing detailed analyses. It may be true (and I believe it is) that "works to which we customarily pay attention" all exhibit this kind of incoherence in one way or another, but to analyze the different ways in which particular texts, authors, forms, and periods produce that effect, we need to move beyond the simple opposition of readers and texts to an account of the interplay of coherence and incoherence within the text, identifying the specific principles at work in each and showing how it is structured by the developing tensions between them.[38]

By identifying the double logic of single and multiple focus as the common and distinctive structural problematic of the major Victorian multiplot novels, we can develop analyses that recognize not only the qualities they share but also the individual qualities of each novel and novelist. When we encounter the split in *Bleak House* between the wide-ranging authorial narrative and the narrower focus of Esther's first-person narrative, or the shift in *Middlemarch* from the first ten chapters focused on Dorothea to a multiple narrative in which her story becomes only one among several, we are encountering significantly different forms of a common dialogical tension that require different interpretations. To work out those interpretations we cannot simply rely on broad generic patterns like comedy and romance or satire and apologue; we must pay close attention to

38. Kincaid's earlier essay, "The Forms of Victorian Fiction," *Victorian Newsletter* (Spring 1975), pp. 1–4, offers a comparable theory that deals more directly with form. He considers the Victorian novel as a "mixed" or "dual" form, held in an uneasy suspension between the "closed," "spatial," "rational" form of eighteenth-century fiction and the "open," "temporal," "existential" form of the twentieth century. I question the value of placing these oppositions in such a simplifed historical scheme (the shift from "closed" to "open" form is a cliché of literary history, a crisis that always seems to occur in whatever period happens to be under study), but the notion of conflicting patterns within the text, not just in the reader's interpretations of it, is clearly a kind of dialogical form. Kincaid applies this theory quite fruitfully in *The Novels of Anthony Trollope* (Oxford: Oxford University Press, 1977), where he shows how the conventional patterns of Trollope's plots are complicated or subverted by his narrator's rhetoric and his subplots.

the specific features of each novel's form, following the dialogue of competing coherences through the alternations of its narrative voices and perspectives, the shifts and splits, twists and intersections of its lines of development.

That kind of attention to form also distinguishes the readings I am proposing from more abstract deconstructive interpretations. By considering dialogical form as an unstable tension between determinate patterns and focusing on concrete fictional elements, we can explore the problems of meaning each novel develops without turning them into illustrations of universal philosophical themes. The work of Derrida and other post-structuralists has made it easier to extricate multiplot novels from the restrictions of monological assumptions, but we shall not be making the most of this opportunity if we only use it to rediscover and deconstruct the pervasive system of Western metaphysics in every text we read. Instead, we need to recognize how the processes of narrative perform their own constructions and deconstructions, how the interplay of centering and decentering impulses at work in Dickens' mystery plots or Thackeray's shifting authorial stances, in George Eliot's networks of thematic analogies or the uncertain status of Trollope's protagonists produces very different meanings and effects. Clearly these novelists are not as insistent or as radical in their transgressions and transformations of traditional modes of writing as the avant-garde writers favored by theorists like Kristeva, but it is precisely that difference, that apparent deference to established modes that gives them their special interest. In them we encounter the problems and possibilities developed more explicitly in modern writing but encounter them within the traditional system of representation, a system whose grounds of meaning, such as the stability of personal identity, the intelligibility of cause and effect, the authority of the authorial voice, are both exploited and subverted. My readings of these novels will attempt to do justice to their mixed mode by working within the familiar categories of character, plot, and theme, but they will also attempt to show some—and necessarily only some—of the ways in which their double logic composes and decomposes those elements to produce effects of remarkable and irreducible complexity.

As a preliminary example of some of the effects produced by dialogical form, let us briefly consider *Wuthering Heights*. It is neither large nor loose and seems monstrous mainly as a "sport" (as F. R. Leavis calls it), unrelated to other Victorian fiction. Yet in the way it plays double- against single-focus narrative and holds both patterns open to alternative interpretations it closely resembles several other longer novels of the period, while its formal compression permits a more concise analysis. As a single-focus narrative it appears to center in the figure of Heathcliff, who is certainly the most important character and whose career runs from the beginning to the end of the novel. But this pattern is disrupted by several discontinuities: time-shifts which reverse the order of cause and effect, gaps such as Heathcliff's three-year absence and radical transformation between chapters 9 and 10, and the shift of emphasis in which he is progressively displaced by the second Catherine and Hareton. In the course of this displacement he assumes the role of opponent and blocking figure between the young lovers which Hindley played between himself and Catherine, a shift from "hero" to "villain" which indicates a sharp reversal of perspective.[39] For all the appearance and importance of a single focus, the novel eventually requires us to recognize a dual pattern. As William Empson observes, "*Wuthering Heights* is a good case of double plot in the novel . . . telling the same story twice with the two possible endings."[40] This pattern of repetition and difference involves not only parallels between characters but a detailed counterpoint of events, such as the first Catherine being "captured" in the Grange (7) and the second in the Heights (27). The movement of doubling is also at work in the repetition and recombination of names, the doubling and merging of identities (Catherine declares, "I am Heathcliff" [9]; he calls her his "life" and "soul" [16]), and in the doubled narration of Lockwood and Nelly,

39. If one were to attempt a schematic structural description of the novel's "syntax," Heathcliff would not be represented as the constant subject undergoing successive predicative transformations (the pattern of single-focus narrative) but as a "shifter," whose meaning changes with its context.

40. *Some Versions of Pastoral* (1935; rpt. Norfolk, Conn.: New Directions, 1960), p. 84. Empson's study of double plots in Elizabethan drama is less preoccupied than most with establishing unity, and his conception of "double irony" involves conflicts of meaning similar to those produced by what I call dialogical form.

whose obvious biases and limitations require us to redouble their accounts with alternative interpretations; it assumes the most inclusive thematic form in the opposition between the worlds of the Heights and the Grange, or between the energy of natural or supernatural forces and the restraints of civilized order and reason.

These thematic oppositions have often been discussed in commentaries on the novel and need not be pursued here. My main concern is with the possibilities of interpretation produced by the interaction of single and dual focus, linear progression and binary alternation. Like the decrepit house adjoining the Gimmerton chapel, its "two rooms threatening speedily to determine into one" (3), the double narrative can be construed as two phases merging into a single, continuous history, organized by a precise chronology. But the actual narrative order, with its initial departure from chronology (Lockwood begins very near the "end") and subsequent shifts backward and forward, makes the two plots unfold concurrently. As reconstructed sequence, *Wuthering Heights* traces a cycle of disruption and renewal, a tragic metaphysical love story followed, complemented, and reversed by a comic counterplot in which less extreme versions of the original tormented lovers converge to restore civility. This is the version presented by Lockwood and Nelly, with its final note of peaceful resolution.

But against this closed, linear pattern, in which conflict is resolved by the elimination of Catherine and Heathcliff, we can set another, suggested by the belief of "the country folks" that they still walk the moors, in which they and their violent, visionary world remain as a perpetual alternative, coexisting with the more normal, conventional world of the second generation as the two plots coexist. This tension between structural principles is expressed within the novel in Heathcliff's and Catherine's struggles to break out of an irreversible linear sequence and (re)gain their private eternity, and in those moments, like Lockwood's dream, when the past or another world breaks into the present. It is likewise expressed in the many readings of the novel which attempt to assert one extreme of its polarized values against the other, to privilege one plot and subordinate the other, or to encompass their opposition in some sort of dualism. Both the dramatic conflicts and the conflicting possibilities of interpretation arise from the novel's dialogical form.

The dual logic of *Wuthering Heights* cannot be mastered by critical concepts of center, hierarchy, and totality, by either choosing one interpretation or imposing a fixed order on alternative interpretations, by any strategy that attempts to enclose and stabilize the text's production of meaning. This instability is quite clearly not the result of formal "looseness." The devices of analogical and causal connection, metaphoric and metonymic links between the novel's double plots (devices which are always, and always differently at work in every multiple narrative, however large or loose) produce a high degree of formal coherence, but they are all subject to the play of shifting perspectives, a movement of continual substitution which exceeds and resists any monological formulation. We can observe this movement even in the final lines of *Wuthering Heights,* as Lockwood wonders "how anyone could ever imagine unquiet slumbers, for the sleepers in that quiet earth." His words declare the end of the narrative's movement, the end of all its stormy conflicts in a mood of permanent calm, yet they also ironically invite us to remedy his deficient imagination, to conceive what he cannot, and so to begin again the substitution of perspectives.[41]

To consider *Wuthering Heights* and other Victorian multiplot novels as dialogical forms requires us to follow the movement in which meaning is continually produced and effaced. To read them in this way is not to claim mastery of their complexity or to unmask their latent contradictions but to continue the process of setting one perspective against another in which the novels themselves are already engaged, a process which the conventions

---

41. The unresolvable instability of *Wuthering Heights* can also be seen by comparing it with its monological sibling, *Jane Eyre,* where we find a powerfully centripetal organization around a single focus (characters and events gain significance only as they contribute to Jane's development), reinforced by the protagonist's own, thoroughly reliable narration. Conflicts of self-assertion and submission, of the forces of passion or desire with those of repression or renunciation, are expressed not as dialogical tensions but as a dialectical progression in the alternating stages of Gateshead and Lowood, Thornfield and Moor House, which arrives at a final, stable synthesis in the union of Jane and Rochester at Ferndean. Any reading of *Jane Eyre* that seeks to dismantle this synthesis will have to work against the logic of its form, not by following it as we have followed the double logic of *Wuthering Heights.*

neither of narrative nor of critical argument can ever bring to more than a provisional conclusion.

What do such large loose baggy monsters artistically mean? The answer I have begun to give stresses not what but how they mean, but from this beginning, as provisional conclusion to this introduction, we can also anticipate further possibilities of interpretation that are suggested by correspondences between the opposition of single and multiple focus and other typological oppositions. One of these is Edwin Muir's distinction between the novel of character, in which groups of essentially unchanging figures are "continuously redistributed in Space," and the dramatic novel, which traces the development of individuals. Each type implies different perspectives on the world: "The values of the character novel are social . . . the values of the dramatic novel individual or universal, as we choose to regard them. . . . These two types of the novel are neither opposites, then, nor in any important sense complements of each other; they are rather two distinct modes of seeing life: In Time, personally, and in Space, socially."[42] Another, more abstract and far-reaching set of terms is proposed by Edward Said, who opposes the principle of succession, of linear development or dynastic sequence, and that of adjacency, of parallelism or complementarity.[43] These principles underlie different modes of producing meaning, not only in the relationship between elements within a text, but in its relation to other texts, author, reader, and reality. Said regards the "classical" nineteenth-century novel, organized by the career of its protagonist, as the epitome of succession; modern texts free themselves from the increasingly untenable notions of an absolute origin and continuous development by inventing non-narrative forms.

But both principles are at work in the Victorian multiplot novel. As we have already seen, the double plot of *Wuthering Heights* can be construed as either successive or adjacent sequences; similarly, in Muir's terms, the two plots oppose the

---

42. *The Structure of the Novel* (London: Hogarth Press, 1928), p. 63. Muir's account of a differential relation that cannot be understood as logical contraries or complements closely recalls Bakhtin's account of dialogical oppositions.

43. Edward Said, *Beginnings: Intention and Method* (New York: Basic Books, 1975).

individual or universal values of Heathcliff and the first Catherine and the social values reestablished in the courtship of
Hareton and the second. In each case, opposed terms which
theoretically describe extremely different narrative modes or
structural principles prove applicable to the same text; together,
they help to confirm and elaborate the concept of dialogical
form, allowing us to interpret the structural tensions of Victorian
multiple narratives as tensions between the perspectives of the
individual and the social group, between temporal development
and spatial comprehension. Here structures can be related to the
manifest thematic concerns of Victorian fiction: the large loose
baggy monsters mean many things and in many different ways,
but one thing they repeatedly mean to do is to transcend the
limitations of the individual point of view and envision the life of
the whole community.[44] Yet in every case we can observe, not
the realization of a secure and comprehensive vision but a
continual, shifting, unstable, and unpredictable confrontation
between single and plural, individual and social, particular and
general perspectives.

By elaborating and refusing to resolve these incompatible
meanings, Victorian multiplot novels also come to "mean"
themselves, to present not a direct vision of the world but a
dramatization of the process and problems of making sense of it.
This reflexiveness, which is not only articulated in passages of
self-conscious reflection but implied throughout in the constant
construction and deconstruction of meaning, makes Victorian
fiction double in yet another sense, for while it energetically
addresses the novel's traditional concern with the relation of the
individual and society, it also, like our most self-conscious, self-
referring "modern" fictions, discloses the inevitable mediations
of knowledge.

44. J. Hillis Miller stresses the importance of the omniscient narrator as an
embodiment of a "collective consciousness," "a generative presupposition determining form and meaning in Victorian fiction." See *The Form of Victorian Fiction*
(Notre Dame, Ind.: University of Notre Dame Press, 1968), pp. 53–90. The
inclusive knowledge which such a narrator proposes can also be elaborated in the
developmental structure of multiple narrative.

✤ ONE ✤

Dickens:
He Mounts a High Tower in His Mind

The great multiplot novels of Dickens' maturity, *Bleak House*, *Little Dorrit*, and *Our Mutual Friend*, will be our main concern, yet their achievement can best be understood in relation to several features and developments, artistic possibilities and purposes, which run through his whole career. Where then should we begin? Dickens himself, a master of beginnings, confronts at the opening of each of his major novels a similar problem of introducing several issues at once, and nowhere does he manage this with greater force and compression than in the brilliant first paragraph of his last novel, *The Mystery of Edwin Drood*, in which we can observe nearly all the features that will concern us. Let us begin there.

An ancient English Cathedral Town? How can the ancient English Cathedral Town be here! The well-known massive grey square tower of its old Cathedral? How can that be here! There is no spike of rusty iron in the air, between the eye and it, from any point of the real prospect. What is the spike that intervenes, and who has set it up? Maybe it is set up by the Sultan's order for the impaling of a horde of Turkish robbers, one by one. It is so, for cymbals clash, and the Sultan goes by to his palace in long procession. Ten thousand scimitars flash in the sunlight, and thrice ten thousand dancing-girls strew flowers. Then, follow white elephants caparisoned in countless gorgeous colours, and infinite in number and attendants. Still the Cathedral Tower rises in the background, where it cannot be, and still no writhing figure is on the grim spike. Stay! Is the spike so low a thing as the rusty spike on the top of a post of an old bedstead that has tumbled all awry? Some vague period of drowsy laughter must be devoted to the consideration of this possibility.

23

The passage superimposes the images of three different places: Cloisterham Cathedral, the London opium den, and the Sultan's palace, carrying to an extreme of condensation the device of juxtaposition which is a basic method in all of Dickens' fiction. It creates a magical perspective, available to no actual spectator but only to the imagination, in which places or events widely separated in space or time can be grasped synoptically. Seen in this paratactic fashion, these images produce an effect of grotesque contrast, and yet they may also possess significant similarities. The barbarous execution of the robbers, the symbolic sacrifice enacted in the cathedral, and Jasper's private ceremonies of escape are analogous, through hardly equivalent forms of ritual. By plunging the reader directly into Jasper's drugged vision without explanatory preparation, the passage also suggests the ambiguous relation of appearance and reality: all three places are equally real or illusory until the subsequent narrative establishes a provisional resolution.

Corresponding to these features of perspective is the type of developmental structure toward which this passage opens out. It does not merely begin the narrative, it forces an opening, creates a disturbance, a puzzle. As a beginning now forever deprived of a consonant end, it reveals even more clearly than any of Dickens' completed novels the temporal form of the mystery plot. The cognitive tension established here between the different worlds inhabited by Jasper's divided self could be fully resolved only by the conclusion which, according to Forster, was to confront them with each other again in the condemned cell.[1] Such a conclusion would not only solve the murder mystery but, in its reconstruction of causal links, would also reveal the past which led up to the beginning moment of juxtaposition, the personal history explaining the simultaneous presence of these images in Jasper's mind. The opening passage thus proposes a circular movement whose progression into the future will ultimately return to its point of departure by way of a prior moment in the past and so, as Dickens urged himself to do in his

1. John Forster, *The Life of Charles Dickens*, 2 vols. (London: Dent, 1966), 2: 366.

notes for *Little Dorrit*, "run the two ends of the book together."[2]

Further investigation "must be devoted to the consideration" of the possibilities inherent in all these features. The following chapter will consider the function and significance of Dickens' mystery plots; here we shall be concerned with his use of juxtaposition, the perspectives that present it, and the effects of the similarities and differences it produces.

The elementary process of juxtaposition, the mere contiguity of heterogeneous elements, is a basic constituent of all Dickens' fiction. As it does in the opening of *Edwin Drood*, juxtaposition precedes any connections of theme or plot and implements the powerful expansive impulse that produces Dickens' remarkable multiplicity, the proliferation of characters and worlds, the dense texture of descriptive detail, and the coexistence of different modes. The later multiplot novels give more complex and subtle expression to this impulse, but even in the early novels, which often employ the simpler eighteenth-century form of picaresque "adventures," there are frequent breaks and shifts that produce sharp contrasts. Both the interpolated tales of *Pickwick Papers* and Oliver Twist's alternations between the worlds of Fagin and Mr. Brownlow and the Maylies disrupt linear progression and display a similar concern with yoking contraries together, juxtaposing disparate worlds that challenge and comment on each other. Dickens' preface to *The Old Curiosity Shop* claims as the novel's underlying conception not a story but a set of striking juxtapositions: "in writing the book, I had it always in my fancy to surround the lonely figure of the child with grotesque and wild, but not impossible, companions, and to gather about her innocent face and pure intentions, associates as strange and uncongenial as the grim objects that are about her bed when her history is first foreshadowed." This principle of intensifying contrast organizes not only the encounters between Nell and her "grotesque and wild" companions but also the narrative alternations between her adventures and those of Quilp or Dick Swiveller, juxtaposing pathos with melodrama or comedy. In-

2. See Paul D. Herring, "Dickens' Monthly Number Plans for *Little Dorrit*" *Modern Philology* 64 (1966): 51.

deed, since the plot connection of flight and pursuit is so weakly motivated, these juxtapositions remain the dominant pattern.

Such extreme or incongruous juxtapositions can also become the basis of satire, an important development because it points toward the ironic social panoramas of the later novels.[3] Satiric contrasts seldom organize the large-scale structures of the early novels, but they do appear in isolated, emblematic scenes that represent larger possibilities, such as the passage in *Nicholas Nickleby* describing the hero's arrival in London. As the coach "rattle[s] on through the noisy, bustling, crowded streets," Nicholas and Smike are confronted with a paratactic succession of objects and people that represent the city's multiplicity.

Streams of people apparently without end poured on and on, jostling each other in the crowd and hurrying forward, scarcely seeming to notice the riches that surrounded them on every side; while vehicles of all shapes and makes, mingled up together in one moving mass like running water, lent their ceaseless roar to swell the noise and tumult.

As they dashed by the quickly-changing and ever-varying objects, it was curious to observe in what a strange procession they passed before the eye. Emporiums of splendid dresses, the materials brought from every quarter of the world; tempting stores of everything to stimulate and pamper the sated appetite and give new relish to the oft-repeated feast; vessels of burnished gold and silver, wrought into every exquisite form of vase, and dish, and goblet; guns, swords, pistols, and patent engines of destruction; screws and irons for the crooked, clothes for the newly-born; drugs for the sick, coffins for the dead, churchyards for the buried—all these jumbled each with the other and flocking side by side, seemed to flit by in motley dance like the fantastic groups of the old Dutch painter, and with the same stern moral for the unheeding restless crowd.

Nor were there wanting objects in the crowd itself to give new point and purpose to the shifting scene. The rags of the squalid beggar-singer fluttered in the rich light that showed the goldsmith's treasures; pale and pinched-up faces hovered about the windows where was tempting food; hungry eyes wandered over the profusion

3. By examining Dickens' use of the term, Sylvia Manning has shown how his conception of satire stresses the ironic implications of incongruous juxtapositions. See *Dickens as Satirist* (New Haven: Yale University Press, 1971), pp. 5–6, 232–33. Alexander Welsh also discusses the importance of satiric conventions in Dickens' presentation of the city. See *The City of Dickens* (Oxford: Clarendon Press, 1971), pp. 3–15.

guarded by one thin sheet of brittle glass—an iron wall to them; half-naked shivering figures stopped to gaze at Chinese shawls and golden stuffs of India. There was a christening party at the largest coffin-maker's, and a funeral hatchment had stopped some great improvements in the bravest mansion. Life and death went hand and hand; wealth and poverty stood side by side; repletion and starvation laid them down together. [32]

From generalized indications of diversity, the passage progresses through extended catalogues to a series of ironic juxtapositions that resolve into the abstract oppositions of the conclusion. It replaces the confused experience of the characters with a more detached, controlled, and penetrating vision, moving through the traditional conventions of the dance of death to the final formal antitheses, which encompass the whole range of human life yet also eliminate all vital movement and particularity. Beyond displaying this tension between the possibilities of incoherent diversity and schematic patterns, the passage performs a transformation of linear succession into simultaneous adjacency which corresponds to a movement from surface to underlying meaning. These factors are involved in all of Dickens' fiction: the rapid panorama provided by the moving coach is a concentrated, accelerated version of the picaresque, the adventures of the protagonist whose wandering movement organizes the main developmental structure of most of the early novels (a movement which the later novels also internalize in the protagonist's psychological development); the simultaneous perception of opposites set "side by side" represents the attempt both to comprehend the city's multiplicity and to reveal its hidden coherence through a perspective that will be fully realized only by moving from single- to multiple-focus narrative.

The move toward multiple narrative is more systematic in the later novels, but it also occurs earlier whenever the focus shifts from one line to another, and those moments are often marked by self-conscious reflections on the conventions which permit them. Thus the narrator of *Barnaby Rudge* asserts that "Chroniclers are privileged to enter where they list, to come and go through keyholes, to ride upon the wind, to overcome, in their soarings up and down, all obstacles of distance, time, and place" (9). Such comments celebrate the power conferred by narrative omniscience, but they also betray uneasiness in the need to justify discontinuities—and to mask them with brief distractions in front of the curtain during scene changes.[4] This theatrical metaphor is the basis for Dickens' most elaborate reflection of the validity and significance of narrative shifts and contrasts, the well-known passage that begins chapter 17 of *Oliver Twist.*

> It is the custom on the stage, in all good murderous melodramas, to present the tragic and the comic scenes, in as regular alternation, as the layers of red and white in a side of streaky bacon. The hero sinks upon his straw bed, weighed down by fetters and misfortunes; in the next scene, his faithful but unconscious squire regales the audience with a comic song. We behold, with throbbing bosoms, the heroine in the grasp of a proud and ruthless baron; her virtue and her life alike in danger, drawing forth her dagger to preserve the one at the cost of the other; and just as our expectations are wrought up to the highest pitch, a whistle is heard, and we are straightway transported to the great hall of the castle: where a grey-headed seneschal sings a funny chorus with a funnier body of vassals, who are free of all sorts of places, from church vaults to palaces, and roam about in company, carolling perpetually.
>
> Such changes appear absurd; but they are not so unnatural as they would seem at first sight. The transitions in real life from well-spread boards to death-beds, and from mourning weeds to holiday garments, are not a whit less startling; only, there, we are busy actors, instead of passive lookers-on, which makes a vast difference. The actors in the mimic life of the theatre, are blind to violent transitions and abrupt impulses of passion or feeling, which, presented before the eyes of mere spectators, are at once condemned as outrageous and preposterous.

4. Similar comments sometimes emphasize the awkwardness of abrupt shifts and the incongruities they may produce, such as the ironic assertion in *Martin Chuzzlewit* that "from Mr. Moddle to Eden is an easy and natural transition" (33). Others deny the narrator's power and responsibility, for example, in *Nicholas Nickleby:* "The course which these adventures shape out for themselves, and imperatively call upon the historian to observe, now demands that they should revert to the point they attained previous to the commencement of the last chapter, when . . . " (56); cf. *The Old Curiosity Shop,* chap. 38. Serial publication increased the difficulty of coordinating separate plot lines because it required frequent alternation to keep all the important elements before the audience, and it is not surprising that Dickens' notes for each installment are mainly concerned with determining which characters and events will be included, which postponed. See John Butt and Kathleen Tillotson, *Dickens at Work* (London: Methuen, 1957), pp. 27–29.

These two paragraphs not only deal with extreme contrasts but themselves juxtapose contrasting and apparently incompatible conceptions of art. The first presents an affective account of the way popular art manipulates the audience's response, stressing the element of artifice and delightfully absurd unreality; the second shifts to mimetic terms and asserts a correspondence with "real life." This tension runs through Dickens' whole career. It appears most clearly in his defense of the realistic accuracy of his most extravagant creations, such as Krook's death by spontaneous combustion, one of several polemical skirmishes between "the poet and the critics of probability."[5] It is not just a theoretical conflict but a tension within Dickens' narratives between the centripetal force of formal patterns such as intensifying contrasts that develop according to their own inner logic and the effort to present them as models of reality; it occurs not just in isolated discursive passages but repeatedly in the representational significance assigned to the intricately contrived plot patterns of the later novels.

A more immediate concern is the question of perspective which this passage raises. It appears to urge identification with the perspective of the actor on the stage or in real life, "claiming that in both cases the only true view is the participant's: we must ourselves participate in order to feel the truth of the thing and not merely appraise it from outside."[6] But the passage cannot be reduced so easily to a monological reading. Just as Dickens asserts both the artificiality and the truth of art, so he shows the necessity of a double logic of perspective. Even though the detachment of the audience is liable to make these transitions seem "outrageous and preposterous," it also permits the perception of juxtapositions, of simultaneous suffering and joy to which the participants are "blind." Dickens stresses the claims of involvement and so disparages the passive stance of "mere spectators," yet as his work grows in ambition and complexity it increasingly requires a mobile, distanced, inclusive perspective.

5. See George H. Ford, *Dickens and His Readers* (Princeton: Princeton University Press, 1955), pp. 129–35.

6. John Bayley, "*Oliver Twist*: 'Things as They Really Are,' " in *Dickens and the Twentieth Century*, ed. John Gross and Gabriel Pearson (London: Routledge, 1962), p. 55.

The later novels attempt to present both the truth of individual experience and a comprehensive vision of the world that transcends the limits of individual points of view, perspectives which can inform the same text but can never coincide. Their necessity and incongruity are displayed most openly in the double narrative of *Bleak House*, which separates the restricted participant's view offered by Esther Summerson from the wide-ranging impersonal account of the authorial narrator. There are efforts from both sides to bridge the gap between them, in Esther's struggle to work out the larger meaning of her experience and in the narrator's rhetorical efforts to involve the reader through his use of the present tense, questions, and direct appeals, but the disparity between the two visions persists.

Bleak House presents an instance of dialogical form precisely as Bakhtin describes it, an unresolved opposition between "independent and unmerged voices and consciousnesses," but even where it is not articulated so explicitly, the tension between individual and general perspectives, between, in Muir's terms, the vision of life "in time, personally, and in space, socially," persists in all the major multiplot novels. We shall return to the question of the participant's experience in considering Dickens' developmental structures, but first I want to examine some less direct manifestations of dialogical tension in the ambivalence associated with his more distanced and inclusive perspectives.

The transformation from linear succession to simultaneous adjacency we have observed in the passages from *Nicholas Nickleby* and *Oliver Twist* involves only immediate juxtapositions and contrasts; the later multiplot novels display this shift of perspective on a larger scale. Multiple narratives, considered as completed forms, usually imply an effort to comprehend the fictional world as a pattern of coexisting people, places, and events. The component plots follow their own lines of development and must be considered sequentially, but the coordination of several lines, and the causal intersections or thematic parallels between them, can also lead to a sense of the whole as a complex spatial pattern. This aspect of multiple narrative becomes especially important in Dickens. As he composed his later novels, he came to think of himself as the creator of spatial designs, and he urged his serial readers to consider the completed novels in this way. The preface to *Little Dorrit* begins by stressing the need to view it as a whole: "as it is not unreasonable to suppose that I may have held its threads with a more continuous attention than anyone else can have given them during its desultory publication, it is not unreasonable to ask that the weaving may be looked at in its completed state, and with the pattern finished." The post-script to *Our Mutual Friend* repeats the image of a tapestry: Dickens hopes the novel's readers will, now that "they have it before them complete, perceive the relations of its finer threads to the whole pattern which is always before the eyes of the story-weaver at his loom." Such directions for reading are not, of course, confined to Dickens' prefaces and postscripts. They also appear within the novels in repeated signals, such as the images of travelers on converging roads in *Little Dorrit*, which anticipate the completion of a spatial pattern.[7]

The composition produced by "the story-weaver at his loom" is not simply an aesthetic pattern; it is a form of knowledge. It results from an attempt to discover a hidden pattern that both unifies the novel's form and expresses its significance, that permits an understanding of the fictional world denied to any of its inhabitants. The effort to achieve such comprehension is not only reflected in the structure of interwoven plots, it is also dramatized in passages which attempt to concentrate the significance of the total pattern in moments of synoptic vision. The most elaborate of these is the well-known passage in chapter 47 of *Dombey and Son* where Dickens urges his readers to recognize the contiguity of their own comfortable world with the hidden world of poverty, "lying within the echoes of our carriage wheels and daily tread upon the pavement stones. Look round upon the

7. Cf. the project Dickens described to Forster at the time he was writing the early parts of *Little Dorrit:* "It struck me that it would be a new thing to show people coming together, in a chance way, as fellow-travellers, and being in the same place, ignorant of one another, as happens in life; and to connect them afterwards, and make the waiting for that connection a part of the interest" (*Life of Dickens*, 2: 182). As this image clearly shows, the sense of a spatial pattern is always dependent on a structure of temporal development; the simultaneous coexistence either of locations and events in the representational space of the fictional world or of analogous elements in the space of the text can be realized only by an effort of reconstruction. To stress the importance of that effort in Dickens' multiplot novels is not to regard them as static spatial forms but rather to identify one dynamic impulse in his dialogue of structural perspectives.

world of odious sights—millions of immortal creatures have no other world on earth—at the lightest mention of which humanity revolts, and dainty delicacy living in the next street, stops her ears, and lisps 'I don't believe it!' " Dickens goes beyond simple juxtaposition to stress the hidden causal connections between these worlds.

> Those who study the physical sciences, and bring them to bear upon the health of man, tell us that if the noxious particles that rise from vitiated air were palpable to the sight, we should see them lowering in a dense black cloud above such haunts, and rolling slowly on to corrupt the better portions of a town. But if the moral pestilence that rises with them, and in the eternal laws of outraged Nature is inseparable from them, could be made discernible too, how terrible the revelation!

To avert this retribution, the members of society must recognize the organic connections that bind them together; they must imagine their world as if seen from a magical, elevated perspective: "Oh for a good spirit who would take the house-tops off, with a more potent and benignant hand than the lame demon in the tale, and show a Christian people what dark shapes issue from amidst their homes, to swell the retinue of the Destroying Angel as he moves forth among them!"

The causal connections between apparently isolated worlds which this passage condenses into a synoptic image can also be unfolded in a narrative development. Curiously, although the plot of *Dombey and Son* forms several links between high and low, it does not display the sort of relationships envisioned here. It is rather in *Bleak House*, Dickens' next panoramic social novel, with its complexly interwoven plots and its literal and metaphorical use of disease, that this potential is realized. Its comprehensive spatial vision is imaged in the opening description of the pervasive fog which rapidly notes the coexistence of several widely separated places, presenting a comprehensive view that would be impossible for any of the inhabitants of this fog-bound world. The multiple plot does, however, employ several characters to help expose the pattern of hidden connections between people and places, and it is appropriate that at the novel's climax the most eminent of these detectives, Inspector Bucket, emulates the narrator's elevated vision as he begins the search for Lady

Dedlock: "he mounts a high tower in his mind, and looks out far and wide. Many solitary figures he perceives, creeping through the streets; many solitary figures out on heaths, and roads, and lying under haystacks. But the figure that he seeks is not among them." The narrator must take over to remedy his failure: "On the waste, where the brick-kilns are burning with a pale blue flare . . . there is a lonely figure with the sad world to itself, pelted by the snow and driven by the wind, and cast out, it would seem, from all companionship" (56).

The multiple narrative of *Bleak House* unfolds in time the pattern of interconnections which the moments of synoptic vision present simultaneously. Considered as models of social interconnection, these patterns fulfill the didactic intention stated in *Dombey and Son,* to "show a Christian people what dark shapes issue from amidst their houses," to enlarge their moral vision and so lead them to "apply themselves, like creatures of one common origin, owing one Duty to the Father of one family, and tending to one common end, to make the world a better place." And yet, for all the elevating purpose of this elevated vision, it seems to involve ambiguities like those found earlier in the "mere spectators' " detachment in *Oliver Twist.*

"Oh for a good spirit who would take the house-tops off, with a more potent and benignant hand than the lame demon in the tale." The demon's name is Asmodeus, and the tale is Le Sage's *Le Diable boiteux.* Don Cleofas Zambullo, who releases Asmodeus from a spell and so earns his grateful services, may well have been among the "glorious host" of eighteenth-century heroes who attended Dickens in childhood.[8] Whenever he first read it, Le Sage's satiric fantasy clearly made a strong impression, and the power of Asmodeus to fly through space and reveal the secrets of the city became associated with the privileges of narrative omniscience. Thus, in shifting scenes in *The Old Curiosity Shop,* "the historian takes the friendly reader by the hand, and springing with him into the air, and cleaving the same at a greater

8. Cf. *David Copperfield:* "Roderick Random, Peregrine Pickle, Humphrey Clinker, Tom Jones, the Vicar of Wakefield, Don Quixote, Gil Blas, and Robinson Crusoe, came out, a glorious host, to keep me company. They kept alive my fancy, and my hopes of something beyond that place and time,—they and the *Arabian Nights,* and the *Tales of the Genii*" (4). Forster (1: 11) indicates that this passage is autobiographical and adds other eighteenth-century works to the list.

rate than ever Don Cleophas Leandro Perez Zambullo and his familiar travelled through that pleasant region in company, alights with him upon the pavement of Bevis Marks" (33). And as late as *Bleak House,* another of Asmodeus' traits is involved in the efforts to follow Lady Dedlock's movements made by "the fashionable intelligence—which, like the fiend, is omniscient of the past and present, but not the future" (2), a restriction that also seems to characterize the present-tense authorial narrator.

In *Le Diable boiteux* Asmodeus entertains and instructs his master by taking him to the highest point in Madrid and then rendering all the city's roofs transparent, allowing Le Sage to present a series of satiric vignettes that expose human vices and follies. Dickens dreams of exercising Asmodeus' power, but he wants to eliminate its element of aggressive malice, an association which becomes clear in his account of scurrilous journalism in *American Notes,* "dealing in round abuse and blackguard names; pulling off the roofs of private houses, as the Halting Devil did in Spain; pimping and pandering [Asmodeus' province is the union of illicit lovers] for all degrees of vicious taste, and gorging with coined lies the most voracious maw" (6).[9] Dickens wants to create a white magic equivalent for this demonic omniscience and to extend its range, so he invokes "a good spirit . . . with a more potent and benignant hand."

But the notion of white magic is always somewhat suspect: it is hard to dissociate it completely from its dark counterpart. In the passage from *Dombey and Son,* where organic connections replace Le Sage's isolated vignettes, the tone is one of fervent benevolence, yet there is also a hint of satisfaction in the spectacle of "tremendous social retributions" which confirm the narrator's vision of relationship and from which his elevated point of view protects him. And despite the claim made through this persona that he only observes the action of impersonal physical and moral

9. A positive version of this power in journalistic form appears in Dickens' original conception for the magazine that became *Household Words.* It was to employ the convention of "a certian Shadow, which may go into any place . . . and be supposed to be cognizant of everything, and go everywhere, without the least difficulty," in order to expose abuses and incite reform. "I want him to loom as a fanciful thing all over London," he wrote to Forster, "a sort of previously unthought-of power going about." Forster comments that "hardly anything more characteristic survives him" than this idea (2: 63–64).

laws, the author is always implicated in the plot he has constructed: he assumes the power of the Destroying Angel as well as
that of the good spirit. These ambiguities in the elevated, synoptic
vision may be taken in part as reflections of a problem we shall
encounter again in the providential meaning that Dickens sometimes attributes to his complex plots: the anxiety of authorial
responsibility. But whether or not this inference is admitted,
there can be no doubt that Dickens repeatedly associates narrative elevation with danger and destructive violence.

Early examples abound in *Barnaby Rudge,* the first novel in
which Dickens consistently employs the historian's superior,
panoramic vision, the power of chroniclers "to overcome, in their
soarings up and down, all obstacles of distance, time, and place"
(9). One repeated motif is that of a superior vision brooding over
nighttime scenes of crime and violence. The extended panorama
of the darkened London streets that begins chapter 16 modulates
into reflections on the pervasive threat of criminal attack they
harbor and then focuses on the sinister figure (later identified as
the elder Rudge) who wanders through these scenes in guilty
solitude, "looking . . . over his shoulder from time to time, and as
he did so quickening his pace," sensing, correctly, that he is
observed. Earlier, when Barnaby and Gabriel Varden discover
Ned Chester lying robbed and wounded in the dark street,
Barnaby notes the watching stars: "Whose eyes are they? If they
are angels' eyes, why do they look down here and see good men
hurt, and only wink and sparkle all the night?" (3). And near the
end, the construction during the night of the scaffold on which
Hugh and Dennis are to be hanged is presided over first by Time,
"that Great Watcher with the hoary head, who never sleeps or
rests"; then by a figure stationed atop the prison ("ever and anon
a solitary watchman could be seen upon its roof, stopping to look
down upon the preparations in the street. This man, from
forming, as it were, a part of the jail, and knowing or being
supposed to know all that was passing within, became an object
of as much interest, and was as eagerly looked for, and as awfully
pointed out, as if he had been as spirit"); and finally by the
narrator himself: "All was brightness and promise, excepting in
the street below, into which (for it lay in shadow) the eye looked
down as into a dark trench, where, in the midst of so much life,

and hope, and renewal of existence, stood the terrible instrument of death" (77). Most important is the violence of the riots, which is often observed from roofs or high windows by different characters, such as Gashford (54), Akerman (64), or Haredale, who looks down from the roof of the vintner's house at the attacking mob: "It was but a glimpse, but it showed them the crowd, gathering and clustering round the house: some of the armed men pressing to the front to break down the doors and windows, some bringing brands from the nearest fire, some with lifted faces following their course upon the roof and pointing them out to their companions, all raging and roaring like the flames they lighted up" (67).

The moments of elevated vision in *Barnaby Rudge* are not charged with the didactic social purpose of the later novels. Here the need for shifting narrative focus to present simultaneous events in separate places arises more directly from the historical subject: "events so crowd upon each other in convulsed and distracted times" (61).[10] Yet it is also significant that the moments which epitomize this need for a distanced, inclusive point of view present scenes of threatening yet fascinating violence: the need for distance is psychological as well as epistemological. The intensity with which the riots are presented implies an element of identification with their anarchic energy, but both Dickens' rhetoric and his elevated perspectives work to establish distance. This ambivalence, like the moral ambiguity that surrounds Asmodeus as a model of narrative privilege, appears again at several moments in later novels which associate synoptic vision with menace or violence.

10. Dickens' method as "chronicler" may reflect the influence of Carlyle's *The French Revolution* in its efforts to deal with the problem of the narrative historian which Carlyle formulated: "Narrative is *linear,* Action is *solid.*" Carlyle also invokes Le Sage in Book 6, chapter 6, "The Steeples at Midnight," which presents an elevated nighttime view of Paris on the eve of insurrection: "Could the Reader take an Asmodeus' Flight, and waving open all roofs and privacies, look down from the Tower of Notre-Dame, what a Paris were it!" On Carlyle's use of synoptic perspectives—and his awareness of the falsification they might produce—see H.M. Leicester, "The Dialectic of Romantic Historiography: Prospect and Retrospect in *The French Revolution,*" *Victorian Studies* 15 (1971): 5–17. On other narrative conventions shared by Carlyle and Dickens, see Jonathan Arac, "Narrative Forms and Social Sense in *Bleak House* and *The French Revolution,*" *Nineteenth-Century Fiction* 32 (1977): 54–72.

In *Dombey and Son*, the passage which most fully anticipates the elevated vision of chapter 47 comes at the end of the railroad journey, where rapid linear movement is again replaced by static contemplation.

> Everything around is blackened. There are dark pools of water, muddy lanes, and miserable habitations far below. There are jagged walls and falling houses close at hand, and through the battered roofs and broken windows, wretched rooms are seen, where want and fever hide themselves in many wretched shapes, while smoke and crowded gables, and distorted chimneys, and deformity of brick and mortar penning up deformity of mind and body, choke the murky distance. As Mr. Dombey looks out of his carriage window, it is never in his thoughts that the monster who has brought him there has let the light of day in on these things: not made or caused them. It was the journey's fitting end, and might have been the end of everything; it was so ruinous and dreary. [20]

Here the question of point of view is more difficult. In the later passage, Dombey represents the self-enclosed individual who is blind to the reality of his world; here he participates in the penetrating downward vision "through the battered roofs and broken windows" but apparently misses its significance. The agent of perception is the locomotive, "the monster who has brought him there," not a "good spirit" but, as the preceding paragraphs repeatedly insist, "a type of the triumphant monster, Death," yet this identification may be only a projection of Dombey's desolate mood after the death of his son. These implications cannot be clearly sorted out; the moment which represents the discovery of a hidden reality remains entangled in suggestions of error, of moral failure or subjective distortion. The element of danger is similarly ambiguous. The divided world of the two nations contains, like the riots of *Barnaby Rudge*, the threat of destructive violence, so that the sinister associations might seem to arise from what is being observed, but here the actual violence is produced by the agent, not the object of vision. ("Louder and louder yet, it shrieks and cries as it comes tearing on resistless to the goal.") Whether this is a transference or disclosure of attributes, it strengthens the association of danger with the exercise of narrative omniscience, again reflected in the denial of responsibility: "the monster . . . has let the light of day in on these things: not made or caused them."

In *Bleak House*, where much more of this work of discovery is delegated to the characters, the most sinister agent of such perceptions is the lawyer Tulkinghorn, collector and "silent depository" of secrets (2). "Dwelling among mankind but not consorting with them" (42), he maintains a distance even from the aristocratic families he serves. As he relentlessly pursues the secret of Lady Dedlock's past, he also helps to expose the novel's hidden pattern of relationships, but in Tulkinghorn this activity is separated from any altruistic social purpose. As Lady Dedlock observes, he has no "pity or compunction . . . and no anger. He is indifferent to everything but his calling. His calling is the acquisition of secrets, and the holding possession of such power as they give him, with no sharer or opponent in it" (36). As much a detective as Inspector Bucket, Tulkinghorn mounts not a metaphorical tower in his mind, but the literal tower of Chesney Wold, where his room is appropriately located, and it is there that Lady Dedlock must come to hear his terms after he has learned her secret. As she stands at the open window, Tulkinghorn has "an instant's misgiving that she may have it in her thoughts to leap over, and dashing against ledge and cornice, strike her life out upon the terrace below" (41). In the end, this is what she will do, casting herself down from her social elevation ("at the top of the fashionable tree" [2]) to the very bottom, the foul pauper's graveyard where she dies. But before that fall comes Tulkinghorn's own. Dickens leads up to the moment of his murder with a passage which, like the novel's opening perspective or the view from Bucket's mental tower, expands the narrative focus in a wide panorama:

> A very quiet night. When the moon shines very brilliantly, a solitude and stillness seem to proceed from her, that influence even crowded places full of life. Not only is it a still night on dusty high roads and on hill-summits, whence a wide expanse of country may be seen in repose, quieter and quieter as it spreads away into a fringe of trees against the sky, with the grey ghost of a bloom upon them; not only is it a still night in gardens and in woods, and on the river where the water-meadows are fresh and green, and the stream sparkles on among pleasant islands, murmuring weirs, and whispering rushes; not only does the stillness attend it as it flows where

houses cluster thick, where many bridges are reflected in it, where
wharves and shipping make it black and awful, where it winds from
these disfigurements through marshes whose grim beacons stand
like skeletons washed ashore, where it expands through the bolder
region of rising grounds, rich in cornfield, wind-mill and steeple,
and where it mingles with the ever-heaving sea; not only is it a still
night on the deep, and on the shore where the watcher stands to see
the ship with her spread wings cross the path of light that appears
to be presented to only him; but even on this stranger's wilderness
of London there is some rest. Its steeples and towers, and its one
great dome, grow more ethereal; its smoky house-tops lose their
grossness, in the pale effulgence; the noises that arise from the
streets are fewer and are softened, and the footsteps on the
pavements pass more tranquilly away. In these fields of Mr.
Tulkinghorn's inhabiting, where the shepherds play on Chancery
pipes that have no stop, and keep their sheep in the fold by hook
and by crook until they have shorn them exceeding close, every
noise is merged, this moonlight night, into a distant ringing hum, as
if the city were a vast glass, vibrating.

What's that? Who fired a gun or pistol? Where was it? [48]

The sudden descent from the elevated perspective links it again
with violence. Here one might construe the association as an
implied repudiation of the inhuman detachment and presump-
tion of Tulkinghorn's mode of perception: his pride of elevated
knowledge, like Lady Dedlock's pride of elevated status, is
punished by a precipitous fall. His detective powers have failed to
perceive Hortense's potential for violence or to recognize the
warning of the painted figure looking down from his ceiling. The
physical violence he suffers is the counterpart of the moral
violence he has inflicted in his search for knowledge and power,
but his death does not exorcise the sense of knowledge as
violation.[11]

Dickens' fullest presentation of the dangers of elevated vision
appears in the description of the view from the roof of Todgers'
boarding house in *Martin Chuzzlewit*:

11. Another association of elevated vision with impending disaster comes in
Little Dorrit after Merdle's suicide. An extended panorama shows the news
spreading throughout London during the following day and the growing realization that Merdle's enterprises, in which so many are involved, have perished with
him, until "a solitary watcher on the gallery above the dome of St Paul's would
have perceived the night air to be laden with a heavy muttering of the name of
Merdle, coupled with every form of execration" (2: 25).

After the first glance, there were slight features in the midst of this crowd of objects, which sprung out from the mass without any reason, as it were, and took hold of the attention whether the spectator would or no. Thus, the revolving chimney-pots on one great stack of buildings seemed to be turning gravely to each other every now and then, and whispering the result of their separate observation of what was going on below. Others, of a crook-backed shape, appeared to be maliciously holding themselves askew, that they might shut the prospect out and baffle Todgers's. The man who was mending a pen at an upper window over the way, became of paramount importance in the scene, and made a blank in it, ridiculously disproportionate in its extent, when he retired. The gambols of a piece of cloth upon the dyer's pole had far more interest for the moment than all the changing motion of the crowd. Yet even while the looker-on felt angry with himself for this, and wondered how it was, the tumult swelled into a roar; the hosts of objects seemed to thicken and expand a hundredfold; and after gazing round him, quite scared, he turned into Todgers's again, much more rapidly than he came out; and ten to one he told M. Todgers afterwards that if he hadn't done so, he would certainly have come into the street by the shortest cut; that is to say, head-foremost.[9]

Dorothy Van Ghent has, in a well-known essay, taken this passage as a key to "the Dickens world," a demonic world created by the "transposition of attributes . . . between things and people."[12] J. Hillis Miller agrees that "this is a text of capital importance for the entire work of Dickens," yet he stresses not the world revealed here but the perspective of the perceiver: "Dickens here most explicitly expresses the dangerous end point to which his characters can be brought by the attitude of passive and detached observation."[13] Both interpretations are possible, and there seems to be no way to decide between them, or even to decide whether they are contradictory or complementary, since the relation between world and perceiver here is so uncertain.

The vertigo which threatens the hypothetical observer may only be the consequence of his attempt to gain a superior perspective; the passage might then be taken as a fantastic elaboration of the falsifying effects which *Oliver Twist* attributes to

12. "The Dickens World: A View from Todgers's," *The Sewanee Review* 58 (1950): 419–38.

13. *Charles Dickens: The World of his Novels* (Cambridge, Mass.: Harvard University Press, 1959), p. 116.

the "mere spectator's" detachment. But the danger also seems to arise from the scene to which this perspective exposes us, as if we had suddenly stumbled on a sinister secret hidden from "busy actors" involved in ordinary life. The preceding description of the approach to Todgers' stresses the bewildering, incomprehensible complexity of its neighborhood: "Todgers's was in a labyrinth, whereof the mystery was known but to a chosen few." The natural way to comprehend the pattern of a labyrinth is to view it from above, but here the elevated perspective reveals not a coherent pattern but chaos. It may be that the secret order remains hidden, perhaps obscured by forces which "maliciously" conspire to "baffle" the investigation, or it may be that the secret is precisely that there *is* no secret order. That interpretation is the possibility Dickens always most anxiously avoids, or allows us to glimpse only briefly and obliquely. Even a malicious order or an incomprehensible plenitude is preferable to a void, and this may be why the "blank" produced by the disappearance of the man at the window assumes "ridiculously disproportionate" importance. It hints at the absence of any intrinsic meaning, an underlying blankness so intolerable that it is immediately covered up by the proliferating "host of objects" as the world is reappropriated by humanizing language.

This is one extreme to which Dickens develops the association of elevation and danger; the opposite extreme involves a movement toward escape or transcendence. An early example occurs in *The Old Curiosity Shop*, when Nell's flight from the city is nearing its goal of final escape in the funereal village. After a period of tranquilizing meditation on death among the tombs of the old church ("It would be no pain to sleep amidst them"), she climbs the dark, winding stair of the church tower. "At length she gained the end of the ascent and stood upon the turret top. / Oh! the glory of the sudden burst of light; the freshness of the fields and woods, stretching away on every side, and meeting the bright blue sky. . . . It was like passing from death to life; it was drawing nearer Heaven" (53). Here all danger has been left behind; the panoramic view itself contains no threat ("all, everything so beautiful and happy!"), but the idyllic world it reveals is not accessible as actual living experience; it serves only to offer a promise of salvation.

A far more complex version of this elevated transcendence appears in *Our Mutual Friend*, in Jenny Wren's imaginative transfiguration of Riah's shabby house-top. "We are thankful to come here for rest," she tells the incredulous Fledgeby.

> "It's the quiet, and the air. . . . it's so high. And you see the clouds rushing on above the narrow streets, not minding them, and you see the golden arrows pointing at the mountains in the sky from which the wind comes, and you feel as if you were dead."
>
> The little creature looked above her, holding up her slight transparent hand.
>
> "How do you feel when you are dead?" asked Fledgeby, much perplexed.
>
> "Oh, so tranquil!" cried the little creature, smiling. "Oh, so peaceful and so thankful! And you hear the people who are alive, crying, and working, and calling to one another down in the close dark streets, and you seem to pity them so! And such a chain has fallen from you, and such a strange good sorrowful happiness comes upon you!"

She dismisses Fledgeby: "Get down to life!" and summons Riah to return: "Come back and be dead!"

> As he mounted, the call or song began to sound in his ears again, and, looking above, he saw the face of the little creature looking down out of a Glory of her long bright radiant hair, and musically repeating to him, like a vision: "Come up and be dead! Come up and be dead!" [II, 5]

Again the stress is on escape; vision is no longer directed downward, but unlike the more conventional ascent "from death to life" in *The Old Curiosity Shop*, this scene suggests the possibility of a transcendence which is still connected to the novel's lower world of bondage, a liberating imaginative distance which offers not superior impersonal knowledge but individual spiritual renewal. The ascent to Riah's rooftop mirrors the perilous descent to the depths of the river in which other characters also achieve renewal.

In these examples elevation no longer serves as a means or metaphor for synoptic comprehension, for a spatialized narrative omniscience which attempts to create a collective social consciousness. Instead, the figure is taken up by the other side of Dickens' structural dialogue, the perspective of the isolated individual. This is particularly clear in *Our Mutual Friend*, where, as we shall see, multiple narrative is no longer directed so intently toward the discovery of a hidden pattern and there is more emphasis on the perceptions and developments of the characters. In this case, as in the others we have examined, the significance of elevated vision is partly determined by narrative context, but these passages also reveal a complex of associations which persists throughout Dickens' career. (The association of synoptic vision and danger is still present, in a powerful and concentrated form, in the opening of *Edwin Drood* with which we began.)

It is easier to demonstrate the presence of this complex than to interpret it; to pursue some of its implications would lead us away from questions of structure into a general study of Dickens' narrative imagination. But the examples we have already considered enable us to recognize some of the tensions that inform his multiple narratives. The elevated perspective, the view from the tower of the mind which reveals and represents the inclusive order unfolded in multiple narrative is associated with both power and fear; the effort to disclose a hidden reality is linked to the threat of violence either suffered or inflicted by the agent of knowledge. These ambiguities express the underlying dialogical tension between individual and general perspectives. The unifying pattern of relationships between characters and worlds can offer a positive vision of social interdependence, but from the perspective of the individual it may instead be experienced as a violation of moral autonomy; the simultaneous spatial vision may falsify the temporality of individual development. When we turn to the developmental structures of Dickens' multiplot novels, we shall find a fuller articulation of these oppositions. Beyond the overt movement from appearance to reality, from disordered surface to underlying pattern, they will lead us to further complications and reversals.

Before taking up those complex movements, however, we should consider another aspect of perspective. Synoptic views spatialize narrative through the metonymic relationships of immediate contiguity or revealed causal connections, but a similar perspective, addressed to textual rather than representational space, arises from metaphorical relationships. In all the major novels of Dickens' maturity the unfolding development presents the formation and detection of an elaborate network of plot connections, but at the same time, another network emerges through the formulation of analogies, which can also become objects of detection. In *Bleak House*, for example, after Esther's first encounter with Mr. Turveydrop, she says, "I began to inquire in my mind whether there were, or ever had been, any other gentlemen, not in the dancing profession, who lived and founded a reputation entirely on their Deportment. This became so bewildering, and suggested the possibility, of so many Mr. Turveydrops, that I said, 'Esther, you must make up your mind to abandon this subject altogether'" (14). These reflections provide directions for reading that function like the authorial narrator's anticipation of plot connections a few pages later:

> What connexion can there be, between the place in Lincolnshire, the house in town, the Mercury in powder, and the whereabout of Jo the outlaw with the broom, who had that distant ray of light upon him when he swept the churchyard-step? What connexion can there have been between many people in the innumerable histories of this world, who, from opposite sides of great gulfs, have, nevertheless, been very curiously brought together! [16]

With his broader range of available references, the reader can take up the subject which Esther abandons; Mr. Turveydrop, with his aristocratic pretensions and adherence to the past ("We have degenerated. . . . A levelling age is not favourable to Deportment") becomes an analogue for Sir Leicester Dedlock and his circle. The two characters have no connection on the level of plot, yet here they are brought together from opposite sides of a great gulf to confront each other as analogous social fossils and parasites.[14] *Bleak House* contains a large number of such analogies, many left for the reader to detect, some formulated explicitly by the narrator or the characters themselves, such as the equation between the Lord Chancellor and Krook: "There's no great odds betwixt us," Krook explains. "We both grub on in a muddle" (5). As they multiply, these metaphorical identifications constitute a system of relationships which, though revealed through the narrative sequence, are essentially spatial, simultaneous and reversible.

14. Dickens prepares for this recognition by satirizing the Dedlock values as forms of "Dandyism" in chapter 12.

The importance of analogy in Dickens' fiction has often been recognized, and he himself seems to have considered it one of his strongest traits: "I think it is my infirmity to fancy or perceive relations in things which are not apparent generally."[15] Like the detection of plot connections, such perceptions disclose a hidden meaning, one that may be as tightly focused as the reductive satiric equations of *Bleak House*, or more open and suggestive, as in the same novel's metaphor of infection. My particular concern here is with the way analogies can function as an alternative to causal connections within and between narrative lines. As the parallel between Mr. Turveydrop and Sir Leicester indicates, such connections can replace direct dramatic relations between characters and worlds. Theoretically, the substitution could become virtually complete, producing a narrative sequence of episodes related only by implied similarities and contrasts. And indeed, when critics concentrate on the thematic organization of Dickens' novels and consider the narrative sequence of *Little Dorrit*, for example, as a serial display of analogous forms of imprisonment, they implicitly assume that analogy has become the dominant principle.[16]

Of course, Dickens' major multiplot novels develop extensive causal as well as thematic connections, and it may not seem necessary or even possible to choose between them; but even when the two principles are working quite closely together, they never coincide. As Jakobson observes, "A competition between both devices, metonymic and metaphoric, is manifest in any symbolic process," and that competition sets up a resistance to readings which attempt to integrate both types of connection.[17]

15. Forster, *Life of Dickens,* 2: 273. Cf. Wordsworth on the "observation of affinities / In objects where no brotherhood exists / To passive minds" (*The Prelude,* 1850, 2: 384–86). Such metaphorical connections offer one way of revealing what Dickens calls, in the preface to *Bleak House,* "the romantic side of familiar things."

16. The spatializing effect of such reading appears quite clearly in John Wain's essay on *Little Dorrit,* which considers the novel to be "built up on two metaphors, the prison and the family," and so finds that "its development is by means of outward radiation rather than linear progression. . . . It is an intricate labyrinth, designed so that the reader, on whatever path he sets out, will always be brought back to the point where one or other of the two principal metaphors is confronting him." *Dickens and the Twentieth Century,* p. 175.

17. "Two Aspects of Language and Two Types of Aphasic Disturbances," in Roman Jakobson and Morris Halle, *Fundamentals of Language* (The Hague: Mouton, 1956), p. 80.

An instance in which both types are quite clearly involved is the first shift of focus in *Bleak House*. As the narrator conducts us from Chancery to the world of fashion, he stresses the parallel between them: "Both the world of fashion and the Court of Chancery are things of precedent and usage" (2). At the same time, a plot link is formed by Lady Dedlock's involvement in Jarndyce and Jarndyce, which has brought Tulkinghorn from one world to the other. But the two types of connection cannot carry equal value. If we focus on thematic implications, the analogy, which marks the affinities between the established political system represented by the Dedlocks and the legal system of Chancery, will seem far more important, since it implements the novel's fundamental social criticism. Establishing another connection by making Lady Dedlock a minor party to Jarndyce and Jarndyce will seem irrelevant or redundant, especially since little is made of her involvement afterwards. But if we focus on the causal chain of the mystery plot, that small link will become crucial, since Lady Dedlock's recognition of Hawdon's handwriting on the document Tulkinghorn brings her sets the lawyer off in pursuit of her secret. Even when both types of connection are present, they are inversely related to each other.

That relation is more apparent when one principle is clearly predominant. Dickens' early uses of multiple narrative, which depend less on causal interconnections, are experiments in analogy. In *The Old Curiosity Shop*, after Nell and her grandfather leave London, the action is always divided between their adventures and simultaneous events in London, which are in turn subdivided several times. Narrative alternations between the separated actions not only produce the general effect of intensifying contrast but at times yield sustained sequences of parallel and counterpoint. After Quilp moves into his "bachelor's" den on the wharf, for instance (50–51), we see Nell moving into her equally idiosyncratic new quarters, the ancient little house by the churchyard (52). The two episodes are strongly contrasted in mood, yet each figure is, by his or her change of residence, moving a step closer toward death. Only Nell grasps this significance: to her the house is "a place to live and learn to die in," while sudden death (whose contrivance depends on maneuvering Quilp to the wharf) will take the dwarf unprepared.

Transposition of a theme from one plot line and mode to another can produce rather surprising effects. Chapter 55 ends with Nell being taken by the sexton down into the crypt to gaze into the well which "looks like a grave itself"; it is the last time we see her alive. This scene is immediately followed by a shift to Dick Swiveller, who is discovered decorating his hat with black crepe. "Having completed the construction of this appendage, he surveyed his work with great complacency, and put his hat on again —very much over one eye, to increase the mournfulness of the effect." This performance is inspired by his loss of Miss Wackles: "I never nursed a dear Gazelle, to glad me with its soft black eye, but when it came to know me well, and love me, it was sure to marry a market-gardener" (56). His theatrically comic mourning parodies the elegiac mood that surrounds Nell and announces a narrative movement toward new life.

The development of separated, analogous lines of action is carried much further in Dickens' next novel, *Barnaby Rudge*, in which the emerging pattern displays no less than four pairs of fathers and sons in various degrees of conflict or separation, to which the conflict of Sim Tappertit and his master Gabriel Varden adds a fifth analogue.[18] Again, narrative transitions juxtapose parallel events, such as the ruptures between both Joe Willet and Ned Chester and their fathers (30–31 and 32), the union of each with the girls they love (78 and 79), and the arrests of both the elder Rudge and Barnaby (56 and 57). The supervening historical action of the Gordon riots overtakes and involves all these characters, but the coherence of the novel depends much more on its analogies, in which the riots appear as the public equivalent of the private conflicts between fathers and sons or masters and servants. By relying so heavily on analogy, *Barnaby Rudge* tests and reveals its limits as a structural principle. Even after recognizing the novel's thematic continuity, one may well agree with Forster's complaint about "defects . . . in the management of the plot. The interest with which the tale begins, has ceased to be its interest before the close; and what has chiefly taken the reader's fancy at the outset, almost wholly disappears

---

18. Steven Marcus takes this pattern as the focus of his study of the novel in *Dickens from Pickwick to Dombey* (New York: Basic Books, 1965), pp. 184–204.

in the power and passion with which, in the later chapters, the great riots are described."[19] By comparison with Dickens' later multiplot novels, one can see what is missing here. The metaphorical extension of the family (an important theme and figurative vehicle in most of Dickens' fiction) may provide a thematic focus, but there is no corresponding narrative focus, no protagonist whose development can articulate this significance in terms of personal experience. Instead of presenting a dialogue between perspectives or principles, the novel slackens dialogical tension by dispersing the individual and the linear into the general and adjacent order of analogy.

In *Martin Chuzzlewit* Dickens attempts for the first time to combine the patterns of single- and multiple-focus narrative in a manner like that of the later novels. Again, there is an inclusive analogical scheme in the proposed anatomy of selfishness which Dickens describes in his preface: "I set out . . . with the design of exhibiting, in various aspects, the commonest of all the vices." At the same time, the theme is given a developmental focus in the story of Martin's conversion from selfishness. Unfortunately, Dickens' execution of this design is the least successful aspect of the novel. Martin's transformation remains only a sketchy, schematic outline, while the comic energy released by Pecksniff and Mrs. Gamp, or the melodramatic intensity produced by Jonas Chuzzlewit's story, dissolves the tenuous conceptual links between them and the other characters; they are more significant individually than as illustrations of a general theme.[20] Neither the pattern of multiple focal points related by analogy nor that of a single focus of continuing development is effectively realized in *Martin Chuzzlewit*; the structural dialogue between them remains only a latent possibility.

These earlier experiments can help us to appreciate the achievement of Dickens' later multiplot novels, where structural analogies are highly developed. In *Bleak House, Little Dorrit,* and

19. *Life of Dickens,* 1: 144.

20. H.M. Daleski argues that *Martin Chuzzlewit* fails to achieve thematic unity because of "a false analogy in the novel between self-seeking and self-centred-ness." *Dickens and the Art of Analogy* (London: Faber & Faber, 1970), p. 107. Barbara Hardy presents a broader argument against interpretations which claim formal or thematic coherence for the novel, in *Dickens and the Twentieth Century,* pp. 107–20.

Our Mutual Friend they become not only a means of connection but of expansion; the multiplication of figures and situations related by similarities or contrasts does not simply produce repetitive illustrations of a general theme but large and variegated clusters, groupings linked by family resemblance rather than a single common denominator. Recognizing such interconnections can enable us to consider each moment in the narrative as the intersection of analogies radiating outward in several different directions. To return to our initial example of Mr. Turveydrop, we can recognize not only the clearly prepared resemblances to Sir Leicester but several others as well. As Martin Price observes, "Old Turveydrop appears as a selfish parent like Mrs. Jellyby, a preserver of dead forms like Sir Leicester Dedlock, an infantile egocentric, like Harold Skimpole. These characters gain their full meaning from the structure of which they are a part; no single character exists without his counterpart or contrast, and none fails to participate at some level in one of those unifying themes that are stated and restated in various keys—comic, pathetic, satiric—throughout a work."[21]

From the perspective of the detached observer, these emerging relationships offer an experience of increasing comprehension like that produced by the recognition of plot connections, a satisfying sense of combined unity and diversity, of a complex coherence. But the perspective of the participant reveals a very different aspect, in which the multiplication of analogies is experienced not as an increase but as a loss of understanding, a disruption of coherence. Thus for Esther the thought of "so many Mr. Turveydrops" becomes "so bewildering" that it must be repressed, and the disturbing force of such recognitions later increases to nightmarish intensity in the experience of Jo when, having already encountered both Lady Dedlock and her double Hortense, he meets Esther, who also resembles her mother. "Is there *three* of 'em then?" he asks in a feverish daze (31). A similar but more extended experience of disorientation is presented in *Little Dorrit* when the Dorrits are translated from poverty to riches and attempt to suppress their past. To Amy the scenes of their Continental tour seem "unreal. . . . all a dream—only the old

21. Introduction to *Dickens: A Collection of Critical Essays* (Englewood Cliffs, N.J.: Prentice-Hall, 1967), p. 3.

mean Marshalsea a reality" (II, 3), and she comes to see the society in which they now live as "a superior sort of Marshalsea" (II, 7), an analogy that she works out in extended parallels.

These are all moments of transgression, in which the perspectives of observer and participant converge and subvert each other. We can, of course, regard them simply as instances of authorial manipulation: Dickens uses Esther to direct us to find counterparts of Turveydrop, just as he uses Little Dorrit to explicate the analogy between the Marshalsea and Society, while he uses Jo to reinforce an important link in the mystery plot. (The ability to see the resemblance between Esther and Lady Dedlock is apparently a rather special talent: Jo recognizes it immediately, while Jarndyce and Ada can see the two together without perceiving it [18].) But to consider these moments only as convenient thematic or plot contrivances does not account for the mood of dream or nightmare, the disturbing loss of meaning which the characters experience. For them analogy is a form of disruptive repetition, subverting the sense of individual identity and developmental continuity. As in the threatening aspect of synoptic vision, the individual perspective poses a counterinterpretation to the unifying claims of the general, inclusive pattern. The intersecting and overlapping analogies which increase coherence from one perspective disperse it from the other, and the moments when the two converge most clearly reveal their incommensurability.

Each of these structural perspectives has its corresponding principle of narrative development, and both are at work in the major multiplot novels. As their developmental structures disclose a pattern of causal connections or follow the multiplying analogical cross-references, they work to unfold predominantly spatial systems that reach out to include every element in their expanding networks. Yet the same novels which attempt to achieve this simultaneous comprehension of their worlds are also deeply concerned with the problems and possibilities of individual development dramatized in the careers of their protagonists. Presented less vividly than those who surround them, uncertain in their own sense of themselves, these characters never securely occupy the organizing center of the composition; they are all subject to the question which David Copperfield formulates in his first words: "Whether I shall turn out to be the hero of my own life." But as protagonists such as Esther Summerson or Arthur Clennam struggle to make their way between an unhappy past and a doubtful future, their experience of life "in time, personally," offers a resistance and an alternative to the vision of life "in space, socially."

The narrative movement of Dickens' multiplot novels is therefore neither the elaboration of a spatial pattern nor the development of an individual but contains both and is energized by the tension between them. At some points, the protagonist's career gains prominence and claims the structural function of a main plot to which others are subordinated as causal tributaries or parallels and contrasts; at others, it recedes and appears as only one among several focal points, its faltering momentum dispersed into adjacent, analogous actions or assimilated into a larger system of causes and effects. Each novel presents a different version of this dialogue of shifting perspectives, but the dialogue itself continues from novel to novel and never reaches a stable resolution.

⇌ TWO ⇌

Dickens: Machinery in Motion

The double logic in Dickens' multiplot novels is worked out most fully through the pattern of the mystery plot, a form which enables him both to trace an elaborate system of interconnections and to present the story of a subdued protagonist within the same narrative. Mysteries and the process of solving them play a part in several of the earlier novels, and in *Bleak House* the pattern comes into the foreground and serves to articulate a sweeping social vision, bringing together many characters and narrative lines "from opposite sides of great gulfs." At the same time, from the perspective of characters caught in the focus of the mystery plot, it assumes the temporal form of a reconstructed development, reforging broken links between past and present, connections that may be eagerly sought or feared and avoided. The pattern reappears in different forms in all of Dickens' later novels from *Little Dorrit* to *The Mystery of Edwin Drood*, and its changing functions and significance mark important changes in his interpretation of both collective and individual existence. But while mystery plots serve different purposes at different points in Dickens' career, they always exert the strong imaginative appeal of a narrative movement directed toward the discovery of secrets, the revelation of a hidden coherence.

The secrets toward which mystery plots are directed have a double location, in the minds of others and in the past. Lady Dedlock's secret, for example, has a psychological dimension—the desolation, guilt, and fear hidden behind her cold, closed manner, "so long accustomed to suppress emotion, and keep down reality" (55)—but it also has an independent life, as her past affair with Hawdon produces continuing effects, clues leading to her exposure. The mysteries in Dickens' early novels stress the secret past rather than the secret inner reality. In *Oliver Twist*, the revelation of a secret past prior to the novel's action solves the mystery of Oliver's identity and provides the means of permanently rescuing him from the claims of both the workhouse and Fagin's criminal world. The confrontations between Mr. Brownlow and Monks in chapters 49 and 51 enact the typical dénouement of a mystery plot, presenting a crowded summary of events preceding the narrative and elucidating the villain's mysterious role. But although there has been some dramatized detection leading up to these revelations, they appear essentially as an inserted explanation, rationalizing Oliver's immunity from the evil influences to which he has been subjected. Dickens accomplishes the intention stated in his preface, "to show, in little Oliver, the principle of Good surviving through every adverse circumstance, and triumphing at last," but he does so by contrivances that amount to a deus ex machina. Oliver survives because he is, as we realize at the end, made in his father's virtuous image; he triumphs when others establish this fact, not through his own efforts. *Oliver Twist* illustrates the use of a mystery plot to provide an imposed resolution and its tendency to confine the protagonist to a passive role, problems that persist in Dickens' later novels.

If the mystery plot provides salvation in *Oliver Twist*, it works retribution in *Nicholas Nickleby* through the revelation, after Smike's death, that he was actually the son of his persecutor Ralph Nickleby, who was not aware of his identity. "I have been made the instrument," says Brooker (as indeed he has), "of working out this dreadful retribution upon the head of a man who, in the hot pursuit of his bad ends, has persecuted and hunted down his own child to death" (60). Here the discovery of secret connections completes the overthrow of the villain, precipitating Ralph into the fit of "frenzy, hatred, and despair" in which he goes home to hang himself "on an iron hook immediately below the trap-door in the ceiling—in the very place to which the eyes of his son, a lonely desolate little creature, had so often been directed in childish terror, fourteen years before" (62).

The nemesis which overtakes Ralph Nickleby might seem to be an isolated piece of plot machinery, but however mechanical it may be, it is not entirely isolated. It is instead related to a recurrent theme of the loss or preservation of connection with the past. Ralph and Smike present melodramatic and pathetic versions, but these have comic analogues as well. The comedy of Mrs. Nickleby's monologues depends on her tendency, at the slightest provocation, to plunge at random into her detailed but undiscriminating memories. Her egocentric free associations of past and present are largely innocent, but occasionally Dickens introduces moral criticism of her self-indulgent mode of recall by stressing her failure to be true to her dead husband's memory. An early example is her first interview with Ralph, who, appropriately, tempts her to falsify the past:

> To tell the truth, the good lady's opinion had been not a little influenced by her brother-in-law's appeal to her better understanding, and his implied compliment to her high deserts; and although she had dearly loved her husband, and still doted on her children, he had struck so successfully on one of those jarring little chords in the human heart (Ralph was well acquainted with its worst weaknesses, though he knew nothing of its best), that she had already begun seriously to consider herself the amiable and suffering victim of her late husband's imprudence. [3]

Later, Dickens confronts her with the example of her daughter Kate being strongly moved by her father's memory, so that even the shallow Mrs. Nickleby "began to have a glimmering that she had been rather thoughtless now and then, and was conscious of something like self-reproach" (43). Few readers would not prefer Mrs. Nickleby considering why a warm day with the birds singing reminds her of roast pig, but for Dickens more solemn and pious memories also have a high value.

> It is an exquisite and beautiful thing in our nature, that when the heart is touched and softened by some tranquil happiness or affectionate feeling, the memory of the dead comes over it most powerfully and irresistibly. It would almost seem as though our better thoughts and sympathies were charms, in virtue of which the soul is enabled to hold some vague and mysterious intercourse with the spirits of those whom we dearly loved in life. Alas! how often and how long may those patient angels hover above us, watching for the spell which is so seldom uttered, and so soon forgotten! [43]

Mrs. Nickleby's comic nemesis comes through her dalliance with the lunatic neighbor who makes love and casts vegetable offerings to her over the garden wall. Like Smike, who at the same time is making his own horticultural love offerings to Kate, he is a more extreme example of severance from the past (though in his case the transformation is an improvement). When, after struggling down the chimney, he suddenly switches his allegiance to Miss La Creevy, whom he has never seen before (" 'Aha!' cried the old gentleman, folding his hands, and squeezing them with great force against each other. 'I see her now, I see her now! My love, my life, my bride, my peerless beauty. She is come at last—at last—and all is gas and gaiters!' " [49]), Mrs. Nickleby is humiliated by a grotesquely heightened version of her own infidelity.

These themes are carried through to the end; the novel concludes with a reaffirmation of fidelity to the past.

> The first act of Nicholas, when he became a rich and prosperous merchant, was to buy his father's old house. As time crept on, and there came gradually about him a group of lovely children, it was altered and enlarged; but none of the old rooms were ever pulled down, no old tree was ever rooted up, nothing with which there was any association of bygone times was ever removed or changed. [65]

The last paragraph, like the last illustration, shows Nicholas' and Kate's children visiting their cousin Smike's grave.

In this context, the mystery plot connecting Ralph and Smike emerges as one manifestation of a general concern with the past, which becomes a ground of meaning and value. Fidelity to the past is rewarded, falsification or denial of it punished; indeed, in these terms, the rescue of Oliver Twist appears as a reward for the unconscious fidelity to his origins implied by his adherence to "the principle of Good," just as Monks is punished for his attempts to destroy Oliver's connection with that past. The orientation toward the past also appears in the regressive movement of Nell's flight in *The Old Curiosity Shop*, while in *Barnaby Rudge* the mystery of Haredale's murder provides repeated instances of the past not as refuge but as curse. Mystery plots usually involve some such transgression, either a crime committed in the past or, as in *Oliver Twist*, the suppression of the past. But even more basic than the association with guilt and victimization is the inherent tendency of this developmental pattern to ascribe a special authority to the past, to define the significance of the narrative action in terms of its relation to a hidden origin.

Despite the recurrent expressions of this tendency, it never dominates the early novels. The meaning of the past becomes a central concern only when Dickens begins to treat it not just as anterior but as interior reality through the autobiographical narrative of *David Copperfield*. The structural feature by which Dickens' first-person retrospective narratives are most clearly related to his mystery plots is their disruptions of temporal continuity, the breaks and regressions experienced not only by David Copperfield but also by Esther Summerson in *Bleak House* and Pip in *Great Expectations*. David tells of many such disruptions in his early years. The first comes when he is sent away to Yarmouth and returns to find his mother married to Murdstone (3), the second when he is confined for five days as punishment for biting his stepfather: "The length of those five days I can convey no idea of to any one. They occupy the place of years in my remembrance" (4). After this he is sent off to Salem House, enforcing his sense of separation from his former self: on his way to London he tries, "in a confused blind way, to recall how I had felt, and what sort of a boy I used to be, before I bit Mr. Murdstone: which I couldn't satisfy myself about by any means, I seemed to have bitten him in such a remote antiquity" (5). The death of his mother completes David's estrangement from his early childhood: "The mother who lay in the grave, was the mother of my early infancy; the little creature in her arms, was myself, as I had once been, hushed for ever on her bosom" (9). Further disruptions occur when he is sent to work at Murdstone and Grinby's and then runs away to Dover, where Betsy Trotwood gives him a new identity: "Thus I began my new life, in a new name, and with everything new about me. Now that the state of doubt was over, I felt, for many days, like one in a dream. . . . The two things clearest in my mind were, that a remoteness had come upon the old Blunderstone life—which seemed to lie in the haze of an immeasurable distance; and that a curtain had for ever fallen on my life at Murdstone and Grinby's" (14).

A similar break in time occurs in *Bleak House* when Esther falls ill:

> I lay ill through several weeks, and the usual tenor of my life
> became like an old remembrance. But this was not the effect of

time, so much as of change in all my habits, made by the helplessness and inaction of a sick room. Before I had been confined to it many days, everything else seemed to have retired into a remote distance, where there was little or no separation between the various stages of my life which had been really divided by years. In falling ill, I seemed to have crossed a dark lake, and to have left all my experiences, mingled together by the great distance, on the healthy shore. [35]

And in *Great Expectations* Pip's development is also marked by several sharp breaks, only some of which he notes at the time, such as his first visit to Satis House: "That was a memorable day to me, for it made great changes in me" (9).

As Pip's reflection indicates, these breaks play an important part in the development of the protagonist, disrupting continuity and complicating his sense of identity. In the developmental structure, they not only mark the stages of a linear progression but also contribute to a more complex pattern of reversion. Segmented by such disruptions, suddenly cut off and distanced, the past is not simply left behind. Instead, it seems to be encapsulated, preserved in separate compartments that may be entered again, often unexpectedly and inadvertently. Time is thus structured by divisions and rearrangements that resemble Dickens' other juxtapostions. The possibility of a return to the past is most apparent in David Copperfield's recollections, which, more than Esther's or Pip's narratives, stress the active process of memory. For David, past moments can return with full immediacy, whether deliberately summoned or through the spontaneous associations of particular sensations. This recapturing of the past does not have the explicit thematic significance it acquires in Proust, but it generally carries a positive value, allowing David to appear in the active role of reviving his past instead of being passively determined by it. Yet there are also suggestions that David is subject to a determinism he cannot recognize. His mistaken marriage to Dora, who, as many readers have observed, closely resembles his mother, involves a more troubling form of return to the past. Not only is David unconsciously attempting to regain the childhood paradise from which he was prematurely cut off, but in his inability to accept Dora as she is, in his efforts to improve her and "form her mind" (48), he reenacts the violation his mother suffered. "And when you had made sure of the poor little fool . . . you must begin to train her, must you? begin to break her, like a poor caged bird, and wear her deluded life away, in teaching her to sing *your* notes?" (14). Betsey's accusation of Murdstone could also be applied to David's treatment of his "child-wife." The bitter irony of this analogy, this repetition of the past, subverts the claims of linear development.

The threatening return of the past is only a disturbing undercurrent in David's story, but it produces central dramatic crises in the stories of Esther and Pip. The return of Esther's childhood insecurity that comes with the discovery of her origins, the return of Magwich and Pip's discovery of the source of his great expectations, threaten their sense of identity and force them to redefine the meaning of their lives. Here the pattern of reversion to the past assumes a form like the mystery plot in its revelation of a hidden origin.[1] In these narratives the protagonist's development is subjected to a process of division and multiplication that makes different moments, different versions of the self, coexist side by side, like the alternate versions generated by analogy. Both forms of multiplication challenge the sense of an integral self and organic growth. In the novels that follow David Copperfield, mystery plots reappear and assume new importance. They shape the presentation of both social panoramas and inner conflicts through narrative movements that turn on the discovery of a hidden reality in both the world and the self.

---

1. Reversion to the past is not confined to Dickens' first-person narratives. It also appears in various forms in characters of the later third-person novels, most spectacularly in the sudden relapses into a repressed past life experienced by William Dorrit and Dr. Manette: in a moment the sense of freedom and a new life vanishes, and they are once more in prison. The experiences of all these characters, of course, invite comparison with that of their creator, who reveals in the autobiographical fragment he wrote for Forster the power of his own secret past. Describing the anguish he felt during his days in the blacking factory, Dickens notes their persisting hidden reality for him: "My whole nature was so penetrated with the grief and humiliation of such considerations, that even now, famous and caressed and happy, I often forget in my dreams that I have a dear wife and children; even that I am a man; and wander desolately back to that time of my life" (*Life of Dickens*, 1: 23). Critics usually consider Dickens' concern with the past in this biographical context. See, for example, K.J. Fielding, "Dickens and the Past," in *Experience in the Novel*, ed. R.H. Pearce (New York: Columbia University Press, 1968), pp. 107–31.

Bleak House is the first novel in which Dickens fully exploits this dual potential of mystery plotting. The double narrative separates the inclusive spatial vision of the authorial narrator from Esther's personal temporal account, but the split perspective does not correspond to the main developmental division between the plot complexes of Jarndyce and Jarndyce and Lady Dedlock's secret. The result is an intricate interplay between impulses of division and connection: the two narratives articulate radically different visions of the world, but they also present complementary parts of the main actions.[2] The novel's form thus holds in suspense alternative versions of meaning, the sense of emerging unity and the sense that every event or relationship is subject to opposed interpretations.

The mystery plot which turns on Lady Dedlock's secret past develops the most extensive set of connections and the clearest case of equivocal meaning. As the separate investigations by Guppy and Tulkinghorn expose the hidden connections between Lady Dedlock, Hawdon, and Esther, more than a dozen other characters become involved either in the process of detection or in the relations it reveals. Because these connections bring many characters together from opposite sides of the gulfs separating social classes, they symbolize the bonds of interdependence that join all members of society, replacing the initial survey of isolated, self-enclosed worlds with a vision of organic interrelationship. The outline of Lady Dedlock's story resembles that of Dicken's earlier mystery plots: as in the case of Ralph Nickleby, a character is cut off from the past, leaving a child whose existence and identity are unknown, and the connection is reestablished to work out a harsh retribution.

But the comparison also reveals important differences. The downfall of Lady Dedlock is not simply poetic justice: she is more victim than villain, and as the new prominence of the mystery plot places more emphasis on the process of detection, we see how dubiously it is motivated. Tulkinghorn is concerned only with "the acquisition of secrets, and the holding possession of such

2. The double opening clearly demonstrates this relation: the authorial narrative moves rapidly through space while Esther's first chapter, "A Progress," traces her story up to the same point in space and time, the foggy November afternoon in Lincoln's Inn Hall, where the novel begins.

powers as they give him, with no sharer or opponent in it" (36); Guppy hopes to advance his suit for Esther by establishing relations between her and the aristocracy; the Chadbands and Smallweeds hope to profit by blackmail. Mrs. Snagsby, whose paranoid suspicions of her husband parody the other detectives, shows the destructive tendency of such pursuits even aside from deliberate intention. As Bucket observes, she "has done a deal more harm in bringing odds and ends together than if she had meant it" (54). In *Bleak House* the mystery plot becomes a central artistic strategy for forming and revealing connections, for dramatizing the organic unity and moral interdependence of society, yet both the means to this end and the consequences of pursuing it are clearly suspect.

The case of Jarndyce and Jarndyce provides another set of connections that overlaps the Dedlock mystery and shares much of its logic. It involves not only the unwilling parties to the suit but the much larger group of characters who form the world of Chancery. The pernicious effects of these connections are evident from the beginning: "How many people out of the suit, Jarndyce and Jarndyce has stretched forth its unwholesome hand to spoil and corrupt, would be a very wide question" (1). Like the Dedlock mystery, the suit illustrates the destructive influence of the past, its power to corrupt and immobilize the life of the present, and in working out the answer to the "wide question" of Chancery's effects, Dickens engages in another kind of detection. Tracing these effects back to their source involves the plot in a form of causal explanation; Jarndyce and Jarndyce becomes in another sense what it is called at the beginning, "the cause." This explanatory process is most apparent in the direct effects of Jarndyce and Jarndyce on individual characters, especially on Richard Carstone, and his dramatized corruption by the suit is generalized by the presentation of other victims of Chancery, such as Miss Flite, whom he gradually comes to resemble.

In addition to following such lines of development, the Chancery plot complex also involves the revelation of hidden connections that attributed the bleakness of the novel's entire world to this unique cause. The main example of such indirect causation is Tom-all-Alone's, the focus of social decay and the source in turn of the crime and disease by which "Tom has his revenge" on society (46). Dickens carefully plants the clues that link Tom-all-Alone's to Chancery. When Mr. Jarndyce explains the history the suit to Esther, he mentions "some property of ours . . . meaning of the Suit's" in London.

> It is a street of perishing blind houses, with their eyes stoned out; without a pane of glass, without so much as a window-frame, with the bare shutters tumbling from their hinges and falling asunder; the iron rails peeling away in flakes of rust; the chimneys sinking in; the stone steps to every door (and every door might be Death's Door) turning stagnant green; the very crutches on which the ruins are propped, decaying . . . . These are the Great Seal's impressions, my dear, all over England. [8]

After this preparation, the narrator can add to his first description of Tom-all-Alone's the explanation of its ruinous state: "This desirable property is in Chancery, of course. It would be an insult to the discernment of any man with half an eye, to tell him so" (16).

The hyperbolic form of causal explanation that makes one institution, and even one lawsuit seem to be responsible for the corruption of a whole society has obvious symbolic power, enabling Dickens to dramatize the plight of a world caught in the dead hand of the past. Chancery expands to mythic dimensions, emboying a secularized original sin and intimating eventual apocalypse ("I expect a judgment," says Miss Flite. "On the Day of Judgment" [3]). But the logic of this strategy displaces individual responsibility and grants priority to remote impersonal forces; from a different perspective, the emphasis on an ultimate origin or goal may seem mistaken. The problem of misdirected causal explanation appears in the introductory presentation of John Jarndyce, who attributes the "uncomfortable sensation" he experiences at news of Mrs. Jellyby's or Skimpole's derelictions to the influence of the east wind. Esther soon recognizes that this device is "characteristic of his eccentric gentleness": "Ada and I agreed . . . that this caprice about the wind was a fiction; and that he used the pretense to account for any disappointment he could not conceal, rather than he would blame the real cause of it" (6). Chancery is a similar fiction. Dickens relies on Jarndyce as an important vehicle for his indictment of the Court, citing the harm it has caused and warning of its danger to anyone who becomes involved in it. Although this attribution of responsibility is angry rather than gentle, it may also be misdirected, focusing on what is only a symptom of moral disorder and leaving "the real cause" obscure. Dickens seems to be in the equivocal position of endorsing a mode of explanation while he also suggests that it is somehow false.

Bleak House draws much of its imaginative power from the sense of hidden causes, the threatening past, and the complex, inexorable mechanism through which they exert their effects. But this comprehensive vision allows little scope for individual moral freedom and little hope for improvement, and so, at the same time that the novel elaborates its vast impersonal systems of causation, it also pursues a different logic in its stories of individual development. This counterplot focuses on the careers of Esther and Richard (though Caddy Jellby provides another, minor analogue in her modestly successful struggle to escape the blighting influence of her chaotic home). Richard's story also shows the equivocal effects of the novel's double logic. It offers the fullest demonstration of Jarndyce and Jarndyce as an inherited curse, a situation imposed by the past, and his fate of being born into an endless suit may even be taken as "a symbol . . . of what it is to be in the world at all."[3]

But Esther's account stresses Richard's complicity in his fate; from this perspective Jarndyce and Jarndyce represents the fatal temptation to define one's life in relation to an external source. Richard blames his series of abandoned professions on the suit: "one can't settle down while this business remains in such an unsettled state" (23), and gradually comes to depend on it to establish the position he is unable to create for himself. In yielding to this temptation, he surrenders to the claim of the past, devoting all his energies to solving the mystery of the suit's incomprehensible complexities. This obsessive commitment to the past in hope of future reward destroys the value of life in the present: "There's no now for us suitors," he tells Esther (37). Significantly, the eventual "solution" to the mystery of Jarndyce and Jarndyce, the new will discovered among Krook's rubbish, is irrelevant; resolution comes not through such a deus ex machina

3. Miller, *Charles Dickens*, p. 196.

but through the futile exhaustion of resources, both of money and life. Richard's deterioration and death confirm the error of seeking a basis of meaning in the past and thus repudiate the premise of the mystery plot.

In the perspective that makes Richard a cautionary figure, Esther becomes the main representative of personal responsibility, "the duties and accountabilities of life" (6); but in her story responsibility is deeply entangled with guilt. She recognizes Richard's errors, is immune to the fascination of the suit, and does not even attempt to discover her own origins. When Jarndyce offers to tell her what he knows of her past, she declines: "I am quite sure that if there were anything I ought to know, or had any need to know, I should not have to ask you to tell it to me" (8). And yet, more than Richard or Lady Dedlock, Esther's story dramatizes the urgent pressure of the past and the struggle against its power to determine the course and define the meaning of life in the present. The account of her childhood at the beginning of her narrative presents in a few pages the source of the inner conflict underlying her later development.[4] Her problem is not a question of fact but of interpretation, not her illegitimate birth but the significance ascribed to it by the Calvinistic Miss Barbary: "It would have been far better, little Esther, that you had had no birthday; that you had never been born." Taught to feel guilt for her existence, to believe that she is marked by a curse, "set apart," she resolves "that I would try, as hard as ever I could, to repair the fault I had been born with (of which I confessedly felt guilty and yet innocent), and would strive as I grew up to be industrious, contented, and kind-hearted, and to do some good to some one, and win some love to myself if I could" (3).

Jarndyce's benevolence and the new life of Bleak House provide the opportunity for carrying out this program of compensation. Esther devotes herself to her duties and succeeds in winning love, but that love must be continuously earned, and she can never quite believe she deserves it. Her life must be a

---

4. The psychological effects of Esther's childhood are analyzed by both William Axton, "The Trouble with Esther," *Modern Language Quarterly* 26 (1965): 545–57, and Alex Zwerdling, "Esther Summerson Rehabilitated," *PMLA* 88 (1973): 429–39.

continuing effort to overcome the past and replace its devastating meaning. But the past returns and brings back her childhood insecurity. Seeing Lady Dedlock for the first time, Esther is astonished to find that haughty face becoming "in a confused way, like a broken glass to me, in which I saw scraps of old remembrances." She trembles with "unaccountable agitation" as the vision of "little Esther Summerson, the child who lived a life apart, and on whose birthday there was no rejoicing—seemed to arise before my own eyes, evoked out of the past by some power in this fashionable lady" (18). When she learns that Lady Dedlock is her mother and is threatened with ruin by the discovery of their relationship, the sense of being cursed returns with new power.

> I hope it may not appear very unnatural or bad in me, that I then became heavily sorrowful to think I had ever been reared. That I felt as if I knew it would have been better and happier for many people, if indeed I had never breathed. That I had a terror of myself, as the danger and the possible disgrace of my own mother, and of a proud family name. That I was so confused and shaken, as to be possessed by a belief that it was right, and had been intended, that I should die in my birth; and that it was wrong, and not intended, that I should be then alive. [36]

The sentence of guilt passed on her in childhood comes back with "new and terrible meaning," and when she is drawn to Chesney Wold and hears her echoing footsteps on the terrace, she suddenly feels "that there was a dreadful truth in the legend of the Ghost's Walk; that it was I, who was to bring calamity upon the stately house; and that my warning feet were haunting it even then. Seized with an augmented terror of myself which turned me cold, I ran from myself and everything" (36).

This is the crisis of Esther's story, at which she is poised between two interpretations of her life. The sense of being part of a coherent but terrible design seems to be confirmed, but she seizes on the evidence of Jarndyce's and Ada's love for her and asserts a different meaning.

> For, I saw very well that I could not have been intended to die, or I should never have lived; not to say should never have been reserved for such a happy life. I saw very well how many things had worked together, for my welfare; and that if the sins of the fathers were sometimes visited upon the children, the phrase did not mean

what I had in the morning feared it meant. I knew that I was as
innocent of my birth as a queen of hers; and that before my
Heavenly Father I should not be punished for birth, nor a queen
rewarded for it. [36]

Esther never completely succeeds in throwing off the burden of
the past. The scars left by her illness, whose extent remains
ambiguous to the end of the novel, correspond to the continuing
insecurity betrayed by the hesitant and apologetic tone that
recurs in her narrative. But she also has the strength to transform
the negating forces that threaten from both the past and within
herself into acts of love and service and so to deny their
determining power.

Before considering Esther's reinterpretation further, we can
note other ways in which the pattern of the mystery plot is
reinterpreted. Along with the multiple detective investigations
which expose the hidden past, there are repeated probing movements into hidden areas of the present, the unknown world of the
poor. The first of these occurs when Esther and Ada accompany
Mrs. Pardiggle on the visit to the brickmakers in chapter 8. They
can observe the hardship and squalor of poverty, but they remain
cut off. "We both felt painfully sensible that between us and these
people there was an iron barrier, which could not be removed by
our new friend." (Esther's image is later given literal form in the
iron gate of the pauper's graveyard, another hidden world.) Here
the barrier is crossed by their spontaneous compassion at the
death of Jenny's baby, and the handkerchief that Esther leaves to
cover it becomes the focus of a continuing minor plot line, a
strand connecting rich and poor, mothers and children, living
and dead. The scene works to reveal not only the deprivation of
the poor but their resources of mutual support: "I think the best
side of such people is almost hidden from us. What the poor are
to the poor is little known, excepting to themselves and God."

The second such investigation, making much the same point, is
conducted by Jarndyce when he seeks out Neckett's children and
finds Charley supporting her younger brother and sister. "Look
at this," he urges his companions and the reader. "For God's
sake look at this" (15). By these movements of detection Dickens
takes the house-tops off to reveal another kind of hidden reality.
Here the emphasis falls not on causal explanation or impersonal

determinism but on the possibility for individual moral initiatives to form positive connections. In themselves, these acts are clearly significant, but in terms of the novel's larger systems of cause and effect their power remains slight. Esther herself later observes with "wonder and regret" that Jarndyce's "benevolent disinterested intentions had prospered so little" (35). To reinforce the limited power of the individual, Dickens attempts to enlist the logic of impersonal mechanism in the cause of justice and progress. Thus the narrator attributes Krook's death to a moral determinism that will overtake corrupt institutions as well as individuals: "The Lord Chancellor of that Court, true to his title in his last act, has died the death of all Lord Chancellors in all Courts, and of all authorities in all places under all names soever, where false pretenses are made, and where injustice is done. . . . Spontaneous Combustion, and none other of all the deaths that can be died" (32). Lady Dedlock's downfall seems to serve a similar purpose in causing Sir Leicester's collapse and symbolically breaking the Dedlock hold on England. The last chapter of the authorial narrative, showing the enfeebled baronet among the family tombs, offers the hope that the old order he represents has been destroyed, that a beneficent power greater than individuals or institutions ultimately determines human destinies.

This is of course Esther's characteristic mode of interpretation. Her ability to repudiate her sense of an inherited curse depends on her faith in an objective moral order, a benevolent providence directing human affairs: "I saw very well that I could not have been intended to die, or I should never have lived" (36). Esther repeatedly asserts this view when confronted by disturbing experiences. The pattern appears in symbolic form with the violent storm that leads to her first meeting with Lady Dedlock; it causes Esther to think "with awe of the tremendous powers by which our little lives are encompassed, to consider how beneficent they are, and how upon the smallest flower and leaf there was already a freshness poured from all this seeming rage, which seemed to make creation new again" (18). She will need to cling tenaciously to that faith through the storm overtaking her life, as she does in her emotional interview with her mother, discovering a providential purpose in her disfigurement: "I felt, through all my tumult of emotion, a burst of gratitude to the providence of

God that I was so changed as that I could never disgrace her by any trace of likeness" (36). She calls on the same faith to convince herself that she should accept Jarndyce's proposal, which she interprets as the culmination of a providential pattern: "It came upon me as the close of the benignant history I had been pursuing, and I felt that I had but one thing to do" (44).

Despite the support Esther derives from this positive version of an inclusive design, it remains in tension with her deepest, unacknowledged needs. Her faith in ultimate justice, "gratitude" for being disfigured, and belief that she should marry the fatherly Jarndyce all help her try to renounce the hope of normal human fulfillment and thus rest on the damaging premise that she is indeed "set apart." The threatening and reassuring meanings which stand opposed at the crisis of Esther's story are actually interchangeable; the interpretation she rejects will fit the Dedlock mystery as well as the one she embraces, since she does contribute to her mother's destruction.[5] The providential design offers only a mirror image of the mystery plot's insistence on the explanatory and determining power of the past; like black and white magic, they are two sides of the same coin. Both are hidden patterns which locate meaning in a remote origin, and both are opposed to individual autonomy.

Bleak House depends heavily on this kind of meaning, but its interplay of perspectives also permits us to consider such comprehensive interpretations as mystifying fictions. The fictiveness of Esther's providence emerges when it is confronted by Harold Skimpole's. Like an extreme metaphysical optimist, Skimpole dissolves the problems of suffering and evil into a fanciful "system of harmony." In his blithe view, Gridley's ruin by Chancery or the Necketts' poverty become the source of cheering thoughts: "it was really very pleasant to see how things lazily adapted themselves to purposes" (15). Esther's illness has the beneficent effect of making him appreciate his own health the more, and Richard's enslavement by the suit offers the pleasure of "the brightest visions of the future, which he evokes out of the darkness of Chancery. Now that's delightful, that's inspiriting, that's full of poetry!" (37). Even slaves have their place in the great plan:

5. Dickens avoids making her directly responsible, however, by interposing the surrogate daughter Rosa to precipitate Lady Dedlock's break with Tulkinghorn.

I dare say they are worked hard, I dare say they don't altogether like it, I dare say theirs is an unpleasant experience on the whole; but, they people the landscape for me, they give it a poetry for me, and perhaps that is one of the pleasanter objects of their existence. I am very sensible of it, if it be, and I shouldn't wonder if it were! [18]

Skimpole's providential interpretations clearly proceed from his selfishness, just as they serve to rationalize his sponging: "I take it that my business in the social system is to be agreeable; I take it that everybody's business in the social system is to be agreeable. It's a system of harmony, in short" (18).

It might seem unlikely that Dickens would grant this parasitical Pangloss much subversive power, but it can hardly be an accident that Skimpole's discourse on social harmony and the poetry of slaves immediately precedes Esther's providential interpretation of the storm. For all their obvious moral differences, both versions of providence emerge as individual creations and imply the fictiveness of all objectified moral orders. The same implication appears at Esther's first meeting with Skimpole. Immediately after receiving the basket of housekeeping keys which become the emblem of her dedication to duty, she encounters this gaily irresponsible figure and becomes "confused . . . in endeavoring to reconcile anything he said with anything I had thought about the duties and accountabilities of life (which I am far from sure of)" (6). These confrontations offer glimpses of a different hidden truth, more disturbing than a sinister mechanism: the absence of any intrinsic meaning. Jarndyce attempts to close the gap that reveals this void in his advice to his wards: "Trust in nothing but Providence and your own efforts. Never separate the two" (13). But one can hardly reconcile the orders of providential design and human effort except by an act of faith that begs the question of their relation.[6] Esther can continue her

6. An earlier confrontation between these two orders of interpretation appears in *David Copperfield*. J. Hillis Miller has noted the double pattern of David's story, appearing as both the fulfillment of a providential design and a process of self-creation. He finds the latter aspect in the constitutive power of memory, but it would seem more reasonable to locate it in David's continuing efforts to make his way in the world, in his childhood acts of self-assertion and the "earnestness" and hard work to which he attributes his success as a writer. The pattern of a preestablished destiny involves both the fates of Emily, Ham, and Steerforth and David's eventual union with Agnes. Miller finds that "Dickens contrives to have

own difficult efforts to do good and win love because of her trust in providence, and the happy ending of her story may seem to confirm her faith, but the novel also allows us to see that trust as another form of effort rather than as the recognition of an objective moral order.

The division of *Bleak House* into two narratives is thus only the most obvious expression of its double logic. That strategy produces the expansiveness of relativity, permitting the coexistence of different visions that persists to the end, with Esther declaring the happy completion of her progress in the new Bleak House, finding new evidence "of the goodness and the tenderness of God" (67), and the authorial narrator surveying the gloomy stagnation of Chesney Wold, now held more firmly than ever in the grip of the past. But the novel's drama of meaning achieves its greatest subtlety and intensity when its perspectives confront and reinterpret each other. The wider knowledge of the authorial narrative touches many moments of Esther's account with dramatic irony: she can never grasp the inclusive systems of plot connections and analogies of which her limited experience forms only a part, and from this perspective it is appropriate that the pursuit of Lady Dedlock, which is both the climax of the novel and the point where the two narratives draw most closely together, also produces Esther's greatest bewilderment. But on the other hand, it is precisely through her moments of disorientation that Esther produces the most forceful reinterpretations of the novel's inclusive systems. For the detached observer, the connections revealed by the interlocking lines of detection may

---

it both ways," showing David "to be both self-determining *and* justified and determined from the outside" by letting the providential pattern emerge only in retrospect. "David, then, has both made himself and escaped the guilt which always hovers, for Dickens, over the man who takes matters into his own hands" (*Charles Dickens*, pp. 155–59).

Yet this "solution" only disguises the tension between "Providence and your own efforts." As in Esther's providential interpretations, we can observe David replacing one version with another in the moment of vision when, after he and Agnes have at last declared their love, they stand together and look out the window. "Long miles of road then opened out before my mind; and, toiling on, I saw a ragged way-worn boy, forsaken and neglected, who should come to call even the heart now beating against mine, his own." David replaces the figure of the lonely boy struggling on his own with that of a hero destined to win the angelic heroine, "the source of every worthy aspiration I had ever had; the centre of myself, the circle of my life" (62).

offer a vision of total coherence, a symbolic demonstration of social interdependence or divine control, but for the characters caught up in this mysterious network it assumes a very different meaning. For Jo it is the experience of being arbitrarily "moved on" and pursued: "they're all a-watching and a-driving of me" (31); for Mr. Snagsby it is the comic delirium of being drawn into Tulkinghorn's and Bucket's intrigues and pursued by his wife's implacable suspicions, until he believes he may somehow be responsible for the "dreadful mystery" of Krook's death. "He has had something—he don't know what—to do with so much in this connection that is mysterious, that it is possible he may even be implicated, without knowing it, in the present transaction"(33).

Esther resists this infectious sense of persecution and guilt with her dedication to duty and trust in providence, but she also reveals the threat to individual integrity and autonomy posed by the logic of the mystery plot. The episode of her illness offers the most intense expression of this view. On the way to her meeting with Jo, who passes the infection to her, she has a brief sense of dissociation: "I had for a moment an indefinable impression of myself as being something different from what I then was" (31). It is an appropriate premonition, for as she subsequently falls into fevered dreams and nightmares her sense of identity becomes confused and dispersed; her experience is transposed into a spatial mode in which the stages of her life no longer form a linear progression but coincide.

> While I was very ill, the way in which these divisions of time became confused with one another, distressed my mind exceedingly. At once a child, an elder girl, and the little woman I had been so happy as, I was not only oppressed by cares and difficulties adapted to each station, but by the great perplexity of endlessly trying to reconcile them. [35]

In this perspective the dutiful efforts by which she has tried to give meaning to her life become futile repetition: "I laboured up colossal staircases, ever striving to reach the top, and ever turned, as I have seen a worm in a garden path, by some obstruction, and labouring again." At last all that remains is the sense of being trapped in a system of torment.

> Dare I hint at that worse time when, strung together somewhere in great black space, there was a flaming necklace, or ring, or starry

circle of some kind, of which *I* was one of the beads! And when my only prayer was to be taken off from the rest, and when it was such inexplicable agony and misery to be a part of the dreadful thing?[7]

The background of "great black space" suggests the void that human orders try to fill or hide; the fiery ring conflates the interchangeable patterns of heavenly design and infernal machine, and Esther's prayer "to be taken off from the rest" voices the desperate desire of the individual to escape from such inclusive systems.

These implications are restated even more clearly in the nightmares that accompany Pip's illness in *Great Expectations*, which again express the terror of being assimilated into a vast impersonal system. He dreams "that I was a brick in the house wall, and yet entreating to be released from the giddy place where the builders had set me; that I was a steel beam of a vast engine, clashing and whirling over a gulf, and yet that I implored in my own person to have the engine stopped, and my part in it hammered off" (57). The timing of both these episodes is curiously out of phase with the psychological rhythm: Esther's illness comes before the crisis of her story, Pip's well after. The dislocations confirm the sense that these dreams express not just psychological but structural conflicts, the irreducible tension between individual and general perspectives. In *Bleak House*, Dickens' heavy use of mystery plotting allows more scope to inclusive patterns; the claims of the individual are asserted more strongly in isolated moments of reversal and reinterpretation than in continuous developments. His later novels attempt to redress the balance.

Little Dorrit appears at first to depend even more heavily than *Bleak House* on the developmental pattern of the mystery plot.[8] The mystery of the Clennam family secret runs through the whole novel. It is introduced at the beginning when Arthur returns to

7. The importance of this image as a definition of Esther's condition is confirmed by Dickens' note, "necklace and the beads," the only figurative image specified in his number plans for *Bleak House*, which are reprinted in *Renaissance and Modern Studies* 9 (1965): 66–85.

8. Victor Shklovsky even takes the novel as his main example for a technical analysis of mystery plotting. See "The Mystery Novel: Dickens's *Little Dorrit*," in *Readings in Russian Poetics: Formalist and Structuralist Views,* ed. Ladislaw Matejka and Krystyna Pomorska (Cambridge, Mass.: M.I.T. Press, 1971), pp. 220–26.

London and asks his mother about a possible past wrong; it is developed through his investigations, the sequence of chapters presenting Affery's "dreams" and the increasing involvement of Rigaud-Blandois with the family; and it is resolved at the end when Mrs. Clennam is forced to reveal the suppressed truth. Other mysteries contribute to the brooding atmosphere of secrecy and menace which envelops this plot sequence, such as Mrs. Clennam's paralysis, the meaning of the motto "Do Not Forget," the noises Affery hears, and Flintwinch's double—all of which are explained in the dénouement. As in *Bleak House,* the mystery plot provides a means of tracing and forming connections between disparate worlds. Arthur's suspicion of a hidden link between his family and the Dorrits takes him to the Marshalsea, and further investigations lead to the Circumlocution Office and Bleeding Heart Yard. Moreover, other secrets and investigations or exposures establish parallel mysteries in the other plot lines, such as the discovery of the Dorrits' inheritance or the nature of Mr. Merdle's "complaint," which make the pattern all the more prominent.

All these mysteries rest on the sense of meaning as an objective truth awaiting eventual discovery, an original or final cause that determines the significance of all its manifold, mysterious effects. It may be hidden in the past, like the secrets of Arthur's birth and the suppressed codicil, or it may be hidden in the future as a design to be fulfilled, a mysterious destiny drawing separate narrative lines together:

> Strange, if the little sick-room fire were in effect a beacon fire, summoning some one, and that the most unlikely some one in the world, to the spot that *must* be come to. Strange, if the little sick-room light were in effect a watchlight, burning in that place every night until an appointed event should be watched out! Which of the vast multitude of travellers, under the sun and the stars, climbing the dusty hills and toiling along the weary plains, journeying by land and journeying by sea, coming and going so strangely, to meet and to act and react on one another; which of the host may, with no suspicion of the journey's end, be travelling surely hither? [I, 15]

But while the novel repeatedly proposes these versions of a fixed meaning determined by an origin or goal, it also keeps in play a sense of highly variable meaning, of a text open to numerous, even opposed interpretations, like Cavalletto's all-purpose expression "altro," which becomes, "according to its Genoese emphasis, a confirmation, a contradiction, an assertion, a denial, a taunt, a compliment, a joke, and fifty other things" (I, 1). The mysteries of *Little Dorrit* are similarly equivocal, subject to the play of shifting emphases and always "altro," other than they seem.

Arthur is the main focus of this play in the Clennam mystery, as the emphasis alternates between his roles of detective and of troubled protagonist. As detective, he is the agent of truth and justice, determined to trace hidden connections, to discover and set right past wrongs, the man who repeatedly insists, "I want to know" (I, 10). But this resolute figure who devotes himself to "the storming of the Circumlocution Office" also appears as a despondent middle-aged man who feels his life has been irreparably blighted and declares "I have no will" (I, 2). In the presentation of Arthur as protagonist, the emphasis shifts from the results to the motive of detection, and the mystery plot becomes a means of dramatizing his problematic relation to the past. The narrator repeatedly insists that Arthur's character has not been determined by his harsh upbringing, "because he was a man who had, deep-rooted in his nature, a belief in all the gentle and good things his life had been without" (I, 13),[9] but though he has not adopted his mother's dark creed, its effects are apparent in his suspicion that his family is somehow guilty. Raising the question of some wrong done to another seems at first to serve as an indirect accusation for the wrong done to himself, and his persistent investigations seem to be motivated less by a conscious desire for knowledge than by an unconscious desire for justification: like his mother's paralysis, they reflect a hidden sense of guilt.

Esther Summerson struggles against a disabling sense of inherited guilt by attempting to deny it, Arthur by attempting to locate it elsewhere. He thus becomes increasingly obsessed with Blandois, whose mysterious relation with his mother seems to be

9. The solution of the mystery offers an explanation for this innate immunity by revealing that he is not actually Mrs. Clennam's child but, as Lionel Trilling notes, "a child of love and art." *"Little Dorrit,"* in *The Opposing Self* (New York: Viking, 1955), p. 61. Even this late in Dickens' career, we can observe a vestige of the same logic that worked to resolve *Oliver Twist*.

bound up with the mystery of a hidden transgression: "how could he separate it from his old vague fears, and how believe there was nothing evil in such relations?" (II, 23). The only wrong of which he can actually accuse Blandois, however, is that he has "purposely cast a dreadful suspicion on my mother's house" (II, 28), which is essentially what Arthur himself has done in his own thoughts. As in the story of Oedipus, the roles of detective and criminal become interchangeable. While the plot continues to present Arthur as the hero pursuing the villain, Dickens' remarkable extended simile for his obsession tells a different story:

> As though a criminal should be chained in a stationary boat on a deep clear river, condemned, whatever countless leagues of water flowed past him, always to see the body of the fellow-creature he has drowned lying at the bottom, immovable, and unchangeable, except as the eddies made it broad or long, now expanding, now contracting its terrible lineaments; so Arthur, below the shifting current of transparent thoughts and fancies which were gone and succeeded by others as soon as come, saw, steady and dark, and not to be stirred from its place, the one subject that he endeavoured with all his might to rid himself of, and that he could not fly from. [II, 23][10]

There is thus much point to the maddening words with which his mother rejects his efforts to intervene: "It is you, Arthur, who bring here doubts and suspicions and entreaties for explanations, and it is you, Arthur, who bring secrets here" (II, 23).

The strange shifts and reversals which mark the development of the Clennam mystery are matched by its strange conclusion. Though Arthur's suspicions have seemed to become more significant as psychological symptoms than as narrative anticipations, they turn out at last to have been essentially correct: there is indeed a family secret which involves a wrong done to one of the Dorrits. But by the time this solution emerges it has become largely irrelevant to Arthur's story. His investigations have contributed little; he is absent when the secrets are revealed and never learns of them. Despite this disjunction, the culminating scenes of the mystery plot take the form of an intense climax, asserting their claim to central significance. The long-anticipated

10. At the end, this reversal even takes over on the level of plot: Arthur is imprisoned and Blandois performs the detective's function of exposing the Clennam secrets.

pattern of convergence is fulfilled in the confrontation of Blandois and Mrs. Clennam, and there are dramatic triumphs of truth as Mrs. Clennam confesses, charity as she begs and receives Little Dorrit's forgiveness, and justice as the house collapses on Blandois. But the melodrama of this climax is hollow. The secrets are revealed in such a confused mass of exposition that they remain unclear, yet they add so little to the novel's significance that this hardly matters.[11] Blandois's violent death is equally irrelevant: for all the emphasis on his villainy, he remains as ineffectual as the secrets he helps to expose. The whole sequence thus ends in a resounding anticlimax, in a sense of ironic disproportion between effects and their supposed cause. As Chesterton observes, "The secrecy is sensational; the secret is tame. The surface of the thing seems more awful than the core of it." But this discrepancy may not indicate, as Chesterton supposes, that the "real secret" remains hidden as a deeper core of meaning;[12] it may rather reveal that the real secret is an absence of determinate, objective meaning which the elaborate machinery of the mystery plot can no longer quite hide, a void in which it spins its wheels, going nowhere. The anticlimactic ending would then work to demystify the mystery plot, to discredit its explanatory claims and thus help to reinterpret the novel's structure of development.

The same process can be observed more clearly in the parallel mystery of the Dorrits' inheritance, which is resolved by the middle of the novel. Here Pancks and Rudge serve as detectives, establishing a hidden connection with the past that will supposedly transform the Dorrits' lives. But the purpose of trans-

11. The obscurity of these explanations has even prompted one recent editor, John Holloway, to add an appendix summarizing them in more intelligible form. (Harmondsworth: Penguin, 1967), pp. 896–97. Dickens' number plans give the strong impression that he himself did not know the secret before the time came to write the last number. He had to use two extra sheets of notes, "Retrospective" and "Prospective," to work out the details of the Clennam secret and the connection with the Dorrits, to determine how Blandois has learned all this, and to make this information consistent with the earlier narrative. The manuscript furthermore shows heavy rewriting of Mrs. Clennam's revelations. See Herring, "Dickens' Monthly Number Plans for *Little Dorrit*," pp. 56–61.

12. "It seems almost as if these grisly figures, Mrs. Chadband and Mrs. Clennam, Miss Havisham and Miss Flite, Nemo and Sally Brass, were keeping something back from the author as well as from the reader. When the book closes we do not know their real secret. They soothed the optimistic Dickens with something less terrible than the truth." *Charles Dickens* (New York: Dodd, Mead, 1906), pp. 168–69.

lating them from "Poverty" to "Riches" is actually to expose the illusion of movement measured on the outward scale of wealth and social status: William, Tip, and Fanny remain spiritually imprisoned; Amy remains the innocent and self-sacrificing child of the Marshalsea. The ironic character of this plot sequence is not only apparent in retrospect; it is implied from the beginning in the title of chapter 23 of Book 1, "Machinery in Motion." The phrase applies most obviously to the machinery of Doyce's factory, in which Arthur here begins his partnership; but this chapter also presents the beginning of Pancks's investigation of the Dorrits. The puffing steam-tug tells Arthur he wants to learn everything about them. "This comprehensive summary of his desires was not discharged without some heavy labouring on the part of Mr Pancks's machinery." Pancks is the engine of the Dorrit mystery plot, a creaky contrivance whose processes are merely mechanical, not organic.[13] The emerging irony which controls this plot machinery turns it back on itself with a self-destructive intent like that ascribed to the factory's literal "straps and wheels, which, when they were in gear with the steam-engine, went tearing round as though they had a suicidal mission to grind the business to dust and tear the factory to pieces." This subversion of the mystery plot makes it cancel itself like a suicidal machine, collapse of its own dead weight like the Clennam house. In the space cleared by this demolition, a different kind of plot and meaning can develop.

The development of this counterplot focuses on the stories of Arthur and Little Dorrit and is reinforced and elaborated by thematic connections with the novel's larger social panorama. As we have seen, the emphasis on Arthur's psychological and moral development reinterprets his suspicions as expressions of resentment and guilt, but his preoccupation with the past also appears

13. Another sign of this irony appears in the way Dickens alternates the Dorrit mystery plot with other sequences for an effect of false suspense. The ninth number ends with Pancks saying he has made a discovery about the Dorrits and beginning to reveal it to Arthur (I, 32). This is followed not only by the interval between the original installments but by two chapters dealing with the Merdles and Society, the Barnacles and the Circumlocution Office, further delaying Pancks's revelations. But by shifting the focus from Pancks's secret and the Marshalsea to the "higher" world which the Dorrits' new wealth will enable them to enter, Dickens undercuts the illusion of movement by anticipating its destination, which can already be recognized as "a superior sort of Marshalsea" (II, 7).

in his hope for recovered happiness with Flora: "he had kept the old fancy of the Past unchanged" (I, 13). Their first meeting destroys this hope, partly because of the ways she has changed but even more because of the ways she has not: "Flora, who had been spoiled and artless long ago, was determined to be spoiled and artless now." She presents a brilliantly comic, and at times touchingly pathetic version of bondage to the past, always trying to revive their former relationship and incapable "of separating herself and him from their bygone characters." Arthur's disillusionment with Flora does not prevent him from trying once more to recover the possibility of romantic love with Pet Meagles, but when this tentative effort is also frustrated, he withdraws into the role of "a very much older man who had done with that part of life" (I, 28), a "nobody" whose possibilities for happiness are lost in the past.

Unlike his obsession with the family secret, Arthur's belief that he is too old for love (and that Little Dorrit is too young) consistently appears as a defensive self-deception. Both expressions of his damaged will and self-esteem prolong his fixation on the past and block new development. These defenses are not set against the threat of a hidden determinism; rather, they use notions of determined meaning and closed possibilities against the threat of oppressive freedom, the dreary isolation and emptiness in which he must begin his life again. Only much later can he recognize his self-deception; only when that hope also seems lost can he consider Little Dorrit's love as a source of meaning:

> Looking back upon his own poor story, she was its vanishing-point. Every thing in its perspective led to her innocent figure. He had travelled thousands of miles towards it; previous unquiet hopes and doubts had worked themselves out before it; it was the centre of the interest of his life; it was the termination of everything that was good and pleasant in it; beyond, there was nothing but mere waste and darkened sky. [II, 27]

This vision is comparable to Esther's nightmares as a symbolic representation of Arthur's experience, but here the intuition of a hidden order is produced by the conscious mind and reveals a comprehensible human relationship rather than a terrifying impersonal design, an order created by the characters themselves rather than by a remote, mysterious source. As a spatial, synoptic image of temporal development, it involves a reversible perspective: for Arthur the desolate background represents a hopeless future, but it can also represent his dreary point of departure and, perhaps, the blank background of all human meanings. Arthur's story explores the empty space created or exposed by the breakdown of the mystery plot, but he can experience that emptiness only as loss. Whether in fear, hope, guilt, or despair, he can only keep looking back for a meaning that always eludes him. Without any definite threat or antagonist for him to confront, his story cannot turn on a decisive crisis. Instead, he subsides into "the despondency of low, slow fever" (II, 29) until Little Dorrit returns to bring him back to life.

Little Dorrit's return to Arthur in prison typifies her role as ministering angel, the only role that many readers have allowed her: she has been seen as "the Paraclete in female form," an "incarnation of divine goodness," and "the Bride from Heaven" who is also an angel of death.[14] In this role, like Arthur as detective, she appears as the agent of a remote order of meaning and value, but despite her otherworldly attributes she is also an inmate of "the prison of this lower world" (II, 30) and has to stuggle with its problems. Arthur, reluctantly considering the possibility of love between her and John Chivery, realizes he should not "make a kind of domestic fairy of her" (I, 22), and neither should we. Like Esther, she finds her role in duty and self-denial (though here the problem of guilt is, as we have seen, shifted to Arthur), and like Esther she is sustained but unfulfilled by it. "From her infancy ever so reliable and self-suppressed" (I, 18), she must be both innocent child and responsible "little mother" without ever being a young woman with her own needs and desires. Her littleness may be a sign of sentimental idealization, but it is also a sign of deprivation, of stunted growth.

When the Dorrits are catapulted from poverty to riches, she loses her sustaining role and must face the same disorienting blankness that confronts Arthur at the beginning of the novel. Like him, she can find meaning only in the past: "all that she saw appeared unreal. . . . all a dream—only the old mean Marshalsea a reality" (II, 3). Her nostalgia is the index of an ironic truth:

14. Trilling, *"Little Dorrit,"* p. 65; Miller, *Charles Dickens*, p. 246; Welsh, *The City of Dickens*, pp. 207–09.

devoting themselves to concealing their past, the rest of her family remain possessed by it, but it also marks her own inability to develop further. Both Little Dorrit and Arthur are lost in an empty freedom to which they cannot give meaning until at last they come back together and give each other the chance for new life. In reaching that happy ending, they complete the counterplot to the Dorrit and Clennam mysteries. The most significant secret for them has been hidden not in the past but in the present, the secret of Little Dorrit's unfulfilled love. Arthur is finally able to solve at least that mystery, and Little Dorrit, once her unreal riches are gone, shows a new strength which no longer takes the form of self-denial. As a "charm" for their final departure from the Marshalsea, she has him burn the long-suppressed codicil without learning its contents. "'Does the charm want any words to be said?' asked Arthur, as he held the paper over the flame. 'You can say (if you don't mind) "I love you!"'" answered Little Dorrit. So he said it, and the paper burned away" (II, 34). The gesture declares the irrelevance of the mysterious past: the only significant connection between the Clennam and Dorrit families has been formed by the hero and heroine themselves.

Through the shifting emphases of plot and counterplot Dickens moves toward a narrative structure that allows more importance to the perceptions and choices of individuals than to the revelation of an inclusive design. This shift appears in several other aspects of the novel, such as the increased use of the characters' points of view and stress on the different perspectives each offers (e.g., "This history must sometimes see with Little Dorrit's eyes . . ." [I, 14]). Similarly, the development of multiple focus is no longer devoted so much to displaying the anatomy of a social organism: there are far fewer interconnections between characters and narrative lines than in *Bleak House,* and the most important of these are formed by the characters, neither determined by the past nor (despite all the proleptic asides) fulfilling a predestined pattern.

The shift of emphasis toward the individual is most apparent in the thematic development of the problem of responsibility: though Dickens decided against calling the novel "Nobody's Fault," it remains committed to exposing evasions of responsibility in both public and private life. The pervasive theme of imprisonment thus stresses not victimization but the conditions which characters impose on themselves. Perverse, wilfully isolated figures like Mrs. Clennam or Miss Wade offer the most obvious instances of self-imprisonment, but weaker characters like Merdle or William Dorrit present subtler versions that involve more complex relations with others. As the Father of the Marshalsea, Dorrit cannot sustain his false pride or disguise his selfishness with the energy of his own pretenses and illusions; his role depends on the collaboration of everyone around him, especially Little Dorrit, who must not only work to support the family but maintain the pretense that she does not, "preserving the genteel fiction that they were all idle beggars together" (I, 7).

Little Dorrit presents many such collaborative fictons, and Dickens' repeated use of this term emphasizes the way in which characters create and maintain their conditions.[15] It appears again when Mrs. Gowan asks Mrs. Merdle to confirm her pretense that Henry's marriage to Pet Meagles is unfortunate. "The Priestess of Society" recognizes "that this was a sufficiently good catch. Knowing, however, what was expected of her, and perceiving the exact nature of the fiction to be nursed, she took it delicately in her arms, and put her required contribution of gloss upon it" (I, 33). The varnishing metaphor anticipates the efforts of Mrs. General, who prepares young aspirants to Society by teaching them to "seem to be ignorant of the existence of anything that is not perfectly proper, placid, and pleasant" (II, 5). Whether the novel's illusionists require this sort of conscious collaboration or simply try to impose their pretenses on others (like Blandois's pretense of being a gentleman or Casby's of being a benevolent patriarch), their fictions all depend on collective support.

Society thus no longer appears as a network of hidden connections but as an economy of fictions its members produce and exchange.[16] It may seem to be one vast prison, an impersonal

15. For a survey of the many kinds of fictions the characters produce and an interpretation of their relation to Dickens' own fiction-making, see Janice M. Carlisle, "*Little Dorrit:* Necessary Fictions," *Studies in the Novel* 7 (1975): 175–214.

16. The economic model becomes explicit in the account of the genteel "blinds and makeshifts," "affectations" and "mysteries" in which the inhabitants of

force that represses the individual, but that notion is itself exposed as a convenient fiction. "Society suppresses and dominates us," says its priestess Mrs. Merdle (I, 20), thereby excusing herself for preventing her son from marrying Fanny; and Fanny, dedicating herself to revenge on Mrs. Merdle, later justifies her acceptance of that vacuous son by a comparable fiction of determinism: "It would be the life I am best fitted for. Whether by disposition, or whether by circumstances, is no matter" (II, 14). "Society" and the individual's "fate" are objectified by the same type of projection and displacement that has created the god of Mrs. Clennam's Calvinism, "through its process of reversing the making of man in the image of his Creator to the making of his Creator in the image of an erring man" (I, 13).

Individual and collective responsibility for the state of the novel's world are most apparent in the two plot complexes which involve the most characters, the Circumlocution Office and Merdle's fraud. Like Chancery in *Bleak House,* the Circumlocution Office is a pervasive, impersonal institution which embodies and seems to be responsible for many diverse forms of social wrong, but it has none of the mythic autonomy of Chancery. Its bureaucracy is a system for diffusing and disguising responsibility, but it ultimately depends on the consent of the misgoverned. Ferdinand Barnacle explains to Arthur that the office fulfills the unacknowledged general will "that everything shall be left alone" and satisfies the general appetite for "humbug." He cheerfully demythologizes the symbolic institution:

> "Our place is not a wicked Giant to be charged at full tilt; but only a windmill showing you, as it grinds immense quantities of chaff, which way the country wind blows."
>
> "If I could believe that," said Clennam, "it would be a dismal prospect for all of us."
>
> "Oh! Don't say so!" returned Ferdinand. "It's all right. We must have humbug, we all like humbug, we couldn't get on without humbug. A little humbug, and a groove, and everything goes on admirably, if you leave it alone." [II, 28]

Hampton Court collaborate to disguise their shabby circumstances: "There was no end to the small social accommodation bills of this nature which the gipsies of gentility were constantly drawing upon, and accepting for, one another" (I, 26).

This "best and brightest of the Barnacles" should be well qualified to appraise the career of his fellow humbug Merdle: "A consummate rascal, of course . . . but remarkably clever! One cannot help admiring the fellow. Must have been such a master of humbug." But Dickens has already undercut this myth as well: Merdle is no clever master criminal; he is remarkable only for his exceptional meanness and always appears as the miserable prisoner of his own fraud. His success depends only on the collective desire to believe in the magic of rapid wealth, a "moral infection" (II, 13) which, unlike the symbolic disease of *Bleak House*, spreads not through an impersonal, undiscriminating mechanism but through the collaboration of all who succumb.

The insistent emphasis on responsibility is a corollary of the troubling sense of freedom which Arthur's and Little Dorrit's stories disclose, but here the disturbance is contained by the moral assurance of satire. As in the mystery plot, meaning is conceived as a hidden truth, but it is no longer remote or mysterious and remans hidden only through individual and collective bad faith. As the conclusion approaches, there is an accelerating rhythm of exposure that aligns the multiple plots: Dorrit's collapse and Merdle's, the revelation of the Clennam secrets and Pancks's exposure of Casby are presented as parallel moments of truth. But this triumphant movement of assimilation is disrupted by developments that undermine the opposition of illusion and reality. At the climax of William Dorrit's story, the powerful scene of his collapse at Mrs. Merdle's dinner, the repressed past returns, the hidden truth emerges, yet it takes the form of delusion. In his last days, his return to the truth is marked by the renewal of his close relation with Little Dorrit, yet this restoration also depends on another collaborative fiction.

> When he had been sinking in this painless way for two or three days, she observed him to be troubled by the ticking of his watch— a pompous gold watch that made as great a to-do about its going as if nothing else went but itself and Time. She suffered it to run down, but he was still uneasy, and showed that was not what he wanted. At length he roused himself to explain that he wanted money to be raised on this watch. He was quite pleased when she pretended to take it away for the purpose, and afterwards had a relish for his little tastes of wine and jelly, that he had not had before. [II, 19]

There is as much illusion in the last phase of his life as before, but its meaning has changed. In returning to the Marshalsea, Dorrit's "poor maimed spirit . . . cancelled the dream through which it had since groped," so that the world created by love can briefly replace the world created by social ambition and fear, but as this happens the opposition of illusion and reality is replaced by one between different illusions, different fictions; the triumph of truth remains equivocal. A similar equivocation persists in the happy ending of Arthur and Little Dorrit's story. The burning of the codicil represents the triumph of the meaning created by their mutual love and trust over that determined by the remote past, but this new beginning also repeats Mrs. Clennam's original suppression of the truth, and Little Dorrit becomes her collaborator in hiding it from Arthur. In the absence of objective, transcendent truth, all meanings must be fictions, and though they do not all become equivalent, none can entirely escape the disturbing sense of groundlessness, the taint of equivocation.

The desire to fill or deny that absence persists, however, and prevents any monological resolution. For all its stress on the meanings which the characters themselves produce, *Little Dorrit* is also punctuated with appeals to a remote, transcendent source. The opening chapter anticipates this movement, as its final paragraph shifts from the oppressive, "staring" heat of Marseilles and the equally oppressive atmosphere of the prison to a more distant, nonhuman world.

> The wide stare stared itself out for one while; the sun went down in a red, green, golden glory; the stars came out in the heavens and fire-flies mimicked them in the lower air, as men may feebly imitate the goodness of a better order of beings; the long dusty roads and the innumerable plains were in repose—and so deep a hush was on the sea, that it scarcely whispered of the time when it shall give up its dead. [I, 1]

The whispered intimation of apocalypse, of a predestined ending in which the hidden past will be resurrected, announces the remote determination of meaning that governs the mystery plot, just as the notion of human values as feeble imitations of a higher order announces the logic of Little Dorrit's role as angelic emissary. The novel repeatedly attempts to posit some such ground of truth and value even as it repeatedly exposes pervasive fictiveness. The more hopelessly the characters seem imprisoned in the fictions they have created, the stronger the need for a transcendent rescue, even if it comes only with death, as at the deaths of William and Frederick Dorrit: "The two brothers were before their Father; far beyond the twilight judgment of this world; high above its mists and obscurities" (II, 19).

The anxious need to ground the novel's own fictions appears in Doyce's self-effacement as an inventor, representing an author who does not create but only discovers an objective truth:

> He never said, I discovered this adaptation or invented that combination; but showed the whole thing as if the Divine artificer had made it, and he had happened to find it, so modest he was about it, such a pleasant touch of respect was mingled with his quiet admiration of it, and so calmly convinced he was that it was established on irrefragable laws. [II, 8]

There is no hint of irony in this account, but in the context of so many characters who create their worlds and deny their responsibility, Doyce's modesty looks suspiciously like another, subtler form of bad faith. Forster says that the original conception of "Nobody's Fault" involved a character who would typify such bad faith: "The book took its origin from the notion he had of a leading man for a story who should bring about all the mischief in it, lay it all on Providence, and say at every fresh calamity, 'Well, it's a mercy, however, nobody was to blame you know!' "[17] Dickens, too, may be tempted to "lay it all on Providence," but he also exposes such evasions.[18] The vision of a purely human world is oppressive when that world seems irredeemably lost in its illusions, enclosed in the prisons it has built, but *Little Dorrit* sustains that dark vision and finds its best hope in the relations and meanings the characters themselves create. The dialogue between this perspective and the appeal to a remote, inclusive

17. *Life of Dickens*, 2: 179.
18. See, however, his claim three years later of providential justification for his management of foreshadowing: "I think the business of art is to lay all that ground carefully, not with the care that conceals itself—to show, by a backward light, what everything has been working to—but only to *suggest*, until the fulfillment comes. These are the ways of Providence, of which ways all art is but a little imitation." *The Letters of Charles Dickens*, ed. Walter Dexter (London: Constable, 1938), 3: 125.

order remains unresolved, but the emphasis has shifted to the individual's self-determination.

Little Dorrit, with its beautifully restrained closing juxtaposition of its protagonists, "inseparable and blessed," and the "usual uproar" of the world, marks Dickens' most complex expression of his structural dialogue. His later novels continue the developments we have followed in *Bleak House* and *Little Dorrit,* but their forms become simpler as he assigns more importance to the perspectives of his characters and less to the possibility of an inclusive vision. This change is apparent in *Great Expectations,* Dickens' most strongly centered single-focus novel.[19] Here the pattern of the mystery plot no longer works to trace a network of social connections; instead it is restructured to focus exclusively on the protagonist's development. Pip does not, like Arthur Clennam, attempt to detect a hidden secret; instead the secret past pursues and overtakes him, forcing him to redefine his conception of himself and his history. His story thus presents a revised and concentrated version of Esther Summerson's experience: both are afflicted by a hidden sense of guilt that originates in early life; their moral autonomy is threatened by the discovery of a secret relationship that seems to have determined them, and both must then struggle to reinterpret their experience. But Pip is much more deeply implicated in this nightmare; the emphasis shifts from the guilt imposed on him to the guilt he earns, much as Arthur Clennam earns at least some of his by succumbing to the moral infection of Merdle's speculations. Miss Havisham is exaggerating, as well as evading her own responsibility, when she tells the newly enlightened Pip, "You made your own snares. *I* never made them" (44), but he can nevertheless regain his freedom only by taking responsibility for his life.

As in *Little Dorrit,* Dickens develops the theme of responsibility through multiple instances of initially innocent victims who become accomplices in their own fates and the oppressors of others. Miss Havisham creates her own world by wilfully perpetuating her role as forsaken bride and uses Estella to gain

19. Forster says the novel was originally conceived as a monthly rather than a weekly serial (*Life of Dickens,* 2: 284); in that larger form, secondary characters and narrative lines would probably have acquired more independent interest, as they do in *David Copperfield.*

revenge on all men; Magwitch, having been manipulated and betrayed, seeks compensation by manipulating Pip. With the economy of fable, Dickens makes both patrons originally victims of the mysterious Compeyson, but by keeping the villain in the shadows he shifts the emphasis away from this anterior source toward the continuing action. Pip's experience seems most of all a story of victimization. As a child he is subjected to a series of dominating adults, beginning with the convict who terrifies him into stealing food and a file, thus intensifying the sense of guilt and unworthiness continually imposed on him by Mrs. Joe and Pumblechook. He emerges from their domination only to come under the spell of Miss Havisham, and his great expectations can be realized only by submission to the intimidating Jaggers, who makes him feel "at a disadvantage, which reminded me of that older time when I had been put upon a tombstone" (36). Finally, Magwitch, to Pip the most oppressive of all, reappears to claim possession of him.

But for all the power these figures hold to control and define him, Dickens insists on Pip's complicity. Like Richard Carstone, he is presented less as a victim than as an example of error. He first helps to make his own snares by accepting Estella's judgment of his lower-class origins and learning to regard the life of the forge as "coarse and common," leading to his eager acceptance of the great expectations Jaggers offers. The mystery of their source permits him to impose his own wishful interpretation:

> [Miss Havisham] had adopted Estella, she had as good as adopted me, and it could not fail to be her intention to bring us together. She reserved it for me to restore the desolate house, admit the sunshine into the dark rooms, set the clocks a-going and the cold hearths a blazing, tear down the cobwebs, destroy the vermin—in short, do all the shining deeds of the young Knight of romance, and marry the Princess. [29]

Pip's illusions are doubly deceptive: he not only mistakes the source of his new life but makes the more fundamental mistake of believing that any extraneous source can grant him a valid identity. Circumstances contribute to his error of fact, but the willingness to be directed by an outside force is his own.

The discovery that Magwitch is the actual source of his great expectations works, like the resolution of a mystery plot, to reveal the hidden truth and redefine relationships. But this "solution" is not final; instead, it forces him to assume an active role, resisting the determination of meaning by others and attempting to substitute his own. When Magwitch declares that he has "made" him, Pip is overcome by violent revulsion: "The abhorrence in which I held the man, the dread I had of him, the repugnance with which I shrank from him, could not have been exceeded if he had been some terrible beast." This is less a response to Magwitch himself than to the meaning he conveys. As Pip's "second father," Magwitch links him to a far worse origin than the life he has left behind and makes him recognize his guilt toward his other "father:" "sharpest and deepest pain of all—it was for the convict, guilty of I knew not what crimes, and liable to be . . . hanged at the Old Bailey door, that I had deserted Joe" (39).

Pip's horror at this invasion of his life is at bottom the horrified sense of himself as the instrument of a hidden design, the creation of another; he compares himself to both Frankenstein and his monster: "The imaginary student pursued by the misshapen creature he had impiously made, was not more wretched than I, pursued by the creature who had made me, and recoiling from him with a stronger repulsion, the more he admired me and the fonder he was of me" (40). In her similar crisis, Esther manages to assert a positive meaning through her faith in a benign providence, but Pip must reinterpret his life without such aid. He must, in effect, return to the beginning and resume the responsibility of naming himself ("So, I called myself Pip"), return to the initial encounter with the convict that has seemed to mark his life with the "taint of prison and crime" (32) and recover a different meaning from the act of charity that first formed their relation. Pip reaffirms this meaning by accepting responsibility for Magwitch's safety, and in helping him attempt to escape and standing by him to the end, he finds a comparable new meaning in the man who once seemed to have imposed a curse on him.

For now my repugnance to him had all melted away, and in the hunted, shackled creature who held my hand in his, I only saw a

man who had meant to be my benefactor, and who had felt
affectionately, gratefully, and generously, toward me with great
constancy through a series of years. [54]

"By choosing his servitude to Magwitch, Pip transforms it into
freedom,"[20] or rather, he posits his freedom by refusing a
deterministic interpretation.

But for all its concentrated emphasis on this account of Pip's
errors and recovery, *Great Expectations* retains traces of other
perspectives. Some appear when his retrospective judgments on
himself seem inappropriately harsh, as in his comments on his
failure to confess his theft of the food and file: "In a word, I was
too cowardly to do what I knew to be right, as I had been too
cowardly to avoid doing what I knew to be wrong" (6). The voice
of the mature protagonist is clearly meant to represent the result
of Pip's successful moral education, but in such moments the
distancing impulse becomes excessive and betrays a persistent
sense of guilt which can find no objective justification. The
possibility of a very different version of Pip's story from the one he
presents is suggested most forcefully by the novel's analogies,
especially those between him and Orlick, who may be seen as his
violent double and the instrument of his unacknowledged desire
for revenge on those who have injured him.[21] Such an interpretation cannot master all of Pip's story, but it finds enough support
there to hold open a gap between the narrative of growing
awareness, responsibility, and freedom, and its dark double, the
nightmare of blindness and compulsion which the reinterpretation of the mystery plot attempts to dispel. Through the persistent possibility that Pip remains part of a sinister hidden
design beyond his comprehension, the dialogue of perpectives
continues. Dickens' most compressed single-focus novel condenses without synthesizing divergent meanings that might have
been articulated separately in a multiple narrative. "Pip, dear old
chap," Joe explains, "life is made of ever so many partings
welded together" (27). The double force of divisions that also

20. Miller, *Charles Dickens*, p. 276.

21. This is the interpretation presented by Julian Moynahan, "The Hero's
Guilt: The Case of *Great Expectations*," *Essays in Criticism* 10 (1960): 60–70.
Alexander Welsh also discusses the doubling of hero and villain in *David
Copperfield* and *Little Dorrit*. See *The City of Dickens*, pp. 130–35.

bind together, splitting the self and identifying opposites, disperses the single center of *Great Expectations* into undecidable alternatives. In the novel's alternative conclusions, projecting and effacing the "shadow of another parting," this doubleness persists to the end.

Our Mutual Friend, Dickens' last large multiplot novel, extends the effort to affirm the individual's perspective and power of self-determination. The focus repeatedly shifts among a large number of characters and situations, but instead of establishing an inclusive narrative perspective, Dickens develops the characters' different points of view and stresses the disparities between their worlds.[22] This multiplicity allows for an intricate counterpoint and interweaving of narrative lines as characters meet and interact, group and regroup in shifting relationships, but this complex movement is not directed toward the discovery or fulfillment of any hidden design or unifying pattern. Instead it emphasizes the relations the characters form, the meanings they themselves create, the freedom they exercise, and their responsibility for their fates. In some respects the fluidity of the novel's shifting perspectives and configurations, together with the prominent symbolism of the dust heaps and river, death and regeneration, make it more complex than Dickens' previous multiple narratives, closer to the discontinuity and symbolic modes of modern fiction and poetry. In its elaborate tapestry we can discern the outlines of *The Waste Land.*[23] But in other ways *Our Mutual Friend* is much simpler than *Bleak House* or *Little Dorrit.* Its main narrative lines resolve into the traditional pattern of a double plot based on parallels and contrasts between the stories of two couples, and as this pattern emerges the dialogical tension of the earlier novels is replaced by a predominant emphasis on the development and relationships of individuals.

22. See Miller, *Charles Dickens,* pp. 277–93, for examples of this multiplication of perspectives and related shifts of style and tone between different worlds.

23. The comparison, which had occurred to several modern readers (e.g. Edgar Johnson, *Charles Dickens: His Tragedy and Triumph* [New York: Simon and Schuster, 1952], 2: 1043–44), was corroborated by the publication of Eliot's manuscript, which places the whole poem under the Dickensian rubric, "HE DO THE POLICE IN DIFFERENT VOICES." See T.S. Eliot, *The Waste Land: A Facsimile and Transcript of the Original Drafts,* ed. Valerie Eliot (New York: Harcourt Brace, 1971), pp. 4–5.

The sense of meaning determined by a remote origin or end no longer plays an important part in *Our Mutual Friend;* the power of the past over both action and thought is now only nominal, invoked only in order to be dispelled. This is apparent in the plot device of old Harmon's will. Neither John Harmon nor Bella Wilfer accepts the requirement that they marry each other in order to receive the inheritance; their eventual union is achieved independently. The later wills that are unearthed, like the later Jarndyce will or the Clennam codicil, prove to be ultimately irrelevant. For all the prolonged intrigue centering on them, their only significant effect is to frustrate the dead hand of the past: Harmon eventually assumes possession of the property, as he tells the defeated Wegg, not "through any act of my father's or by any right I have" but "through the munificence of Mr Boffin" (IV, 14), so that the characters themselves determine the final disposition.

Similarly, the characters' inner lives are no longer dominated by obsessions with the past or the struggle to throw off its burden. Harmon appears at first to suffer very obviously from the incapacitating guilt and self-doubt that marked earlier protagonists. His first words are "I am lost!" (I, 3), and at his introduction to the Wilfers he displays "a very bad manner. In the last degree constrained, reserved, diffident, troubled" (I, 4). But these early signs of weakness are later explained as the aftereffects of the drug which nearly caused his death. That trauma condenses all inner conflicts into a brief symbolic episode in which helpless passivity and loss of identity ("I could not have said that my name was John Harmon—I could not have thought it—I didn't know it. . . . There was no such thing as I, within my knowledge" [II, 13]) are quickly followed by the assumption of a new one. Like Esther's and Pip's nightmares, this episode is out of place in the narrative sequence, since it is presented in Harmon's delayed summary, but here the effect of dislocation is not to generalize but rather to encapsulate the disturbance, so that it appears only as a momentary crisis now safely past. Harmon does not even rehearse this dark rite of passage for us until he has already emerged as a strong, self-confident figure, a manipulator of roles and situations. Unlike earlier troubled protagonists, he is never subject to the power of the past, never threatened by impersonal forces or assimilated into a mysterious design.

The decreased concern with a hidden design also appears in the satiric presentation of society through the world of the Veneerings. Their name implies nearly all we need to know about society: it is a set of surfaces without depth, façades with nothing behind them. There are no longer any powerful, oppressive institutions like Chancery or even the Circumlocution Office, no stifling traditions; in this world everything is "bran-new," created by the illusory power of money. Relationships are entirely fictive, so that Veneering's newest acquaintances immediately become his "oldest friends," and all social events, from dinner parties to parliamentary elections, are collaborative charades. The void behind human orders and values is no longer glimpsed as a remote threat; now it looms close, and the "sly, mysterious, filmy" Veneering and his world present only the thinnest "veil" to mask it (I, 2).

The thrust of narrative development is therefore no longer directed toward revealing the secret coherence of society but toward escaping it. Both of the major plot lines focus on the process of escape or rescue from false values and present movements outside the established order. Eugene Wrayburn recognizes the hollowness of this world but is incapable of responding with more than boredom and self-contempt. His slow, troubled movement away from genteel society toward union with Lizzie Hexam produces the most interesting narrative line because it involves the most conflict. Bella, though never part of the Veneering world, is connected with it by her concern with "money, money, and what money can make of life" (III, 4). Harmon is outside this world from the beginning because of his presumed death and resultant freedom to choose his role, just as Lizzie is outside it because of her lower social class. As Wrayburn is drawn toward Lizzie, Harmon, with the Boffins' help, leads Bella away from false social values.

The alternatives to established society are just as fictive as the hollow shell of the Veneering world, just as much individual and collaborative creations as the impervious self-satisfaction of Podsnappery, but they are the creations of imagination and love. Boffin's Bower, the house of the newly married Harmon and

Bella, or the refuge Lizzie and Jenny Wren find on Riah's roof-top are worlds where mutual support makes thought and feeling as substantial as the "hideous solidity" of the Podsnap plate. Bella assures her husband that she has no desire for the luxuries he would provide if they were rich: "your wishes are as real to me as the wishes in the Fairy story, that were all fulfilled as soon as spoken" (IV, 5). As Harmon's story moves into the fairy-tale mode of romance, it enables Dickens to affirm the redemptive and creative power of imagination set free from the mystifying fictions of wealth and status, and that power is reaffirmed in the darker mode of Wrayburn's story when he calls on Jenny's visions to help him return to life (IV, 10).

The novel's affirmation of individual freedom and responsi-bility is most clearly expressed in its transformations of the mystery plot. Instead of turning on hidden connections rooted in the past, mysteries and secrets are now the medium of relations formed in the course of the developing action, as numerous characters make secret compacts, plots, and counterplots. These hidden connections include the benevolent conspiracy of Harmon and the Boffins to reform Bella, the malicious "friendly move" of Wegg and Venus against Boffin, and the "mutual under-standing" reached by the newly wed Lammles when they dis-cover they have deceived each other into marrying for nonexistent wealth: "We agree to keep our own secret, and to work together in furtherance of our own schemes" (I, 10). Secret connections bridge social distances between characters like Riah and Fledgeby or Bradley Headstone and Rogue Riderhood, forming degrading bonds that are either broken or end in destruction, but Dickens stresses the power of self-determination by showing characters entangled in such pacts who resist them by forming counterplots, as Venus does with Boffin or Mrs. Lammle with Twemlow. In both of the main plots, new relations are formed in secret, making them appear as conspiracies against the estab-lished order. Wrayburn's relationship with Lizzie is furtive as long as he thinks of seducing her—or simply refuses to examine his motives: "I have no design whatever. I am incapable of designs" (II, 6).[24] Once he commits himself to marrying her he

24. This chapter's play on the notion of a secret "design" within, not outside the character is juxtaposed with different versions of conspiracy in the next two,

must openly defy social disapproval: "I will fight it out to the last gasp . . . here in the open field" (IV, 16). Harmon must also work in secret. Becoming "dead" to the world he achieves the kind of liberating distance from it that Jenny offers when she urges Riah to "come up and be dead," gaining the freedom to observe the Boffins and Bella and then, with them, to create a new life. Both plots move toward comic resolutions with the final dispelling of mystery as new worlds emerge from the old.

But for all the stress on individual freedom, *Our Mutual Friend,* like *Great Expectations,* is still shadowed by an alternate version, a story of manipulation and compulsion. This double aspect is clearest in Boffin's masquerade as a miser, a sequence in which freedom and bondage change places like partners in a dance. As the golden dustman appears to fall victim to the corrupting power of money, Bella asserts her independence and shows "that she's the true golden gold at heart" (IV, 13). When the deception is at last explained, Boffin emerges as a figure of incorruptible innocence who, like Harmon, has always been in control. But in the same shift from appearance to reality, by a corollary that Dickens seems eager to hide with a great deal of forced gaiety, Bella now appears as the object of manipulation, "the doll in the doll's house" (IV, 5), tested and displayed with proud, patronizing affection by her husband, so that the power of self-determination demonstrated by her moral development is deeply compromised.

Wrayburn's redemption is equally problematic. Here the change of heart is produced not by hidden manipulation but by open violence: he is unable to resolve his conflicting motives until Headstone beats him into a better frame of mind.[25] This resolution, though arbitrary, is also appropriate, for throughout Wrayburn's story compulsion plays as large a part as freedom, and the most intense relation it develops is not his love for Lizzie but his rivalry with Headstone, whom he scorns and torments yet perhaps also envies for the consuming passion of which Wrayburn himself is incapable.

As in *Great Expectations,* this alternate perspective cannot fully determine the meaning of *Our Mutual Friend;* but neither can it be

---

"In Which a Friendly Move is Originated," and "In Which an Innocent Elopement Occurs."

25. Cf. Estella in the second ending to *Great Expectations*: "I have been bent and broken, but—I hope—into a better shape."

excluded. Though such shifts work to subvert the novel's affirmations, they also save it from coercive simplification and help to preserve its structural dialogue. Whenever one perspective appears to gain complete control over one of Dickens' novels, its basis of meaning is threatened. In a dialogical form, perspectives can have no independent value; they gain meaning only through the oppositions and tensions between them. As tension between the sense of individual autonomy and the sense of an inclusive order becomes less important, other oppositions arise to take its place; the self may be threatened less by assimilation than by fragmentation, by inner rather than outer compulsion. But in each case, however powerful the impulse to establish one vision of the world may be, it never completely succeeds. To the end of his career, the most important form of freedom in Dickens' work is displayed not in his characters' self-determination but in the continuing play of perspectives that resists any monological resolution.

⭸ THREE ⭸

Thackeray: Seeing Double

To begin with beginnings was appropriate for dealing with Dickens, since the openings of his novels perform so dramatically the formal gesture of juxtaposing the diverse elements his multiple narratives combine. For Thackeray it might be more appropriate to begin with his endings, which tend to dramatize not the inclusive power of narrative but its arbitrariness and inadequacy. Contemplating the New Palace of Westminster, Thackeray "declared he saw no reason why it stopped; it ended nowhere, and might just as well have gone on to Chelsea."[1] Some contemporary critics perceived the same formal problem in Thackeray's own works: "His conception of a story . . . is incomplete. There is no reason why he should begin where he does, no reason why he should end at all."[2] Modern readers are more likely to praise the realism of such "incompleteness,"[3] but this revaluation of what is perceived as formal looseness fails to confront the more general problem of form in Thackeray. We shall be concerned at several points with moments in his novels that blur the outlines of narrative form: uncertain or multiple beginnings, displaced or muffled climaxes, inconclusive or ironically conventional endings; but these are only more dramatic instances of the way forms ranging from conventions of social

1. Gordon N. Ray, *Thackeray: The Age of Wisdom* (New York: McGraw-Hill, 1958), p. 331.
2. W.C. Roscoe, in *National Review*, January 1856, reprinted in *Thackeray: The Critical Heritage*, ed. Geoffrey Tillotson and Donald Haws (London: Routledge, 1968), p. 271. Tillotson considers Roscoe the best of Thackeray's Victorian critics. See also R.S. Rintoul on the arbitrariness of the ending of *Pendennis*, pp. 99–100.
3. For example, Geoffrey Tillotson, who praises "the bufferless endings of the novels. . . . Thackeray designed them to be loose so that they represent life more truthfully." *Thackeray the Novelist* (Cambridge: Cambridge University Press, 1954), p. 173.

behavior to underlying conceptual structures of thought are continually placed in question by Thackeray's fiction.

Thackeray and Dickens share a strong sense of conventional patterns, types, and forms, but Dickens' symbolic imagination tends to work through inherited forms like the mystery plot, intensifying and reinterpreting them, while Thackeray works against them, resisting their arbitrariness and attempting to displace and discredit them in his effort to reveal a truth they obscure. This process can be more fully observed in Thackeray's development through the early burlesques and parodies,[4] but for our purposes we can begin to define his conception of form and distinguish it from Dickens' by considering the early scene in *Pendennis* where the young hero for the first time attends a play and sees "the Fotheringay," the actress with whom he becomes infatuated. Thackeray suspends the narrative at the moment of her first entrance to comment on the sentimental drama by Kotzebue in which she appears:

> Those who know the play of the "Stranger" are aware that the remarks made by the various characters are not valuable in themselves, either for their sound sense, their novelty of observation, or their poetic fancy.
>
> Nobody ever talked so. If we meet idiots in life, as will happen, it is a great mercy that they do not use such absurdly fine words. The Stranger's talk is sham, like the book he reads, and the hair he wears, and the diamond ring he makes play with—but, in the midst of the balderdash, there runs that reality of love, children, and forgiveness of wrong, which will be listened to wherever it is preached, and sets all the world sympathising. [4]

We can compare this passage with Dickens' comments on the stylized conventions of melodrama in chapter 17 of *Oliver Twist*. Both passages dwell fondly on the absurd unreality of popular drama; both claim that such contrived spectacles nevertheless offer access to an important truth. But for Dickens that truth is manifested through the form of melodramatic artifice, with its

4. These have been studied by James H. Wheatley, *Patterns in Thackeray's Fiction* (Cambridge, Mass.: M.I.T. Press, 1969), pp. 1–28. John Loofbourow, *Thackeray and the Form of Fiction* (Princeton: Princeton University Press, 1964), also begins with the early works to show the importance of Thackeray's manipulation of available forms and styles. Both critics go on to develop versions of the opposition between forms and feeling in Thackeray's later fiction.

pattern of extreme contrasts, while for Thackeray the form of "fine words" and theatrical illusion is simply false: "sham," "balderdash." The truth, or "reality" which is somehow "in the midst" of these shams without being contaminated by them is a truth of inner feeling, the generous sentiment which responds to the display of "love, children, and forgiveness of wrong." Thackeray's art, by implication, will reject the falsified speech and behavior of sentimental drama, just as it rejects those of "silver fork" or "Newgate" novels, but its positive efforts will be aimed at communicating the truth of feeling and at tracing the relation between that inner truth and the false forms which distort it.

To regard this brief passage in isolation as a declaration of artistic principles may seem to assign Thackeray an aesthetic which is sentimental in its uncritical acceptance of generalized stock responses and confused in its failure to recognize, as Dickens does, the connection between form and significance. The passage, however, is not an independent assertion but part of a scene, in which its generalizations perform the function of psychological analysis, helping to explain Pen's response to the play. The relation of commentary to action here, and the relation of this scene to the novel's larger context can serve to illustrate more general principles of structure in Thackeray.

As Emily Costigan, as "Miss Fotheringay," enacts the role of Mrs. Haller, she demonstrates the power of the drama's "sham" to "set all the world sympathising." ("With what smothered sorrow, with what gushing pathos, Mrs. Haller delivered her part!") The multiplication of names here is significant: the actress, appearing under her stage name, plays the part of a character whose intense feelings she communicates without experiencing them herself. Pen falls in love with a double illusion. Not for one moment do we share his delusion; the groundlessness of his adolescent emotion is apparent even before the next chapter, "Mrs. Haller at Home," presents the "real" Emily in all her prosaic domesticity and complacent, amiable stupidity. But, as happens so often in Thackeray, the dichotomy of illusion and reality breaks down here. The passage on the "reality" which appears in the midst of *The Stranger's* sham, as well as the generally sympathetic tone with which Pen's early follies are presented, prepare us to value the sincerity of his feelings and his capacity to experience them, to value feeling in itself, apart from its object. "To love foolishly is better than not to be able to love at all," the narrator comments later. "Some of us can't: and are proud of our impotence, too" (6). The point is subtly reinforced in the theatre scene when, as "Mrs. Haller" reaches the peak of pathos, "little Bows buried his face in his blue cotton handkerchief, after crying out 'Bravo.' " Bows has "made her," "taken her in hand and taught her part after part" by drilling her in mechanical duplication of his example (6), yet he cannot help responding to the sham he has created.

Pen is also acting out a preestablished role. Awaking on the morning after the play, he is delighted to find that "he was as much in love as the best hero in the best romance he ever read" (4), for even before encountering Emily,

> Pen began to feel the necessity of a first love—of a consuming passion—of an object on which he could concentrate all those vague floating fancies under which he sweetly suffered—of a young lady to whom he could really make verses, and whom he could set up and adore, in place of those unsubstantial Ianthes and Zuleikas to whom he addressed the outpourings of his gushing muse. [3]

And as we observe these interchanges of life and art, we should begin to recognize another level, on which Thackeray is contriving this charming fiction of youthful enthusiasm with which he strives to set us sympathizing.

Pendennis is the story not only of a young man's sentimental education but of the growth of a writer. Pen's career illustrates the development of the artist as his position converges with that of the authorial narrator, so that he can in turn become the narrative persona of later novels; but at the same time the story of his "fortunes and misfortunes" offers an implicit account of the motives and methods of narrative. Pen's progress moves through successive stages of error and illusion toward what is presented as eventual enlightenment, the choice of Laura and the domestic pieties she represents. But in an important sense the activity of the narrator moves in the opposite direction, recreating youthful illusions and celebrating the lost capacity to experience them. The principle of this substitution is indicated in a passage of narrative commentary that follows immediately after the con-

clusion of the Fotheringay episode and marks the beginning of
Pen's next stage, his career at the university.

> Every man, however brief or inglorious may have been his
> academical career, must remember with kindness and tenderness
> the old University comrades and days. The young man's life is just
> beginning; the boy's leading-strings are cut, and he has all the novel
> delights and dignities of freedom. He has no idea of cares yet, or of
> bad health, or of roguery, or poverty, or tomorrow's disappoint-
> ment. The play has not been acted so often as to make him tired.
> Though the after-drink, as we mechanically go on repeating it, is
> stale and bitter, how pure and brilliant was that first sparkling
> draught of pleasure!—How the boy rushes at the cup, and with
> what a wild eagerness he drains it! But old epicures who are cut off
> from the delights of the table, and are restricted to a poached egg
> and a glass of water, like to see people with good appetites; and, as
> the next best thing to being amused at a pantomime one's self is to
> see one's children enjoy it, I hope there may be no degree of age or
> experience to which mortal may attain, when he shall become such
> a glum philosopher, as not to be pleased by the sight of happy
> youth. [17][5]

The most obvious implication here is the familiar image of
Thackeray as the exponent of nostalgia ("Thackeray is the
novelist of memory—of our memories as well as his own"),[6] but
equally important is the way the passage indicates the function of
narration, and the motive for the multiplication of narratives, in
the reenactment through mediating surrogates of experience
which is not (or no longer) directly accessible.

Following the original doubling of narrator and protagonist,
the number of surrogates multiplies as the narrative progresses.
In moving toward the position of the author, Pen serves this
function for others, such as Warrington, and eventually arrives at
a point where others must serve it for him. Thus, when he escorts

5. The same image of mediated pleasure appears in the *Roundabout Papers*: "A
pantomime is not always amusing to persons who have attained a certain age; but
a boy at a pantomime is always amused and amusing, and to see his pleasure is
good for most hypochondriacs" ("*De Juventute*").

6. G.K. Chesterton, *The Victorian Age in Literature* (New York: Henry Holt,
1913), p. 126. For a more recent development of this notion, see Myron Taube,
"Thackeray and the Reminiscential Vision," *Nineteenth-Century Fiction* 18 (1963):
247–59. A more general treatment of time and memory in Thackeray is presented
by Jean Sudrann, "The Philosopher's Property: Thackeray and the Use of Time,"
Victorian Studies 10 (1967): 359–88.

Fanny at Vauxhall, he finds himself "pleased with her pleasure . . . . 'What would I not give for a little of this pleasure?' said the *blasé* young man" (46). At this stage, the narrative focus shifts to secondary figures who can provide substitutes for Pen's lost simplicity. Thus chapter 39, "Relates to Mr. Harry Foker's Affairs," focuses on the dissipated young brewer's heir at the point when all his precocious sophistication is swept away by his sudden infatuation with Blanche Amory. A similar shift after the evening at Vauxhall permits us to "peep into Fanny's bed" and "find the poor little maid tossing upon her mattress . . . and thinking over all the delights and events of that delightful, eventful night, and all the words, looks, and actions of Arthur, its splendid hero" (47).

As this passage suggests, there is an element of voyeurism in the effort to repossess these youthful experiences, but it is controlled by the distance Thackeray maintains, an effect that becomes clear when we fill in the ellipses: "Fanny's bed (which she shared in a cupboard, along with [her] two little sisters)"; "tossing upon her mattress, to the great disturbance of its other two occupants." The narrative is never completely dominated by Pen's or Fanny's or Foker's view of their experience, but is always colored by the benign irony of Thackeray's retrospection. Indeed, the whole pattern of doubling between character and narrator rests on the premise that experience can be understood only in retrospect, a truth which the characters' own experience repeatedly demonstrates. Thus the narrator comments on Pen's early life in London: "at this time of his life Mr. Pen beheld all sorts of places and men; and very likely did not know how much he enjoyed himself until long after, when balls gave him no pleasure, neither did farces make him laugh; nor . . ." etc. (36). After the convalescent Pen, Helen, and Laura have left Warrington alone in the chambers they have all shared, he immediately realizes "he had had the happiest days of his life . . . he knew it now they were just gone" (53). And later Laura realizes she has come to love Warrington only when he reveals the secret marriage that makes their love impossible (66).

Yet the clearer view of hindsight is always accompanied by regret for the lost possibilities it identifies; the narrative is marked by several extended passages of nostalgia for "the delightful capacity to enjoy" (30), or more generally for "old times . . . when people were young—when *most* people were young. Other people are young now, but we no more" (52). Even when change brings improvement, such as escape from illusion or obsession, it is still experienced as loss. Pen, realizing as he emerges from his illness that he no longer loves Fanny, is both relieved and ashamed: "It is pleasant, perhaps, but it is humiliating to own that you love no more" (53). The narrative takes the form of a generalized memory, preserving a link with the lost past, but while it reveals an underlying continuity through all the vicissitudes of life, it also reveals our isolation:

> Are you not awe-stricken, you, friendly reader, who, taking the page up for a moment's light reading, lay it down, perchance, for a graver reflection,—to think how you, you who have consummated your success or your disaster, may be holding marked station, or a hopeless and nameless place, in the crowd—who have passed through how many struggles of defeat, success, crime, remorse, to yourself only known!—who may have loved and grown cold, wept and laughed again, how often!—to think how you are the same *You*, whom in childhood you remember, before the voyage of life began! It has been prosperous, and you are riding into port, the people huzzaing and the guns saluting,—and the lucky captain bows from the ship's side, and there is a care under the star on his breast which nobody knows of: or you are wretched, and lashed, hopeless, to a solitary spar out at sea:—the sinking man and the successful one are thinking each about home, very likely, and remembering the time when they were children; alone on the hopeless spar, drowning out of sight; alone in the midst of the crowd applauding you. [59]

The narrator's apostrophes assert the isolation and incommunicability of the self: "Ah, sir—a distinct universe walks about under your hat and under mine . . . you and I are but a pair of infinite isolations, with some fellow-islands a little more or less near to us" (16). But his narrative works against this condition. The retrospective account of typical early experience, the presentation of multiple surrogates, attempt to render simultaneously the perspectives which are in life successive and mutually exclusive stages of experience. This conflation of experience and subsequent understanding constitutes Thackeray's image of community, the shared fictive consciousness that joins the "distinct universes" of author and reader. It is clearly a community that does not and cannot correspond to any actual society but exists only within the narrative structure.

This fictive community of experience, the compound perspective which joins the unique and the typical, may be postulated as the goal of Thackeray's narrative, but the project and the means of fulfilling it repeatedly appear suspect. The corrupt Lord Steyne and his cronies throw an ironic light on the reenactment of youthful experience as they sit, appropriately, in a theatre box and discuss Major Pendennis' absence from town.

> "The secret is out," said Mr. Wenham, "there's a woman in the case."
>
> "Why, d—— it, Wenham, he's your age," said the gentleman behind the curtain.
>
> "Pour les âmes bien nées, l'amour ne compte pas le nombres des années," said Mr. Wenham, with a gallant air. "For my part, I hope to be a victim till I die, and to break my heart every year of my life." The meaning of which sentence was, "My lord, you need not talk: I'm three years younger than you, and twice as well *conservé.*"
>
> "Wenham, you affect me," said the great man, with one of his usual oaths. "By —— you do. I like to see a fellow preserving all the illusions of youth up to our time of life—and keeping his heart warm as yours is. Hang it, sir,—it's a comfort to meet with such a generous, candid creature.—Who's that gal in the second row, with blue ribbons, third from the stage—fine gal. Yes, you and I are sentimentalists." [14]

Closer to the novel's own procedure is the way Pen capitalizes on his first great love for the Fotheringay. At Oxbridge the story of his former passion and the verses which had expressed it contribute to his prestige: "There are few things which elevate a lad in the estimation of his brother boys, more than to have a character for a great and romantic passion" (18). Later he derives more substantial profit from the episode by reworking the manuscript in which he had recorded his experience into his "fashionable" novel, *Leaves from the Life-Book of Walter Lorraine.* Once the written record evokes only "the ghost of the dead feeling," it can be made into commercially successful literature, a process which seems to merit Warrington's scornful comment:

> "That's the way of poets," said Warrington. "They fall in love, jilt, or are jilted: they suffer and they cry out that they suffer more than any other mortals: and when they have experienced feelings

enough they note them down in a book, and take the book to market. All poets are humbugs; directly a man begins to sell his feelings for money he's a humbug." [41]

But this is again an oversimplification, for even the "original" passion was inspired and expressed by the conventional forms of romance. Nowhere can we locate an unmediated source of feeling or value.

If truth cannot be established as an origin, it may be posited as a goal. Thackeray attempts to oppose Pen's progressive emergence from illusion to the continuing confusion of life and art represented by Blanche Amory, who hovers between hypocrisy and self-deception, transposing her emotions into her book of poems *Mes Larmes,* and attempting to act out its sentimental fictions in her life. Thackeray passes a harsh final judgment on Blanche: "this young lady was not able to carry out any emotion to the full; but had a sham enthusiasm, a sham hatred, a sham love, a sham taste, a sham grief, each of which flared and shone very vehemently for an instant, but subsided and gave place to the next sham emotion" (73). Making Blanche represent an irredeemable falsification of experience helps to advance both Pen's and Thackeray's claims for a more honest art: "I ask you to believe that this person writing strives to tell the truth," he writes in his preface. "If there is not that [the truth, or the striving?], there is nothing."

From the mingled "sham" and "reality" of *The Stranger* to the purely "sham emotion" of Blanche Amory we have traced a circle where Thackeray would have us find a more linear development. The issue here is not an interpretation of *Pendennis,* which has not been attempted, but the basic terms in which Thackeray's fiction is defined, terms that lie closer to the surface in this story of writers and actors than in any of his other novels. The problem of mediation, the ambiguous relation of feeling and the forms which express it, of experience and the forms which represent it, is a central concern in all of Thackeray's work. His opposed narrative perspectives—the long view of retrospection, of "philosophic" detachment and generalization, and the view of the immediate experience, blind involvement and particularity—these generate the structural dialogue of all his narratives, though in each the relation between them is different. This type of compound perspective is not inevitably linked to multiple narrative, but we can see in the multiplication of surrogates, in the effort to differentiate and oppose versions of a common theme or situation (e.g., Emily and Blanche: innocent disjunction vs. compromised confusion of acting and feeling), and in the developmental organization of these doubles and opposites to form a narrative argument, the basis for a more fully articulated multiple narrative. It was, of course, such a work which had preceded *Pendennis*.

Vanity Fair is a less intimate novel than Thackeray's later works. It does not ask us to become so closely and continuously involved in its characters' experiences as we do in those of Pendennis, Henry Esmond, or Clive and Ethel Newcome. Of all Thackeray's novels it best exemplifies that "panoramic method" which he represented for Percy Lubbock,[7] the detached, broad survey of space and time that refuses to be confined to a single perspective or line of development, and of all his novels it most fully exploits the compositional possibilities of multiple narrative. In such a work there would seem to be little direct application for those preliminary notions of experience and its mediations we have derived from *Pendennis*. But in turning back to *Vanity Fair* we can recognize not only the same pattern of relationship between the narrator and his narrative but the same terms for representing it. Consider the late, minor scene which occurs during the excursion to Pumpernickel, where, the narrator informs us, "I first saw Colonel Dobbin and his party" at the table d'hôte of the Erbprinz Hotel. Later that evening, he sees them again:

It was what they call a *gast-rolle* night at the Royal Grand Ducal Pumpernickelisch Hof,—or Court theatre: and Madame Schroeder Devrient, then in the bloom of her beauty and genius, performed the part of the heroine in the wonderful opera of Fidelio. From our places in the stalls we could see our four friends of the *table d'hôte*, in the loge which Schwendler of the Erbprinz kept for his best guests: and I could not help remarking the effect which the magnificent actress and music produced upon Mrs. Osborne, for so we had heard the stout gentleman in the mustachios call her. During the astonishing Chorus of the Prisoners over which the delightful voice of the actress rose and soared in the most ravishing harmony, the

7. *The Craft of Fiction* (1921; rpt. New York: Viking, 1957), pp. 93–109.

English lady's face wore such an expression of wonder and delight
that it struck even little Fipps, the *blasé* attaché, who drawled out,
as he fixed his glass upon her, "Gayd, it really does one good to see
a woman caypable of that stayt of excaytement." And in the Prison
Scene where Fidelio, rushing to her husband, cries "Nichts nichts
mein Florestan," she fairly lost herself and covered her face with her
handkerchief. Every woman in the house was snivelling at the time:
but I suppose it was because it was predestined that I was to write
this particular lady's memoirs, that I remarked her. [62]

The immediate function of the scene is to illustrate this stage of
Amelia's experience: "I like to dwell on this period of her life,"
the narrator has just explained, "and to think that she was
cheerful and happy," and he goes on to remark of both Amelia
and Dobbin, "perhaps it was the happiest time of both their lives
indeed, if they did but know it—and who does? Which of us can
point out and say that was the culmination—that was the summit
of human joy?" The ability to perceive such a pattern is of course
developed only in retrospect, but here Thackeray character-
istically superimposes that more distant, superior vision on the
immediate moment. This undramatic episode is the actual
"culmination" for this couple, not, as required by conventional
form, their later, tearful reunion on the pier at Ostend: "Here it
is," the narrator ironically exclaims, "the summit, the end—the
last page of the third volume" (67).

Amelia and Dobbin's idyll at Pumpernickel is thus set in the
context of their previous trials and subsequent anticlimax, and it
is here that "Thackeray" first encounters his characters and
learns their story: "It was on this very tour that I, the present
writer of a history of which every word is true, had the pleasure
to see them first, and to make their acquaintance." The scene at
the theatre, he affirms only half-jokingly, is thus located at the
origin of the entire narrative, and we recognize that its pattern of
doubled response is an emblem of mediated feeling, in which
Amelia becomes the surrogate for more detached observers like
the narrator.

If we consider the relation between Amelia and the writer of
her "memoirs" which is presented here as the "original" relation
between the narrator and characters of *Vanity Fair,* we postulate
a narrative whose figures function first of all as registers of
experience, instruments for establishing a characteristic relation

to the world. This is admittedly an unfamiliar way of describing *Vanity Fair*. It seems more easily applicable to a novel by Henry James, where the characters' inner lives are much more fully developed and there is less discrepancy between their level of consciousness and the narrator's. But the paradox of a narrative which aims to recreate experience that is never directly available is, as our brief consideration of *Pendennis* has suggested, a major constituent of Thackeray's fiction. In *Vanity Fair,* where his irony more clearly reflects on his own authorial activity, we can explore that paradox further. At this point, let us simply note the implications of the theatre scene, which stresses the process of mediation and subordinates the questions of moral judgment that usually preoccupy critical discussion of the novel. We can return to the way the characters register experience after examining the novel's narrative perspectives and developmental structure.

The account of "Thackeray" as a friend of the characters and witness to their experiences is, of course, only one of many authorial images in *Vanity Fair* and stands opposed to the figure of the showman who manipulates his puppets while subjecting them to a constant stream of commentary. Thackeray's shifting narrative stances serve the rhetorical purpose of controlling distance, but they also cast an ironic perspective on the act of narration itself, exposing the problematic process of mediation which conditions all knowledge and evaluation of the fictional world. The possibility of a multiple narrative rests, as we have seen in Dickens, on the convention of narrative omniscience, which permits the shift of focus between concurrent actions. Thackeray frequently exploits this power, as in the famous juxtaposition which concludes chapter 32: "Darkness came down on the field and city: and Amelia was praying for George, who was lying on his face, dead, with a bullet through his heart." The repeated presentation of simultaneous actions creates an awareness that any given event or sequence is only part of a larger pattern and creates an expectation that it will be correlated with others, an expectation on which the narrator can in turn play: "In the autumn evenings (when Rebecca was flaunting at Paris, the gayest among the gay conquerors there, and our Amelia, our dear wounded Amelia, ah! where was she?) Lady Jane would be sitting in Miss Crawley's drawing-room singing sweetly to her" (34).

Yet for all the novel's heavy reliance on this convention, the narrator repeatedly reminds us that it *is* a convention ("novelists have the privilege of knowing everything" [3]) and that his ability to reveal the separate, hidden lives of his characters depends on the assumption of a fictive role:

> I know where [Amelia] kept that packet she had—and can steal in and out of her chamber like Iachimo—like Iachimo? No—that is a bad part. I will only act Moonshine, and peep harmless into the bed where faith and beauty and innocence lie dreaming. [12]

> If, a few pages back, the present writer claimed the privilege of peeping into Miss Amelia Sedley's bed-room, and understanding with the omniscience of the novelist all the gentle pains and passions which were tossing upon that innocent pillow, why should he not declare himself to be Rebecca's confidante too, master of her secrets, and seal-keeper of that young woman's conscience? [15]

Furthermore, the claim to omniscience may just as easily be withdrawn, leaving the narrator uncertain ("My belief is . . ." [16]) or unable to decide on the correct version: "But who can tell you the real truth of the matter?" (2). Later, lacking entrée to the aristocratic world of Gaunt House, he must rely on the reports of "little Tom Eaves" (47), and eventually we are told that much of the novel has been derived from Tapeworm, the Secretary of Legation at Pumpernickel, "who of course knew all the London gossip, and was besides a relative of Lady Gaunt," and who, in response to Dobbin's questions, "poured out into the astonished Major's ears such a history about Becky and her husband as astonished the querist, and supplied all the points of this narrative, for it was at that very table years ago that the present writer had the pleasure of hearing the tale" (66).

The doubtful authenticity of such information is matched by the doubtful authority of the narrator as moral commentator. The general moral perspective imposed by the title is enforced by numerous reflections on the vanity of the world and its distorted values, and "Thackeray" appears to strengthen his criticism by disowning any moral superiority, admitting his own implication in these errors: he is the preacher in cap and bells addressing his "brother wearers of motley." But the more he tries to define his position in relation to his story and audience, the more deeply compromised he becomes:

107

I have heard a brother of the story-telling trade, at Naples, preaching to a pack of good-for-nothing honest lazy fellows by the sea-shore, work himself up into such a rage and passion with some of his villains whose wicked deeds he was describing and inventing, that the audience could not resist it, and they and the poet together would burst out into a roar of oaths and execrations against the fictitious monster of the tale, so that the hat went round, and the bajocchi tumbled into it, in the midst of a perfect storm of sympathy.

At the little Paris theatres, on the other hand, you will not only hear the people yelling out, *"Ah gredin! Ah monstre!"* and cursing the tyrant of the play from the boxes; but the actors themselves positively refuse to play the wicked parts, such as those of *infâmes Anglais,* brutal Cossacks, and what not, and prefer to appear at a smaller salary, in their real characters as loyal Frenchmen. I set the two stories one against the other, so that you may see that it is not from mere mercenary motives that the present performer is desirous to show up and trounce his villains; but because he has a sincere hatred of them, which he cannot keep down, and which must find a vent in suitable abuse and bad language.

I warn my "kyind friends," then, that I am going to tell a story of harrowing villany and complicated—but, as I trust, intensely interesting—crime. My rascals are no milk-and-water rascals, I promise you. When we come to the proper places we won't spare fine language—No, no! . . . .

And, as we bring our characters forward, I will ask leave, as a man and a brother, not only to introduce them, but occasionally to step down from the platform, and talk about them: if they are good and kindly, to love them and shake them by the hand; if they are silly, to laugh at them confidentially in the reader's sleeve: if they are wicked and heartless, to abuse them in the strongest terms which politeness admits of.

Otherwise you might fancy it was I who was sneering at the practice of devotion, which Miss Sharp finds so ridiculous; that it was I who laughed good-humouredly at the reeling old Silenus of a baronet—whereas the laughter comes from one who has no reverence except for prosperity, and no eye for anything beyond success. Such people there are living and flourishing in the world— Faithless, Hopeless, Charityless: let us have at them, dear friends, with might and main. Some there are, and very successful too, mere quacks and fools: and it was to combat and expose such as those, no doubt, that Laughter was made. [8]

The two juxtaposed stories hardly demonstrate the narrator's high motives or moral rectitude. Instead, emerging from a confusion of fictive and "real characters," of commercial and religious values, the claim of "sincere hatred" for vice seems no less an assumed role than the expression at other points of cynical worldly wisdom, where " 'I' is . . . introduced to personify the world in general" (36). Irony infects every moral stance the narrator and his audience may adopt, whether he offers them the pleasures of righteous condemnation ("let us have at them") or of tolerant acquiescence: "It is all vanity, to be sure, but who will not own to liking a little of it?" (51).

As a result, every comment or interpretation which the narrator introduces can exert only conditional authority. His formulations raise but cannot resolve the novel's issues; they must be tested against the implications of the narrative as a whole. A brief example, in which Thackeray again sets two stories "one aginst the other" may be found in chapter 61, "In Which Two Light Are Put Out," presenting the deaths of the two old merchants, Sedley and Osborne. The chapter opens with the well-known meditation on the "second-floor arch," in which that detail of Victorian domestic architecture becomes "a memento of Life, Death, and Vanity," and these general reflections on the common fate soon modulate into more pointed remarks (with glances at the story of Dives and Lazarus) on the best state of mind and worldly condition in which to meet death: "Which, I wonder, brother reader, is the better lot, to die prosperous and famous, or poor and disappointed?" Sedley exemplifies the latter; having become reconciled to his daughter during his final illness, the old bankrupt dies a humble penitent.

The shift of focus to his prosperous enemy Osborne strengthens our expectation that the narrative will now fulfill the illustration of the narrator's general moral contrast:

> "You see," said old Osborne to George, "what comes of merit and industry, and judicious speculations, and that. Look at me and my banker's account. Look at your poor grandfather, Sedley, and his failure. And yet he was a better man than I was, this day twenty years—a better man I should say by ten thousand pound."

But in the following account of Osborne's last days, the simple opposition breaks down. He comes to recognize the virtues of Dobbin, whom he has scorned and avoided since George's marriage, and becomes reconciled with him: " 'Major D.,' Mr.

Osborne said, looking hard at him, and turning very red too—
'You did me a great injury [inducing George to marry Amelia];
but give me leave to tell you, you are an honest feller. There's my
hand, sir.' " Through Dobbin's advocacy, he also becomes
reconciled with Amelia and leaves her an annuity in his will. As
this old tyrant softens and attempts to make restitution at the
end, his story becomes more parallel than opposed to Sedley's. In
this complication of the schematic opposition which the narrator
has formulated we may find an effect of "realism" (life does not
conform to abstract patterns), or we may see instead the substitution of one pattern for another, stressing our common humanity
instead of separating sheep and goats. We may even consider this
shift in purely formal terms as the modification of illustrative
functions by plot functions, since Osborne's will not only provides
for Amelia's independence but informs her of her great debt to
Dobbin. In any case, the episode shows how the significance of
Thackeray's narrative emerges only from the play of all its
elements against each other, and it also illustrates the tendency
which most often directs that play, the decomposition of stylized
antitheses.

We can observe this process not only on the scale of circumscribed episodes but in the developmental structure of the entire
novel, which is also, of course, essentially composed of two stories
set against each other, the careers of Amelia and Becky. By this
doubling Thackeray made *Vanity Fair* "A Novel without a Hero,"
not only in its ironic refusal to embody moral ideals (Pendennis,
as his biographer repeatedly reminds us, is also "not a hero" in
this sense), but more fundamentally in its lack of a center. Its
meaning is produced by the relation between its narrative lines,
and that relation is always changing, like the narrator's shifting
roles and stances. The absence of a single compositional center or
perspective thrusts the problem of formal and thematic coherence
into unusual prominence, so that the question of whether and
how the separate narratives are to be connected becomes an
active concern for the reader as well as the author.

One principle which is offered as a possible basis of connection
is that of cause and effect, but it is repeatedly offered only to be
withdrawn. Becky and Amelia begin the novel together, converge
at the time of their marriages, honeymoons, and the Belgian

expedition, and meet once more near the end at Pumpernickel. These intersections, especially the last, are sufficiently contrived to suggest that much depends on them, but this is not the case. Becky, failing to capture Jos in the opening sequence, must go off to the Crawleys just as she would if the episode had never occurred. The possible effects of Becky's stealing George from Amelia are forestalled by his death in battle, and Amelia goes on to suppress her awareness of this betrayal, devoting her life to the cult of his memory just as she would have done if he had never been unfaithful. The final twist of inconsequence comes when Becky produces George's damning note to persuade Amelia to recall Dobbin—and learns she already has (67). Becky laughs in delight, as may we, for the joke is as much on the reader, who should have realized by this time that the significant relationship between the two heroines will not be one of cause and effect. The episodes in which they confront each other directly simply give more explicit and dramatic expression to the play of similarity and difference between them which is implicit throughout. We do not read *Vanity Fair* as we do Dickens' later novels to discover a network of hidden causal connections, nor as we do George Eliot's to trace the minute links of consequence as they are formed. Thackeray forces us to do much sooner what the others also eventually require, to make connections on a different level.[8]

That effort is both incited and directed by the strongly marked parallels between the two narratives which repeatedly place their heroines in stituations that demand comparison. From the opening, where we observe their different responses to leaving school, through their parallel courtships, double honeymoon, and their behavior as wives and mothers, up to their final reunions with long-time admirers, we constantly interpret them in terms of each other. The pattern of their relationship is, like those we have observed on a smaller scale, initially formulated as an antithesis

8. Another factor that reduces the importance of causality is the extended time scheme, in which whatever changes do occur can be shown gradually and in piecemeal stages. Subplots, on the other hand, *are* causally related to one or other of the two main plots (e.g., the episodes in which Miss Crawley's relatives compete for her favor, or Glorvina O'Dowd attempts to capture Dobbin). The causal independence of the main plots and dependence of subplots reinforces the pattern of double focus and controls the dispersive effects of purely analogical connections.

which polarizes both values and qualities of character. The first important occasion for establishing this pattern as the dominant structural principle comes at the point where the two narratives first diverge. This occurs in chapter 7, when Becky must go off to the Crawleys; she and Amelia remain apart until, along with Rawdon and George, they meet again in chapter 14. In terms of proportion and emphasis, Becky dominates this section. She appears in five of the seven chapters, and although Thackeray devotes a considerable part of them to exposition on the Crawley family, much of this is conveyed through her irreverent letters, while the main action presents her successful strategems for establishing herself at Queen's Crawley, as she makes herself indispensable to Sir Pitt, flatters the older son, flirts with the younger, and finally becomes Miss Crawley's favorite.

When, in chapter 12, the narrator interrupts these lively developments "to inquire what has become of Miss Amelia," he must deliberately frustrate the narrative interest and momentum which have just been created. This tactic becomes the explicit issue on which the transition turns, as the narrator records the objections of a hypothetical reader: "'We don't care a fig for her,' writes some unknown correspondent with a pretty little hand-writing and a pink seal to her note. 'She is *fade* and insipid.'" Amelia's claim to attention is first made a question of sentimental masculine preference: she is an instance of "the kind, fresh, smiling, artless, tender little domestic goddess, whom men are inclined to worship" and other women depreciate. But a more important claim emerges as commentary gives way to narration, and the general tendency for a woman like Amelia "to be despised by her sex" is dramatized in the way she is patronized and slighted by the Osborne sisters (and neglected rather than worshipped by George). Her situation assumes a reciprocal relation to the one we have observed in the preceding chapters: the passivity and inexpressive sentiment which lead to her rejection in Russell Square are both the opposite and comple- ment of those qualities which have enabled Becky to succeed at Queen's Crawley. The period during which they have been separated now appears as the "finishing" education of each in her distinguishing qualities: "We have talked of shift, self, and poverty, as those dismal instructors under whom poor Miss

Becky Sharp got her education. Now, love was Miss Amelia Sedley's last tutoress, and it was amazing what progress our young lady made under that popular teacher."

This comparison indicates an underlying symmetry beneath the disproportion of narrative emphasis. Despite the fact that Amelia's is "not much of a life to describe" while she remains protected "in the paternal nest" and Becky is already "on her own wing," she is undergoing a parallel development. And the antithesis of "self" and "love" as their respective "instructors" further implies that she represents the positive pole of value: while Becky cultivates the arts of appearance and manipulation, the unprepossessing Amelia cultivates the inner truth of feeling. They are thus made to divide the field of feminine nature: "Some are made to scheme, and some to love." But again the antithesis is no sooner formulated than it begins to break down. In practice, Amelia's tuition in love consists of worshipping an idealized image of George and elaborating her feelings in long, often unanswered letters. If Becky deludes others, Amelia deludes herself; if Becky is self-seeking, Amelia is self-indulgent. We may favor one or the other, as the narrator does at different points, but Thackeray will never allow us to rest in a simple conception of the relation between them.

This process of construction and deconstruction, of formulating, breaking down, and reformulating binary oppositions, is carried on throughout the novel's development. It is elaborated in many subsidiary doublings, beginning with the opposition of the two Pinkerton sisters in the opening scene and continuing through numerous parallels and contrasts of character and situation.[9] The local effects of these parallels are various and often quite complex, but their general tendency is toward the assimilation of differences, the merging of oppositions into equivalences. The convention of contrasting protagonists is traditionally the basis for a developmental structure which functions as argument,

9. Two studies of the novel's organization provide many examples: Myron Taube, "Contrast as a Principle of Structure in *Vanity Fair*," *Nineteenth-Century Fiction* 18 (1963): 119–35; Edgar F. Harden, "The Discipline and Significance of Form in *Vanity Fair*," *PMLA* 82 (1967): 530–41. Harden's analysis is the more elaborate, claiming that the novel is composed in parallel blocks of two or three successive serial installments. Even though his whole scheme is not fully convincing, he clearly demonstrates Thackeray's extensive parallelism.

differentiating values by the outcome of the action, whether through poetic justice or its ironic inversion (to which Thackeray seems closer), the misfortunes of virtue and the prosperity of vice.[10] But Thackeray blurs the pattern: both heroines experience prosperity and misfortune; both end in positions of secure respectability that do not provide complete happiness. Thackeray deliberately frustrates conventional expectations of a decisive and satisfying resolution: "I want to leave everybody dissatisfied and unhappy at the end of the story—we ought all to be with our own and all other stories."[11]

Critical commentaries on Thackeray's parallelism typically retrace this movement of assimilation, beginning with contrasts and ending with equivalences. Kathleen Tillotson, after describing the more obvious contrasts between the two heroines' fortunes at different stages, observes that "there are also the subtler running contrasts of Becky's treatment of her son Rawdon, Amelia's of George: subtle because Thackeray is critical both of heartless neglect and passionate possessiveness. Or the likeness within difference of Amelia's stupid fidelity to her husband's memory, and Becky's stupid infidelity to Rawdon. Each is an egoist."[12] And the two most detailed studies of the novel's parallels both conclude with a general impression of sameness: "These contrasts . . . create a sense of the limited possibilities of human existence";[13] "the structure emphasizes that, in spite of the differences in men and their lives, all the inhabitants of Vanity Fair are ultimately circumscribed by an inescapable pattern of sameness."[14]

This would seem to be the conclusion of Thackeray's argument: all differences ultimately dissolve in the vision of common vanity, which includes author and reader as well as characters. It is a conclusion which may seem either profound or reductive, or which may seem rather to abandon all moral censure in favor of

10. Mario Praz points out the model of de Sade's "diptych," the stories of Justine and Juliette, which Thackeray knew through the contemporary version by Soulié, *Les Mémoires du diable*. See *The Hero in Eclipse in Victorian Fiction*, trans. Angus Davidson (London: Oxford University Press, 1956), p. 200.

11. *The Letters and Private Papers of William Makepeace Thackeray*, ed. Gordon N. Ray (Cambridge, Mass.: Harvard University Press, 1945–46), 2: 423.

12. *Novels of the Eighteen-Forties* (Oxford: Oxford University Press, 1956), p. 242.

13. Taube, p. 135.

14. Harden, p. 537.

general compassion. In any case, it is, we must remember, specifically the perspective of the conclusion, the long view taken from the end: "Ah! *Vanitas Vanitatum!* Which of us is happy in this world? Which of us has his desire? or, having it, is satisfied?" But Thackeray mistrusts decisive conclusions, both of plot and argument, and this diminishing perspective, in which all the characters become puppets once more, is not the only one he offers. Against the long view of retrospection and disillusioned wisdom he sets the claim of the irreducible moment; against the simplifying conclusion he sets the greater complexity of his narrative process. Both perspectives are engaged at each point in the narrative, and it is only by considering in some detail the way they interact that we can fully recognize the subtlety he derives from his schematic patterns.[15]

Let us return to the point where we began—where "Thackeray" claims he began—to the double spectacle in which characters, like Amelia at the opera, become both the object of observation and the medium of experience. Thackeray's use of the characters as registers of experience is organized by a characteristic dichotomy between modes of response, formulated in the comments which introduce the auction of Sedley's goods after his bankruptcy: "If there is any exhibition in all Vanity Fair which Satire and Sentiment can visit arm in arm together; where you light on the strangest contrasts laughable and tearful: where you may be gentle and pathetic, or savage and cynical with perfect propriety," it is at such assemblies (17). The basic principles of the novel as spectacle are here made remarkably explicit: its numerous contrasts are exhibited as objects of satire and sentiment, two modes which may on occasion appear

15. Wolfgang Iser, *The Implied Reader* (Baltimore: Johns Hopkins University Press, 1974), also discusses *Vanity Fair* in terms of an opposition between distance and involvement, but in his account both types of response are based on a "predominantly intellectual appeal" (p. 116). Distance offers the reader a sense of superiority to the characters, of seeing through their errors and the false social values they imply, while involvement results from making the reader recognize his similarity to the characters and become implicated in their errors, so that "instead of society, the reader finds himself to be the object of criticism" (p. 119). This analysis overlooks the paradoxical effects of more intimate involvement with the characters as registers of experience, which produces not just a simple redirection of criticism from society to the reader but an unstable, dialogical tension between the detached, comprehensive dual-focus mode and the intermittant presentation of Amelia or Becky as a single focus of interest.

together but which "propriety"—and the separation of plot-lines
—usually keep apart. Becky functions as both object and agent of
satire as she pursues her erratic career in the great world, while
Amelia provides the sentimental interludes, offering an alternative or reproach in her domestic obscurity and suffering.

But these complementary stories are not only observed as
spectacle. They also offer alternative modes of participation, the
means of entering into the individual's perspective and pro-
visionally adopting an active or passive stance toward the world
of Vanity Fair, of imaginatively joining its strenuous game of
power and position or of deliberately withdrawing with those who
live on its margins and dedicate themselves to less glamorous
pursuits. The teleology of the novel's argument may insist on the
equivalent vanity of all the forms of life it presents, but at many
points along the way to ultimate disillusionment we are invited to
enter into the characters' sharply different experiences—in part
for the very reason that they *are* only available in the passing
moment: "What well-constituted mind, merely because it is
transitory, dislikes roast-beef?" (51).

Participation in the adventures of Thackeray's active heroine
comes fairly easily: "The famous little Becky Puppet has been
pronounced to be uncommonly flexible in the joints, and lively on
the wire." We can not only admire her unscrupulous agility but
frequently side with her, since she is most often engaged in an
uneven contest with the established powers of a corrupt society.
She represents the claims of an amoral energy, of vitality,
resilience, and wit. Most of all, she presents a brilliant performance, which we can both observe and join. Her sheer skill
can at times command the admiration even of those she has
duped: "What a splendid actress and manager!" thinks Steyne
after learning how she has deceived him. "She is unsurpassable in
lies" (52). Not that Becky's lies and selfishness are themselves
admirable: she can never evade moral criticism for very long. But
in those moments when the burden of judgment is removed from
both character and reader, her power as a medium of experience
is released. In such moments Becky's powers of invention offer
not lies but creative fictions; her energy and resourcefulness in
sustaining and varying her performance constitute a comic
celebration of the power of art over life's accidents and inequities,

as when her efforts to win favor with Lady Southdown by soliciting both religious and medical advice result in her being forced to take the countess' medicine.

> Lord Steyne, and her son in London, had many a laugh over the story, when Rawdon and his wife returned to their quarters in May Fair. Becky acted the whole scene for them. She put on a night-cap and gown. She preached a great sermon in the true serious manner: she lectured on the virtue of the medicine which she pretended to administer, with a gravity of imitation so perfect, that you would have thought it was the Countess' own Roman nose through which she snuffled. "Give us Lady Southdown and the black dose," was a constant cry among the folks in Becky's little drawing-room in May Fair. And for the first time in her life the Dowager Countess of Southdown was made amusing. [41]

Thackeray's passive heroine can hardly exercise an equally powerful attraction: "the Amelia Doll . . . has had a smaller circle of admirers," but his tactic is, as we have seen, to claim a positive value for this apparent deficiency. Thus, in defending the shift from Becky's intrigues at Queen's Crawley to Amelia's quiet life at home, he links her capacity for feeling with her lack of obvious dramatic interest: "Poor little tender heart! and so it goes on hoping and beating, and longing and trusting. You see it is not much of a life to describe. There is not much of what you call incident in it . . . . the life of a good young girl who is in the paternal nest as yet, can't have many of those thrilling incidents to which the heroine of romance commonly lays claim" (12). These comments recall the terms in which Thackeray has previously defended his own art, with a similar mock apology ("I know that the tune I am piping is a very mild one") and opposition to more popular, factitious modes: "We might have treated the subject in the genteel, or in the romantic, or in the facetious manner" (6), with parodic samples of each alternative. In advising his readers that they "must hope for no such romance," Thackeray claims for his work a negative, or relative, realism: its "truth" is perceived through the displacement of falsifying conventions like the heightened drama of romance—or like the acceptance of marriage as a conclusion ("As his hero and heroine pass the matrimonial barrier, the novelist generally drops the curtain, as if the drama were over then" [26]). Just as

Thackeray the performer is linked with Becky, Thackerary the adherent of unglamorous truth is linked with Amelia: her sensibility seems to offer access to an inner truth which the false forms of Vanity Fair distort and repress.

In terms of moral evaluation, the opposition of false wordly values to the truth of the heart would establish Amelia as the novel's moral norm, an interpretation which has the support of Thackeray's most distinguished biographer:

> Life is redeemed for Thackeray only by affection, by love, by loyalty to the promptings of the heart . . . . Becky's career is admirably suited to illustrate the destructive operation of the standards of Vanity Fair, but Thackeray desired through Amelia's history to show what he would put in their place, the life of personal relations, the loyalty and selflessness inspired by home affections. This recurring contrast was essential to his purpose.[16]

But we have already seen how "this recurring contrast" breaks down into equivalence. Amelia's opposition to Becky offers not so much a standard of judgment as an alternative mode of participation, a perception of Vanity Fair through the experience of its victim, one who is thrust to its periphery by the same forces that enable the more aggressive to move toward the center. This complementarity may be rendered dramatically, as when Amelia silently suffers while Becky charms George, or by structural implication, as when through the central section of the novel, Becky's fortunes rise while Amelia's descend; but it generally invites us to find in the account of Amelia's trials what is absent from Becky's adventures, a depth of feeling which extracts from the world's vanity not comedy but pathos.[17]

Yet as the narrative moves toward Amelia in this search for inner "truth," we repeatedly find the way blocked. The narrator adopts a protective attitude toward her vulnerable sensibility and

16. Gordon N. Ray, *Thackeray: The Uses of Adversity* (New York: McGraw-Hill, 1955), pp. 421–22.
17. The two plots do not, of course, determine a complete segregation of modes. The same kind of contrast can appear within either story, and these transgressions can produce some of Thackeray's subtlest effects. In Becky's story the effect of a sudden note of sentiment is usually accomplished through a character's memory of a lost past, as when Becky's songs lead Lady Steyne to recall her convent childhood (49), or when Rawdon, leaving his son at school, "came away with a sadder, purer feeling in his heart" (52), or when Becky herself, in her later adversity, recalls the husband she has lost: "'If *he'd* been here,' she said, 'those

deliberately limits his omniscience to shield her. Thus, when she seeks religious consolation for the distress of her early married life, the narrator ostentatiously draws the curtain: "Have we a right to repeat or overhear her prayers? These, brothers, are secrets, and out of the domain of Vanity Fair, in which our story lies" (26). The value of such feelings can apparently be preserved only by placing them beyond the range of observation: to present them directly would be an act of betrayal or violation: "Her sensibilities were so weak and tremulous, that perhaps they ought not to be talked about in a book" (38). To invoke qualities which can be properly represented only through their literal absence may seem a mere trick, creating an illusion of depth. We see an instance of such an effect in George Osborne's romantic manner:

> George had an air at once swaggering and melancholy, languid and fierce. He looked like a man who had passions, secrets, and private harrowing griefs and adventures. His voice was rich and deep. He would say it was a warm evening, or ask his partner to take an ice, with a tone as sad and confidential as if he were breaking her mother's death to her, or preluding a declaration of love. [21]

There is a suspicious echo of this effect in the narrator's defense of his claim that Amelia's "simplicity and sweetness are quite impossible to describe in print. But who has not beheld these among women, and recognized the presence of all sorts of qualities in them, even though they say no more to you than they they are engaged to dance the next quadrille, or that it is very hot weather?" (27). But this concerns only the realm of social appearance, however ingenuous, and is offered here in explanation of Amelia's immediate popularity with the young men of George's regiment: "Her simple artless behaviour, and modest kindness of demeanor, won all their unsophisticated hearts." Becky's public performances are deliberately contrived to suggest "the presence of all sorts of qualities" she does not in fact possess,

---

cowards would never have dared to insult me.' She thought about 'him' with great sadness, and perhaps longing—about his honest, stupid, constant kindness and fidelity; his never-ceasing obedience; his good-humour; his bravery and courage. Very likely she cried, for she was particularly lively, and had put on extra rouge when she came down to dinner" (64). Equally effective are the moments when satire invades the domain of sentiment, as in the narrator's sardonic farewell to Amelia: "Grow green again, tender little parasite, round the rugged old oak to which you cling!" (67).

to express emotions she does not feel.[18] In perceiving her disingenuous behavior not just as false but as superbly artful, we
indirectly grasp one of her most important qualities as a potential
surrogate; correspondingly, we can perceive Amelia's "simple,
artless behaviour" as an inadequate expression of the potential
depth of feeling which may be realized through her mediation,
requiring an imaginative effort to grasp what cannot be presented
directly.

Thackeray conveys the sense of a more direct approach to
states of intense feeling and at the same time indicates the
necessity of preserving a distance from them by enacting the
violation of Amelia's privacy through the figures of Dobbin and
Becky. Dobbin contrives to get a last glimpse of her before the
regiment leaves for battle:

> And presently Dobbin had the opportunity which his heart coveted,
> and he got sight of Amelia's face once more. But what a face it was!
> So white, so wild and despair-stricken, that the remembrance of it
> haunted him afterwards like a crime, and the sight smote him with
> inexpressible pangs of longing and pity.
>
> She was wrapped in a white morning dress, her hair falling on
> her shoulders, and her large eyes fixed and without light. By way of
> helping on the preparations for the departure, and showing that she
> too could be useful at a moment so critical, this poor soul had taken
> up a sash of George's from the drawers whereon it lay, and followed
> him to and fro with the sash in her hand, looking on mutely as his
> packing proceeded. She came out and stood, leaning against the
> wall, holding this sash against her bosom, from which the heavy net
> of crimson dropped like a large stain of blood. Our gentle-hearted
> Captain felt a guilty shock as he looked at her. "Good God,"
> thought he, "and is it grief like this I dared to pry into?" And there
> was no help: no means to soothe and comfort this helpless,
> speechless misery. He stood for a moment and looked at her,
> powerless and torn with pity, as a parent regards an infant in pain.
> [30]

Later Becky also intrudes, enabling the narrator both to distinguish his own greater restraint and to reinforce his claim for the

18. Barbara Hardy notes Thackeray's use of "behaviouristic description" in
presenting Becky, restricting his account to her speech, tones, and gestures in a
way that intensifies our ironic awareness that they do not represent her actual
feelings. See *The Exposure of Luxury: Radical Themes in Thackeray* (London: Peter
Owen, 1972), pp. 74–75.

deeper reality of private emotion hidden by the spectacle of dramatic public events:

> Until this dauntless worldling came in and broke the spell, and lifted the latch, we too have forborne to enter into that sad chamber. How long had that poor girl been on her knees! what hours of speechless prayer and bitter prostration she had passed there! The war-chroniclers who write brilliant stories of fight and triumph scarcely tell us of these. These are too mean parts of the pageant: and you don't hear widows' cries or mothers' sobs in the great Chorus of Victory. And yet when was the time, that such have not cried out: heart-broken, humble Protestants, unheard in the uproar of the triumph! [31]

Since such moments do render a powerful sense of Amelia's "helpless, speechless misery," the narrator's claim that her inner qualities are "impossible to describe in print" or "secrets" that lie out of his domain must be recognized as part of Thackeray's strategy rather than literal statements of authorial policy. They serve to intensify awareness of what remains unspoken by an ostentatious reticence that finds its counterpart in the way the narrator draws attention to his decorous refusal to present Becky's more sordid adventures, paying ironic tribute to hypocritical social conventions governing what "ought not to be talked about in a book" (see especially the opening of chapter 64, with its extended simile on the siren's "hideous tail" hidden beneath the water).

In both cases, as on other occasions when we are reminded of the narrator's presence and functions, Thackeray is insisting on the inevitable process of mediation which precludes complete immediacy or direct knowledge.[19] Amelia's role as the primary focus of sentiment does not give her a privileged place in the novel's scheme of values, nor does her tender sensibility represent

19. The same stress on mediation lies behind the vexed question of Thackeray's ability to handle the "big scene," the full dramatic presentation of important episodes (raised by Lubbock and much debated since). In terms of his conception of narrative, such a method would make a false claim to convey unmediated presence. The many ingenious alternatives which Thackeray contrived may be seen in the survey by John A. Lester, Jr., who observes that between "the two poles of author-presentation and dramatic enactment" Thackeray typically employs a variety of "intermediate 'semi-scenes'" in which the process of narrative mediation can still be perceived. See "Thackeray's Narrative Technique," *PMLA* 69 (1954): 402.

a stable inner truth, since her emotions are nearly always implicated in errors of judgment and self-deception. But in using her trials to elicit a sense of pathos, Thackeray opens an alternative means of indirect participation in his fiction. From the detached, inclusive perspective of retrospective evaluation, his two main narratives may cancel each other out, but from the perspective of more intimate involvement, they augment and mediate each other. Their elaborate counterpoint extends the novel's range beyond satire or sentiment into effects of remarkable complexity.

Many of these effects: the interplay of similarity and difference, the expansive force of participation in opposed modes of experience, and the combination of "short" perspective that dwell on the quality of the moment with longer ones that set it in the context of narrative sequence—all may be observed in the brief span of two chapters, 50 and 51, which juxtapose important episodes in each of the two heroines' stories. The first presents Amelia's losing struggle against poverty and final surrender of Georgy to old Osborne; the second presents Becky's triumphant social success in the aristocratic world she has long sought to enter. The effect of their juxtaposition is not just another contrast but the most extreme contrast of the novel, the lowest point in one heroine's fortunes set against the highest in the other's. The pattern produces many obvious ironies bearing on life's injustice, the misfortunes of the humble and loving, the prosperity of the worldly and cynical, which are brought into sharp focus by the two heroines' respective attitudes toward their sons: for Amelia to give up hers is the greatest ordeal she has experienced since her husband's death, while Becky willingly lets hers be sent off to school as a step in her progressive intimacy with Lord Steyne. Other specific parallels between the two chapters elaborate the contrast. Amelia's efforts to make money include the painting of "a couple of begilt Bristol boards," producing "feeble works of art" which are rejected by the Fancy Repository and Brompton Emporium of Fine Arts, and she writes a pleading letter to Jos, "painting in terms of artless pathos" the family's condition. While this "poor simple lady, tender and weak" is vainly trying "to battle with the struggling, violent world," Becky succeeds through her skillful performances in both life and art, disarming and conquering those she meets and, at her peak of acclaim, actually performing in mime and song.

The contrast also serves as a restatement of the antithesis between the outward glitter and excitement of "the great world" and the inner realm of feeling and secret suffering. Becky's penetration "into the very centre of fashion" helps to reveal the hollowness of its glamor: "Her success excited, elated, and then bored her." Amelia's silent struggle appears as only a parenthesis in the account of Becky's conquests; the title of chapter 50, "Contains a Vulgar Incident," offers the characteristic mock apology for descending to such commonplace matters as domestic hardship and love. Again, the narrator insists on the recognition of hidden pathos, like the widows' cries and mothers' sobs drowned out by the chorus of victory after battle as the account of Amelia's painful separation from her son expands into generalization: "The child goes away smiling as the mother breaks her heart. By heavens it is pitiful, the bootless love of women for children in Vanity Fair."

But the juxtaposition of these two chapters also yields a much more profound effect of similarity between the sharply different experiences they present. I do not mean the sort of ironic parallel we might draw by standing back to observe, for instance, that Amelia's blind and overly possessive love for her son is as "vain" and mistaken as Becky's avid desire to enter the great world. I mean the opposite sort of connection which creates greater involvement rather than the reductive abstractness of the "long" view. The most surprising effect of these episodes is the way both momentarily ecape from ironic comparison and allow us to participate in both Amelia's suffering and Becky's elation, to pass from one to the other with a sense of the underlying continuity, the shared intensity of these extremes that draws us more deeply into both experiences. Here the two heroines fully realize their capacity for mediation. Thackeray clearly indicates the element of hysterical excess in Amelia's devotion to her son ("Her heart and her treasure—her joy, hope, love, worship—her God, almost!"), but this does not qualify compassion for her misery. Becky's values are at least equally distorted; we are not asked to approve of her ambitions, but we are induced to participate in her triumph. The narrator has earlier remarked that Becky, "from her wit, talent, and energy, indeed merited a place of honour in Vanity Fair" (34), and here she gains that reward. Wit, talent, and energy can be appreciated for themselves, quite apart from their moral direction, and in Becky's artistic triumph at Gaunt House they appear in a moment of brilliant purity: "She had reached her culmination: her voice rose trilling and bright over the storm of applause: and soared as high and joyful as her triumph."[20]

The bond of intensity between these reciprocating episodes, the double realization of the potential for participation through these characters, is crucial, but it is not the only factor working here. Thackeray still preserves the distance entailed by narrative mediation, a distance which the reader can only try to cross. In presenting Amelia's suffering, the narrator displays the same reticence we have observed earlier: "She could say nothing more, and walked away silently to her room. Let us close it upon her prayers and her sorrow. I thing we had better speak little about so much love and grief." The quality of her experience must, to an important extent, be grasped indirectly, as in the description of the way she leaves Georgy alone with his aunt: "She was trying the separation:—as that poor gentle Lady Jane Grey felt the edge of the axe that was to come down and sever her slender life." Thackeray cited this image in a letter as an example of the way pathos should be "indicated rather than expressed. . . . I say that is a fine image whoever wrote it . . . that is greatly pathetic I think: it leaves you to make your own sad pictures."[21] Inducing this sort of participation is the method of both episodes. Neither offers the illusion of an objective spectacle, and the restriction imposed by the narrator's tact on his presentation of Amelia's suffering is matched by the restrictions supposedly imposed on his knowledge of Gaunt House by his position as "an uninitiated

20. Cf. the later moment of theatrical ecstasy, also located at a "culmination," that produces Amelia's "wonder and delight" observed by "Thackeray" at the performance of *Fidelio:* "the astonishing Chorus of the Prisoners over which the delightful voice of the actress rose and soared in the most ravishing harmony" (62). We can now see this "original" moment of the narrative as a symbolic synthesis of Becky's capacity for expressive performance and Amelia's for intense response. It focuses the problematic status of narrative form in Thackeray, since it figures as a structural center, both origin and ultimate convergence, yet it is also as marginal, as supplementary, as a digression—or a footnote.

21. *Letters*, 2: 425.

man [who] cannot take upon himself to pourtray the great world accurately."[22]

Beyond the factor of narrative mediation, there is the added complication of temporal perspective: both episodes are organized by an opposition between the suspended moment and the continuing sequence. Amelia's protracted struggle and painful act of renunciation are momentous from her own perspective, but Thackeray also sets them in a larger context by including other points of view and continuing the narrative past the separation. Georgy welcomes the change and adapts to it readily; for him, and for the Osbornes, whose side is also sympathetically presented, it is not a loss but a renewal. Like the juxtaposition with Becky's successes in the following chapter, these contrasts intensify the pathos of Amelia's situation, but they also offer alternative perspectives on the same event and allow us to see it as part of a continuing, manifold sequence and not just as an isolated crisis. Becky's triumph is more emphatically framed by commentary and narrative that indicate its transience. It is the narrator's retrospective knowledge that authorizes us to suspend judgment in order to participate in the quality of her experience: "let us make the best of Becky's aristocratic pleasures . . . for these too, like all other mortal delights, were but transitory." The reader is explicitly warned, as the narrator begins his account of the climactic evening at Gaunt House, that "it will be among the very last of the fashionable entertainments to which it will be our fortune to conduct him." Thus a double perspective plays upon Becky's supreme moment: it is "her culmination," both a point of intensity whose quality may be valued for its own sake and the peak of a development which now leads downward.

The title of chapter 51 suggests a double perspective in evaluative as well as temporal terms: "In Which a Charade is Acted Which May or May Not Puzzle the Reader." The longer narrative perspective sheds an ironic light on the roles Becky plays. She achieves her culmination as "the most *ravissante* little

22. Thackeray's refusal to present Becky's triumph at Gaunt House as dramatic scene seemed an artistic failure to Lubbock: "There was a chance of a straight, unhampered view of the whole meaning of his matter; nothing was needed but to allow the scene to show itself, fairly and squarely. . . . Yet the chance is missed, the triumphant evening passes in a confused haze" (*The Craft of Fiction*, pp. 103–04). The point is that for Thackeray "a straight, unhampered view of the whole meaning" is impossible.

Marquise in the world"; even at the peak she can only masquerade as one of the aristocracy. While this charade confines to a circumscribed fiction the role she hopes to play in reality, the other, in which Becky appears as Clytemnestra (for the first time), projects a possibility she may actually realize, a possibility which is underscored by Steyne's aside: "By ——, she'd do it too." Just as the last pages of the previous chapter move on to place its focal event in the context of continuing action, so here Thackeray concludes by giving the narrative a sharp downward turn with Rawdon's arrest for debt as he leaves Gaunt House. The reader may or may not be momentarily puzzled, but it soon becomes clear that this is part of another charade. The conspiracy of Clytemnestra and Aegisthus is replaced by that of Becky and Lord Steyne, and as fiction is transposed from art to life, moral judgment becomes necessary once more. The next intense experience in which we shall be invited to participate will be Rawdon's when he returns home to discover his wife and her patron alone together. But the satisfaction offered by that famous moment of moral retribution will in turn give way to new complications that qualify its claims as the narrative progresses.

This rhythm of approach and withdrawal, setting the arresting interest of the individual and the immediate against the longer perspectives of generality and retrospection, is always at work in Thackeray's narrative, and in the end it is always the longer perspectives which prevail. A concise paradigm may be seen at the end of *Pendennis*, when the hero excitedly returns to Laura with the news that they are now free to marry. Thackeray forces us to pause on the threshold as Pen rushes in to tell her: "May we follow him? The great moments of life are but moments like the others. Your doom is spoken in a word or two. A single look from the eyes; a mere pressure of the hand, may decide it; or of the lips, though they cannot speak" (74). The narrative passes over the scene and then circles back to it, as if it had already taken place, displacing the moment of culmination in order to reaffirm the longer, leveling view and mediating its emotional intensity. In *Vanity Fair*, the end also imposes uniformity: the weak and the strong, the selfish and the generous, the clever and the foolish appear equally implicated in vanity, equally secure and dissatisfied, equally to be pitied and dismissed: "Come children, let us shut up the box and the puppets, for our play is played out."

The final stress on common vanity may be seen as the conclusion of the novel's moral argument, but it can also be seen as a return to the basis of its logic. Its elaborate, restless play on patterns of difference and similarity, exaggerating oppositions in order to collapse them, never allowing the reader a single, stable perspective or standard, this method too rests on *vanitas,* or emptiness, the emptiness which underlies the production of meaning from sheer difference. This ultimate groundlessness makes the novel both reductive and open: if *Vanity Fair* forces us to recognize that all its moments are but moments like the others, each yielding to the next, it also induces us to participate in an expansive process that can have no logical conclusion.

Whether or not *Vanity Fair* is Thackeray's greatest novel, it is certainly the one in which he most fully exploits the dialogical possibilities of multiple narrative. Later works show clear advances in some respects but regression in others. The convention of morally contrasted heroines, for instance, reappears in the opposition of Blanche and Laura in *Pendennis,* of Beatrix and Rachel in *Esmond,* and gives way to a single, divided heroine with Ethel in *The Newcomes.*[23] In this sequence one can observe the evolution of greater complexity in characterization, but there is also a simplification of developmental structure as Thackeray directs his hero toward the definitive rejection of the "bad" heroine and choice of the "good," or, in the case of Ethel, presents the unconditional victory of the good side of her character. Thackeray's allegorical design for the cover of the original parts of *Pendennis* shows his hero ambivalently poised between the two heroines and their opposed attractions, worldly rewards and domestic pieties. But in the end Pen must choose, and, as if to validate this simplification, Thackeray redrew the design for the frontispiece of the book to show his right-minded hero moving in the direction of Laura, home, and duty.[24] Both *Pendennis* and *Esmond* fix the hero's final position with a late scene of revelation that exposes and condemns the false heroine. Pen's

23. Alexander Welsh has discussed this development in the larger context of nineteenth-century "false" and "true" heroines. See "The Allegory of Truth in English Fiction," *Victorian Studies* 9 (1965): 10–12.

24. The change has been noted by Jean Sudrann, "Thackeray and the Use of Time," p. 368.

discovery of Blanche with Harry Foker (73) is primarily comic and merely frees him to carry out the choice of Laura he has already made, but Esmond's discovery of Beatrix with the Pretender supposedly produces a sudden and permanent disenchantment: "The roses had shuddered out of her cheeks; her eyes were glaring; she looked quite old. . . . And as he looked at her he wondered that he could ever have loved her. His love of ten years was over" (III, 13).

These scenes invite comparison with Rawdon's discovery of Becky and Lord Steyne, a moment of equally stark exposure. But in *Vanity Fair* the apparently decisive revelation dissolves into new complexities, not just through the narrator's ambiguous question, "Was she guilty or not?" (53), but through the inclusion of more than one point of view. For Rawdon the discovery of Becky's treachery is clear and decisive, but Becky also experiences her own discovery: "She stood there trembling before him. She admired her husband, strong, brave, and victorious." Her belated recognition of strength, moral as well as physical, in the man she has foolishly underestimated is the obverse of his belated disillusionment; Thackeray's counterpoint yields a subtle irony: "At the moment—the only moment—of appreciation, she loses Rawdon."[25] Becky stands exposed, but not, like Blanche and Beatrix, in order to be summarily dismissed; Thackeray is as much concerned to explore the quality of her experience in defeat as in triumph and to contemplate the emptiness with which it confronts her: "All her lies and schemes, all her selfishness and her wiles, all her wit and genius had come to this bankruptcy." Most important, the scene comes after only three-fourths of the narrative, not at the very end. Rawdon goes on to compromise his position by accepting the appointment Becky's schemes have secured; Becky goes on from this reversal to gain her eventual reward, a booth of her own in Vanity Fair. Thackeray refuses to endorse a simple, decisive resolution.

These differences between *Vanity Fair* and Thackeray's next two novels are closely related to his change of structural principles. The decision to center the narratives of *Pendennis* and *Esmond* in their heroes' careers prevents him from giving independent development to the alternative possibilities represented

25. Barbara Hardy, *The Exposure of Luxury*, p. 26.

by his contrasting heroines. But at the same time the later novels explore other forms of doubleness—and duplicity. *Esmond* is, in fact, an impressive example of the way a double logic can work in a single-focus narrative; like *Great Expectations,* it condenses opposed meanings that might have been articulated separately. The narrative is generated by the initial doubling of Esmond in his twin roles of protagonist and narrator of his story, a division which is stressed by the detached, impersonal manner of his "memoirs," in which he generally refers to himself in the third person. But this doubling of the younger, often deluded, experiencing self and the older, supposedly enlightened, narrating self is common to the autobiographical form and is only the most obvious division. A more important split arises from Esmond's questionable reliability. As several recent critics have shown, it is possible to find in his story quite a different meaning from the one he ascribes to it.[26] Where Esmond presents the account of a development through successive stages of error to eventual wisdom, we can see the cyclical repetitions of oedipal fixation; where he presents an image of modest, self-abnegating virtue, we can see the self-aggrandizing pride of a man who has substituted himself for the series of idols he previously worshipped; where he claims to have achieved lucid retrospective detachment, we can see self-perpetuating blindness. As in the opposition of Amelia and Becky, we can make no final choice between these opposed versions, but neither can we entertain both at once. Alternating between them, we stage our own dialogue of perspectives.

In *The Newcomes* Thackeray returned to the use of multiple narrative. Its slow, expansive account of "the world, and a respectable family living in it" (38) makes extensive use of shifting narrative focus to present the numerous coexisting microcosms that together constitute a broad social panorama. Thematically, however, the multiplication of situations and nar-

26. J. Hillis Miller, *The Form of Victorian Fiction* (Notre Dame, Ind.: University of Notre Dame Press, 1968), discusses both the novel's compound temporal perspectives (pp. 17–25) and "the incompatability between Esmond's interpretation of his own life and the interpretation presented obliquely to the reader" (pp. 97–104). Juliet McMaster, *Thackeray: The Major Novels* (Toronto: University of Toronto Press, 1971), pp. 109–25, discusses Esmond's "moral ambiguity" as indicated by such discrepancies. Barbara Hardy, *The Exposure of Luxury,* pp. 185–87, notes how Esmond's account of Beatrix belies his claims to have outgrown his infatuation.

ratives has a restrictive rather than expansive effect, for its major use is to stress the repetition of the same patterns from one world or generation to another, most importantly the pattern of arranged marriages in which love is sacrificed for wealth or social position. As argument, these parallels contribute to the novel's bitter critique of worldly, "respectable" values, but they also become the occasion for self-conscious reflections on the production of fiction by recreating archetypal patterns. Thackeray's general term for such patterns is "fable," and the novel is framed by opening and concluding sections that directly relate it to the traditional moral apologue. The "Overture" begins with a brilliant pastiche of beast fables that anticipates several themes. To the objections of "the critic" ("What a farrago of old fables is this! What a dressing up in new clothes!"), the narrator replies, "What stories are new? All types of all characters march through all fables: tremblers and boasters; victims and bullies; dupes and knaves," etc. But this insistence on the fictive, conventional basis of his work also supports its claim to significance, since life too is marked by the recurrence of familiar patterns: "There may be nothing new under and including the sun; but it looks fresh every morning, and we rise with it to toil, hope, scheme, laugh, struggle, love, suffer, until the night comes and quiet. And then will wake Morrow and the eyes that look on it; and so *da capo*."

In this stress on repetition we can again see Thackeray imposing the long perspective, in which similarity overwhelms difference. But in *The Newcomes* this perspective is complicated by a method which carries over from *Esmond* some of the problems of mediation that arise from the use of a character as narrator, since the novel is told by Pendennis. Pen (the scribe) is often little more than a transparent authorial persona, but since he is not entitled to conventional omniscience, his narrative is marked by several explanatory asides on the sources of his knowledge that put his authority in question. Some of these appear only as rationalizations for his access to other characters' thoughts: "What young Clive's private cares were I knew not as yet in those days . . . it was only in the intimacy of future life that some of these pains were revealed to me" (35). But this perspective from the "future" involves limitations as well as privileges. The long view of retrospection offers the possibility of greater knowledge and judicious detachment: "This narrative . . . is written maturely and at ease, long after the voyage is over whereof it recounts the adventures and perils." But it also relies on conjecture and invention: "The public must once for all be warned that the author's individual fancy very likely supplies much of the narrative; and that he forms it as best he may, out of the stray papers, conversations reported to him, and his knowledge, right or wrong, of the characters of the persons engaged" (24). Pen justifies his method by analogy with those of historians, archeologists, and paleontologists: "As Professor Owen or Agassiz takes a fragment of a bone, and builds an enormous forgotten monster out of it . . . so the novelist puts this and that together" (47). The fictional narrator claims scientific validity for a narrative that has already been characterized as old fables dressed up in new clothes.

Thackeray frequently plays on this paradox, introducing analogies between his characters and the figures of fable. Ethel, for instance, is the princess courted by three suitors, Kew, Farintosh, and Clive, and manipulated by Lady Kew, the old witch or bad fairy who was not invited to the christening.[27] But the parallels are also ironic, since the narrative does not fulfill the ideal moral norms of fable: the good suffer and the wicked go unpunished. The incomplete applicability of archetypal patterns matches the incomplete knowledge of the "historian"; the apparent contradiction between "scientific" and "fabulous" narration is resolved in their common fictiveness. Both rely on models or heuristic fictions; both can yield only partial and hypothetical knowledge, never direct possession of the particular and immediate.[28]

In Pen's reconstruction of the past Thackeray expresses the aspiration toward complete repossession of experience; each recovered fragment gives hope of total knowledge:

27. These and other uses of fabular patterns are discussed by Jean Sudrann, "Thackeray and the Use of Time," pp. 378–83.
28. Cf. Alexander Welsh's defense of Thackeray's "heuristic use of fiction, which may truly be regarded as scientific," in his introduction to *Thackeray: A Collection of Critical Essays* (Englewood Cliffs, N.J.: Prentice-Hall, 1968), p. 7. If to be "truly scientific" a method must include the possibility of empirical verification, Thackeray's narrative hardly merits that description, since its play of oppositions such as fable and antifable repeatedly returns us to the self-enclosed system of the text.

In the faded ink on the yellow paper that may have crossed and recrossed oceans, that has lain locked in chests for years, and buried under piles of family archives, while your friends have been dying and your head has grown white—who has not disinterred mementoes like these—from which the past smiles at you so sadly, shimmering out of Hades an instant but to sink back again into the cold shades, perhaps with a faint faint sound as of a remembered tone—a ghostly echo of a once familiar laughter? I was looking, of late, at a wall in the Naples Museum, whereon a boy of Herculaneum eighteen hundred years ago had scratched with a nail the figure of a soldier. I could fancy the child turning round and smiling on me after having done his etching. Which of us that is thirty years old has not had his Pompeii? Deep under ashes lies the Life of Youth, the careless Sport, the Pleasure and Passion, the darling joy. You open an old letter-box and look at your own childish scrawls, or your mother's letters to you when you were at school; and excavate your heart. Oh me for the day when the whole city shall be bare and the chambers unroofed—and every cranny visible to the Light above, from the Forum to the Lupanar! [28]

The conceit of excavation results in a remarkable parallel to Dickens' project of removing the house-tops and revealing the pattern of social interconnections. Here the synoptic vision proposes a total, spatial apprehension of time, but the archeological imagery suggests that such omniscience is possible only when the buildings are no longer inhabited, when life has departed.[29] These suggestions are confirmed by the effect of this passage in context. It interrupts an account of the brief period of idyllic happiness Clive and Ethel enjoy together in Baden. Since they are the hero and heroine, whose union is blocked by all the worldly values the novel condemns, its logic would seem to direct us toward sympathetic participation in their experience of intimacy here, but instead of dwelling expansively on this moment, the novel sets it at a great distance. The very expression of desire to recapture the past serves to make it more remote; their happiness appears only through their surviving letters found

29. Esmond also anticipates final, apocalyptic knowledge of the past: "We forget nothing. The memory sleeps, but wakens again; I often think how it shall be when, after the last sleep of death, the *réveillée* shall arouse us forever, and the past in one flash of self-consciousness rush back, like the soul revivified" (III, 7). Here Thackeray more explicitly indicates the impossibility of such knowledge for empirical consciousness.

"among Colonel Newcome's papers to which the family biographer has had subsequent access," reduced to the traces of
"faded ink on the yellow paper."

The novel itself is such a trace. Its hypothetical reconstructions
and rehearsals of old fables can represent experience only as
tokens of its absence, making the individual an instance of the
typical, the moment a reenactment of the perpetual. Thackeray
insists on the mediation that qualifies the authority of his long
perspectives by keeping his patterns incomplete, as he does at the
novel's end by his suspended resolution. After preparing for the
final union of his hero and heroine, first by reforming Ethel and
preventing her marriage to Farintosh, then by rescuing Clive
from his mistaken marriage by killing off Rosey, Thackeray
refuses at the last minute to follow through with a conventional
happy ending. Instead, Pen's narrative stops with the death of
Colonel Newcome, and "Thackeray" himself appears to deliver
the epilogue: "As I write the last line with a rather sad heart,
Pendennis and Laura and Ethel and Clive fade away into Fable-
land." He professes sympathy with the reader's frustrated desire
for a satisfying conclusion and, surveying the fragmentary
evidence which the text provides, offers his own conjecture: "My
belief then is, that in Fable-land somewhere Ethel and Clive are
living most comfortably together." Finally, abandoning even
plausible reconstruction, he surrenders his fiction to the reader's
sentimental preferences:

> Anything you like happens in Fable-land. Wicked folks die *à propos*
> (for instance, that death of Lady Kew was most artful, for if she
> had not died, don't you see that Ethel would have married Lord
> Farintosh the next week?)—annoying folk are got out of the way;
> the poor are rewarded—the upstarts are set down in Fable-land—
> the frog bursts with wicked rage, the fox is caught in his trap, the
> lamb is rescued from the wolf, and so forth, just in the nick of time.
> And the poet of Fable-land rewards and punishes absolutely.

This mock concession recalls the ironic conclusion of *Vanity Fair,*
with its subversion of the happy ending and final stress on
fictiveness. But here the effect is not one of diminution and
dismissal; the character do not dwindle into puppets but recede
beyond our range of observation, preserving their independence
from the "author."

We can derive from this epilogue an effect of "realism" by emphasizing Thackeray's negation of sentimental conventions, confirming the ironic conviction that poetic justice prevails only in fables, not in life, and that *The Newcomes* is really an antifable. But an alternative reading is equally possible, for the epilogue, confirming the promise of the "Overture," locates the entire fictional world in "Fable-land," where "anything you like happens." What has already happened there is thus the result of authorial wish, in this case directed toward the frustration rather than the fulfillment of young love and idealism, the persistent pattern of the parallel narratives. From this perspective it becomes clear that unhappy endings are no more "realistic" than happy ones, though either may fulfill or violate the logic of the preceding narrative. Thackeray leaves the pattern of his narrative incomplete, but this is actually consistent with its logic, since it has repeatedly qualified the authority of its patterns and questioned the validity of its own procedures. Setting one incomplete pattern against another, suspending his narrative between "the world" and "Fable-land," Thackeray preserves the doubleness of his vision.

⇥ FOUR ⇥

George Eliot: Equivalent Centers

Most of George Eliot's novels are multiple narratives. As it had been for Dickens and Thackeray, the form became a means of pursuing some of her most important artistic purposes and articulating some of her deepest imaginative concerns. Her experiments with parallel and converging narrative lines in *Silas Marner, Romola,* and *Felix Holt* each have considerable interest and importance in her development, but they are only preparations for the complex achievement of her two last and most ambitious novels, *Middlemarch* and *Daniel Deronda,* on which I want to concentrate.

Middlemarch, not only George Eliot's greatest novel but in many ways the greatest of all Victorian multiplot novels, is especially distinguished by its power of comprehension, in the sense both of inclusiveness and of understanding. Its broad social scope enables George Eliot "to give a panoramic view of provincial life;"[1] the penetration of its psychological analyses presents an equally sure grasp of individual character, and the steady control of its narrative movement presents both the self and society as "a process and an unfolding" (15) of change and interaction. Its separate plot lines are less tightly linked than Dickens', its parallels and contrasts less sharply stylized than Thackeray's, but this apparent looseness becomes the basis for an attempt at a more complex coherence. "I hope there is nothing that will be seen to be irrelevant to my design," she wrote to her publisher, just as she later asserted that in *Daniel Deronda* "I meant everything in the book to be related to everything else there."[2] Both statements recall her earlier, abstract definition of form as

1. *The George Eliot Letters,* ed. Gordon S. Haight (New Haven: Yale University Press, 1954–55), 5: 241.
2. *Letters,* 5: 168; 6: 290.

"the relation of multiplex interdependent parts to a whole which is itself in the most varied & therefore the fullest relation to other wholes,"[3] but such hints should not be necessary for the reader of *Middlemarch*, who is repeatedly urged to regard the narrative as an intricate web of interrelationships. Much modern criticism has been devoted to describing and celebrating the "wholeness" of *Middlemarch*, and there is no need now to retrace in detail its interwoven strands of action, theme, and image. It should be more useful, rather, to begin by considering the principles and purposes which inform George Eliot's multiple narration and, in light of the structural tensions we have already found in Dickens and Thackeray, to inquire how well it actually fulfills her theory of organic form.

The opening of chapter 29 of *Middlemarch* draws attention to some of the principles that lie behind George Eliot's multiplication of narrative:

> One morning, some weeks after her arrival at Lowick, Dorothea—but why always Dorothea? Was her point of view the only possible one with regard to this marriage? I protest against all our interest, all our effort at understanding being given to the young skins that look blooming in spite of trouble; for these too will get faded, and will know the older and more eating griefs which we are helping to neglect. In spite of the blinking eyes and white moles objectionable to Celia, and the want of muscular curve which was morally painful to Sir James, Mr. Casaubon had an intense consciousness within him, and was spiritually a-hungered like the rest of us.

Perspective is clearly made a moral issue here: shifting narrative focus, interest, and effort at understanding to the less appealing Casaubon becomes an exercise of the moral imagination, a recognition of the existence and claims of another. Like Dorothea, the reader must realize that her husband has "an equivalent centre of self, whence the lights and shadows must always fall with a certain difference" (21). To enforce this awareness, the narrative must present each situation from more than a single

3. "Notes on Form in Art (1868)," in *Essays of George Eliot*, ed. Thomas Pinney (New York: Columbia University Press, 1963), p. 433. The model for this conception is "the human organism," and the passage concludes: "The highest form, then, is the highest organism, that is to say, the most varied group of relations bound together in a wholeness which again has the most varied relations with all other phenomena." See also Darrell Mansell, Jr., "George Eliot's Conception of Form," *Studies in English Literature* 5 (1965): 651–62.

point of view, each character both as he is perceived by others (such as Celia and Sir James) and by himself. From this single, preliminary instance we can begin to see how structure in *Middlemarch* is defined as a set of relations between minds and how the need to represent a multiplicity of minds multiplies both perspectives and lines of development. Each character becomes, in principle, an equivalent center with his own point of view and his own story; each redefines the meaning of the whole narrative "with a certain difference." But while we are asked to recognize these numerous possible points of view, the shifting focus also stresses the limitations and distortions each produces. Equivalent because each is "the centre of his own world" (10), they are also false centers, as the "parable" of the scratched mirror insists:

> Your pier-glass or extensive surface of polished steel made to be rubbed by a housemaid, will be minutely and multitudinously scratched in all directions; but place now against it a lighted candle as a centre of illumination, and lo! the scratches will seem to arrange themselves in a fine series of concentric circles round that little sun. It is demonstrable that the scratches are going everywhere impartially, and it is only your candle which produces the flattering illusion of a concentric arrangement, its light falling with an exclusive optical selection. These things are a parable. The scratches are events, and the candle is the egoism of any person. . . . [27]

The need to recognize both the claims and the distortions of several perspectives creates an especially prominent role for George Eliot's omniscient narrator, as we can also see in the shift from Dorothea to Casaubon. The narrator both offers privileged access to each "intense consciousness" and provides a larger context which contains them all. The narrator appears as an embracing consciousness, capable of relating these partial, incompatible perspectives to each other ("Poor Lydgate! or shall I say, Poor Rosamond! Each lived in a world of which the other knew nothing" [16]) and of relating them to the reader, making us recognize both Casaubon's "difference" and how much he is "like the rest of us." Instead of merely presenting a montage of disparate points of view, the narrator works to establish continuity, here through the brief reflections on the common prejudice favoring youth, a passage from one individual to another by way of inclusive generalizations. This modulation from one perspective to another, moving back and forth between general and particular, similarity and difference, is the basis of George Eliot's narrative method in *Middlemarch,* a method whose principles are formulated in Lydgate's physiological metaphor: "there must be a systole and diastole in all inquiry . . . a man's mind must be continually expanding and shrinking between the whole human horizon and the horizon of an object-glass" (63). This rhythm of expansion and contraction repeatedly carries the narrative from the microscopic scrutiny of particular scenes or states of mind to more general assessments of the characters and beyond to still wider generalizations of their significance, a movement of perspective which corresponds to the developmental structure of separate yet interrelated, distinct yet comparable plot lines.[4]

The narrator's modulations of level, distance, or focus proceed with a firm control that may give the impression of "an incredibly easy effortless manner, the manner of a spinner of tales who passes from one chapter to the next, from one object to another even when remote, without the slightest difficulty,"[5] but the customary smoothness of these shifts should not obscure the difficulties they negotiate. We can recognize Casaubon's point of view as well as Dorothea's, but we can hardly entertain both sympathetically at the same time. Similarly, in moving from particular cases to their larger significance, the narrator must mediate between the competing claims of the individual and the universal, of involvement and detachment. This is most apparent in the application of general moral principles. The narrator of *The Mill on the Floss* warns that "moral judgments must remain false and hollow, unless they are checked and enlightened by a perpetual reference to the special circumstances that mark the individual lot" (VII, 3), and this warning is both repeated and demonstrated in *Middlemarch* in the lesson drawn from an extended analysis of Bulstrode's religious rationalizations for his selfish motives: "There is no general doctrine which is not

4. I have given a more detailed analysis of George Eliot's shifts between levels of concreteness and abstraction in *Scene and Symbol from George Eliot to James Joyce: Studies in Changing Fictional Mode* (New Haven: Yale University Press, 1969), pp. 23–26. See also J. Hillis Miller, *The Form of Victorian Fiction* (Notre Dame, Ind.: University of Notre Dame Press, 1968), pp. 82–84.

5. Walter Naumann, "The Architecture of George Eliot's Novels," *Modern Language Quarterly* 9 (1948): 38.

capable of eating out our morality if unchecked by the deep-seated habit of direct fellow-feeling with individual fellow-men" (61). The generalization defines Bulstrode's moral corruption, but the very terms of this summary judgment require us to preserve our "fellow-feeling" with him, our implication in his failure, which has been the burden of the preceding argument:

> There may be coarse hypocrites, who consciously affect beliefs and emotions for the sake of gulling the world, but Bulstrode was not one of them. He was simply a man whose desires had been stronger than his theoretical beliefs, and who had gradually explained the gratification of his desires into satisfactory agreement with those beliefs. If this be hypocrisy, it is a process which shows itself occasionally in us all. . . .

The narrator's alternation between individual and general is thus not an effortless tracing of connections, not the natural pulsation of an organic rhythm, but a series of small collisions and reversals, a perpetual process of "checking" one perspective against another.[6]

If we contract our focus again to the opening of chapter 29, we can observe signs of strain in the rhetoric that accompanies the effort to make connections. The device of first proposing to continue the previous chapter's account of Dorothea's experience and then breaking it off in mid-sentence is a dramatic way of enforcing Casaubon's claims on our attention, but it is also rather contrived and disingenuous, especially in its imputation of guilt for the "griefs which we are helping to neglect." George Eliot's narrator is really "protesting" against the logic of her own narrative, which has given and will continue to give more attention to Dorothea than to Casaubon, in part for the very reason that she is capable, with painful difficulty, of learning to recognize his "equivalent centre of self," while he can never recognize hers. The thrust of the plot reinforces this preference: the chapter which begins by demanding sympathy for Casaubon's point of view presents as its main incident his heart

6. The tension between these levels is most apparent in George Eliot's conception of tragedy as "the irreparable collision between . . . the individual with whom we sympathize, and the general of which we recognize the irresistible power," in "Notes on the Spanish Gypsy and Tragedy in General," in J.W. Cross, *George Eliot's Life* (London: Blackwood, 1885), 3: 32.

attack, the first step toward eliminating him from the novel in order to give Dorothea a second chance in life. The expansive tendency of treating every character as equivalent is checked by the tendency toward a more centered narrative.

This tension of centering and decentering impulses runs through the whole novel. The shift of focus at the opening of chapter 29 repeats on a small scale the opening movement of the novel in Book 1, which is also based on the pattern of "Dorothea —but why always Dorothea?" Unlike *Bleak House, Little Dorrit, Our Mutual Friend,* or *Vanity Fair, Middlemarch* does not announce its multiplicity from the beginning by discontinuity between its opening chapters or the simultaneous introduction of two centers of interest. Instead it opens with "Miss Brooke," which for the first ten chapters is firmly centered on the story of Dorothea up to her marriage, then shifts in the next two to Lydgate, Rosamond and Fred Vincy, Featherstone and Mary Garth.[7] This delayed expansion of focus in chapters 10 and 11 is more radically disorienting; it forces us to revise our conception of the novel's structure by a break which is not just a rhetorical tactic and whose effects are not just superficial. Indeed, on the surface the movement is far smoother here, as the focus shifts away from Dorothea by a "diastolic" expansion, first in the group scene of Mr. Brooke's dinner party, which introduces several new characters, and then in general reflections which relate such meetings to larger historical movements: "Municipal town and rural parish gradually made fresh threads of connection . . ." (11).[8]

7. This delay could be attributed to the fact that George Eliot originally conceived and began to write the stories of Dorothea and Lydgate separately, but the structural principles by which they are related must still be inferred from the novel itself. See Jerome Beaty, *Middlemarch from Notebook to Novel: A Study of George Eliot's Creative Method* (Urbana: University of Illinois Press, 1960), pp. 1–42, for an account of the way George Eliot joined the original "Middlemarch" and "Miss Brooke."

8. Passages that dilate on the historical context frequently serve to smooth transitions in this way. Chapter 46, for example, begins, "While Lydgate, safely married and with the Hospital under his command, felt himself struggling for Medical Reform against Middlemarch, Middlemarch was becoming more and more conscious of the national struggle for another kind of reform." The following paragraph notes the current state of the reform movement in Parliament and then passes on to a scene between Mr.Brooke and Will Ladislaw as they discuss the political situation. The narrative thus shifts from Lydgate to Ladislaw by a "diastolic" expansion of focus to the national horizon (and at the same time formulates a thematic analogy in the common concern with reform).

The narrative thus maintains continuity as it proposes both new centers of interest and new ways of relating them. We need to consider the principles involved in this process of reorientation before taking up more problematic aspects of the expansion from single to multiple narrative.

The transitional commentary which opens chapter 11 invites us to look for both causal and analogical connections. Introducing Rosamond in opposition to Dorothea, it begins the process of comparing parallel figures and stories while raising the expectation of eventual intersection:

> Certainly nothing at present could seem much less important to Lydgate than the turn of Miss Brooke's mind, or to Miss Brooke than the qualities of the woman who had attracted the young surgeon. But any one watching the stealthy convergence of human lots, sees a slow preparation of effects from one life on another, which tells like a calculated irony on the indifference of the frozen stare with which we look at our unintroduced neighbor. Destiny stands by sarcastic with our *dramatis personae* folded in her hand.

The qualifications "stealthy" and "slow" anticipate the kind of long, continuous developmental structure George Eliot prefers to the dramatic reversals and revelations by which Dickens often connects separate plot lines. She said her "design" in *Middlemarch* was "to show the gradual action of ordinary causes rather than exceptional,"[9] and the narrator frequently stresses this aspect in presenting the unfolding action as a tight fabric of causation requiring close analysis, applying the "strong lens" of a microscope to detect the "play of minute causes" (6), "unravelling certain human lots, and seeing how they were woven and interwoven" (15).

Lydgate's story is the immediate occasion of this last statement of intent and the one that best fulfills it, as George Eliot traces each step in his gradual entanglement by "the hampering threadlike pressure of small social conditions" (18), the determination of his fate by the cumulative effect of numerous small, often inadvertent decisions and lapses. Some of the links between plot lines also involve this fine causal webbing, as when we observe, for example, how Mr. Brooke's political ambitions

9. *Letters*, 5: 168.

lead to renewed prosperity for the Garths ("In watching effects . . . it is often necessary to change our place," the narrator remarks as the focus shifts from Brooke's confrontation with Dagley to the Garth home in chapter 40, where Caleb receives the offer to manage the Freshitt and Tipton estates), an event that will in turn open a new vocational opportunity for Fred Vincy.

But the portentous figure of a sarcastic "Destiny" suggests a very different conception of plot, an emphasis on the result rather than the process of convergence, on an eventual resolution that will determine the meaning of the whole. It may have been this emphasis which led some of the novel's first readers to anticipate the eventual marriage of Dorothea and Lydgate,[10] and although it is easy to see why George Eliot refuses such a pat, conventional resolution, the ways in which these characters may affect each other's lives remain a crucial concern as their largely separate stories unfold. Consideration of this kind of deferred coherence should itself be deferred, however, until we have examined other types of structural relations.

The relative independence of the main plot lines increases the importance of comparisons between them; the distances which separate them on the level of action offer room for a more complex play of analogies than we find in any other Victorian multiplot novel. The decision to join the original "Miss Brooke" and "Middlemarch" seems to have arisen from a recognition of similarities between Dorothea and Lydgate, and the reader reenacts this perception as he compares these two stories of idealistic aspirations frustrated by social restrictions and mistaken marriages. From Book 2 onward, we are prompted to pursue this kind of reading by book titles that direct us to compare "Three Love Problems" or "Two Temptations" and to find multiple applications for rubrics such as "Old and Young" or "The Dead Hand." The perception of such resemblances implies a commanding perspective, just as the observation of gradual convergence is associated with the superior detachment of an aloof "Destiny" or of "Uriel watching the progress of planetary history from the Sun" (41). The "Proem" to *Romola* offers a gloss on this angelic perspective: there the comprehensive

10. See W.J. Harvey's survey of contemporary reception in *Middlemarch: Critical Approaches to the Novel*, ed. Barbara Hardy (London: Athlone, 1967), pp. 128–29.

view of human history is represented by the elevated vision of the "angel of the dawn" passing over the Mediterranean and observing "the broad sameness of the human lot" underlying differences of place and time. Like Thackeray's long retrospectives, this privileged standpoint gives greater emphasis to similarities than to differences. It permits the narrator's formulation of inclusive generalizations and brings into prominence the common concerns of work and love, the problems of vocation, courtship, and marriage which form the grounds of George Eliot's narrative parallelism in *Middlemarch*.

But just as generalizations must be checked by perpetual reference to individual circumstances, so these inclusive themes are checked by differences that resist assimilation.[11] The expansive force of such differences was eloquently registered by Henry James when he considered the "balanced contrast between the two histories of Lydgate and Dorothea."

> Each is a tale of matrimonial infelicity, but the conditions in each are so different and the circumstances so broadly opposed that the mind passes from one to the other with that supreme sense of the vastness and variety of human life, under aspects apparently similar, which it belongs only to the greatest novels to produce.[12]

We should not overemphasize this disjunctive aspect: James's failure to give sufficient weight to the connections established by such a "balanced contrast" led him to conclude that "*Middlemarch* is a treasure-house of detail, but it is an indifferent whole." But the similarities established by George Eliot's thematic analogies in *Middlemarch* are so broad that they leave room for an unusually large range of variation. Unlike more specialized and tendentious analogies such as the various forms of imprisonment in *Little Dorrit* or the various forms of vanity in *Vanity Fair*, they do not in themselves propose an argument. They simply define areas in which we can observe the close and shifting

11. Metaphors of elevated vision are not so strongly charged with a sense of imaginative power or longing in George Eliot as they are in Dickens or Thackeray. Like Dorothea, she is "not at ease in the perspective and chilliness of that height" (34). Cf. the rejection in *Scenes of Clerical Life* of the aloof "bird's-eye station" which misses the "essential truth" of individual lives ("Janet's Repentance," chapter 10).

12. *George Eliot: The Critical Heritage*, ed. David Carroll (New York: Barnes & Noble, 1971), p. 357. James's review first appeared in the *Galaxy*, March 1873.

interplay of similarities and differences, and thus they can always be read with different emphases. One reader may find unity in a balanced contrast while another, like James, may find greater significance in its discrepancies. Considering the many forms in which the novel presents problems of vocation, one of George Eliot's critics emphasizes the expressive power "which makes this formal pattern say insistently that human beings are very like each other,"[13] while another emphasizes differences and concludes that the many instances do not add up to a single general theme: "what emerges is not so much a theme as a set of variations."[14] To isolate and interpret any particular pattern, however, removes us from the actual complexity of the narrative, which, as it expands into full multiplicity, increases the number of possible comparisons until each moment becomes a nexus of intersecting analogies.

This effect can be observed at many points, but it is clearest where the narrator's commentary suggests comparisons, as in the account of Lydgate's bitter discontent as his debts begin to press upon him, his

> sense that there was a grand existence in thought and effective action lying around him, while his self was being narrowed into the miserable isolation of egoistic fears, and vulgar anxieties for events that might allay such fears. His troubles will perhaps appear miserably sordid, and beneath the attention of lofty persons who can know nothing of debt except on a magnificent scale. Doubtless they were sordid; and for the majority, who are not lofty, there is no escape from sordidness but by being free from money-craving, with all its base hopes and temptations, its watching for death, its hinted requests, its horse-dealer's desire to make bad work pass for good, its seeking for function which ought to be another's, its compulsion often to long for Luck in the shape of a wide calamity. [64]

The series of anonymous instances includes some very precise cross-references: "watching for death" recalls the anxious speculations of Peter Featherstone's relatives in chapter 32, a comic demonstration of the way greed and fear constrict the

13. Barbara Hardy, *The Novels of George Eliot: A Study in Form* (London: Athlone, 1959), p. 107.
14. W.J. Harvey, *The Art of George Eliot* (London: Chatto & Windus, 1961), p. 155.

mind. Similarly, "horse-dealer's desire" recalls Fred Vincy's attempts to pay his debts, his groundless confidence "that by dint of 'swapping' he should gradually metamorphose a horse worth forty pounds into a horse that would fetch a hundred at any moment" (23). Lydgate's case is much more serious than these comic versions of "money-craving," but the analogies indicate the way he is being brought by a process of slow attrition to a similar state of egoistic confinement. The implicit comparison with Fred looks forward to the scene two chapters later where Lydgate becomes totally absorbed in the attempt to win money at billiards, "acting, watching, speaking with that excited narrow consciousness which reminds one of an animal with fierce eyes and retractile claws," presenting "a strange reversal of attitudes" with Fred, who is shocked to find him "looking excited and betting, just as he himself might have done" (66). It is a reversal which marks the crossing of two paths, one leading upward, the other down.

These cross-references are only a few of the possible comparisons. Lydgate's and Fred's gambling recalls Farebrother, who is also brought into the billiards scene. (The phrase about "seeking for function" also recalls Farebrother's unsuccessful candidacy for the position of hospital chaplain.) Lydgate had felt distaste at Farebrother's playing cards for money: "he had an ideal of life which made this subservience of conduct to the gaining of small sums thoroughly hateful to him" (18), but he fails to profit by Farebrother's example and advice: "take care not to get hampered about money matters" (45). Farebrother was never so badly hampered or compromised as Lydgate becomes; accepting frustration, he preserves his integrity, but he also escapes from "money-craving" through Lydgate, who recommends him as rector of Lowick, a favor Farebrother later tries unsuccessfully to return. Again the parallels diverge, the paths cross. We could also set Lydgate's plight against the much greater poverty of the Garths and their ability to sustain it without compromising values quite as idealistic as his. (Farebrother cites their example in his first conversation with Lydgate: "a good wife—a good unworldly woman— may really help a man, and keep him more independent" [17]). And on the other hand, we could compare Dorothea, whose superfluous wealth tends to isolate her, not in "egoistic fears" but in "motiveless ease" (54), and who gladly gives it up to marry Will Ladislaw and "learn what everything costs" (83).

Beyond all such specific comparisons of money troubles lies the broader comparison of moral and psychological states that relate all the novel's characters to each other. George Eliot's emphasis on the importance of such "miserably sordid" matters as small debts is part of her inistence on the moral significance of the commonplace, the hidden depth of ordinary experience, including "that element of tragedy which lies in the very fact of frequency" (20). One way she makes us feel this depth is by the range of reference that can be brought to bear on each individual's experience. Lydgate's sense of "his self . . . being narrowed" is echoed by other characters' experiences of isolation and by numerous metaphors of confinement and expansion. We could compare Dorothea's earlier experience of confinement, "struggling in the bands of a narrow teaching, hemmed in by a social life which seemed nothing but a labyrinth of petty courses, a walled-in maze of small paths that led no whither" (3). Casaubon's proposal seems to offer "a fuller life . . . opening before her. . . . She was going to have room for the energies which stirred uneasily under the dimness and pressure of her own ignorance and the petty peremptoriness of the world's habits" (5). But of course Casaubon is "himself . . . lost among small closets and winding stairs," so that "the large vistas and wide fresh air which she had dreamed of finding in her husband's mind were replaced by anterooms and winding passages which seemed to lead nowhither" (20). Dorothea is imprisoned at Lowick, both before and after Casaubon's death, a confinement from which Ladislow offers escape. When it at last becomes clear that they love each other, at a point only a few pages before the passage describing Lydgate's increasing confinement, "it was as if some hard icy pressure had melted, and her consciousness had room to expand" (62).[15]

Many other examples could be added, for the degree and quality of openness and potential for growth or enclosure and limitation are important features of most of the characters, and in

15. Barbara Hardy discusses several of these and other related images in *The Novels of George Eliot*, pp. 221–23.

every case we see the different roles played by intention and circumstance. Lydgate's isolation is not the wilful self-enclosure of a Casaubon, but to see him falling into "a bitter moody state which was constantly widening Rosamond's alienation from him" (64) recalls that other "tale of matrimonial infelicity" in a way that sharpens the irony of his fate. It is his own awareness of what is happening to him that most distinguishes Lydgate and makes his deterioration tragic. He is being cut off from the larger life of "thought and effective action lying around him," but the multiple analogies which define his situation by their overlapping similarities and differences connect him with the larger life of the novel.

This capacity for making connections is even more striking when the novel's thematic analogies reach out to incorporate a minor figure who has previously appeared only in the background. The best example of this effect comes in chapter 74, when Harriet Bulstrode learns of the scandal about her husband: "She locked herself in her room. She needed time to get used to her maimed consciousness, her poor lopped life, before she could walk steadily to the place allotted her." The imagery recalls the account of Lydgate's painful acceptance of Rosamond's unresponsiveness: "The first great disappointment had been borne: the tender devotedness and docile adoration of the ideal wife must be renounced, and life must be taken up on a lower stage of expectation, as it is by men who have lost their limbs" (64),[16] while her situation invites a more general comparison with Dorothea's disillusionment with Casaubon. Mrs. Bulstrode's acceptance of her wretched husband and the humiliation he has brought on her is presented in terms of a hypothetical contrast: "it was not possible to her in any sense to forsake him. There is a forsaking which still sits at the same board and lies on the same couch with the forsaken soul, withering it the more by unloving proximity." As Barbara Hardy points out, this "unloving proximity" is illustrated in the next chapter by Rosamond's cold

16. Cf. Fred Vincy: "I have never been without loving Mary. If I had to give her up it would be like beginning to live on wooden legs" (52); and Will Ladislaw, when he thinks that he has lost Dorothea: "there was no more foretaste of enjoyment in the life before him than if his limbs had been lopped off and he was making his fresh start on crutches" (82).

"sense of justified repugnance" toward Lydgate, who has been implicated in Bulstrode's disgrace, while Mrs. Bulstrode's ritual change of costume before facing her husband is echoed by Dorothea's when she prepares to return to Rosamond in chapter 80.[17] These parallels and contrasts link this private crisis with the novel's major actions and themes, defining and amplifying the significance of Mrs. Bulstrode's subordination of her own suffering to another's need. For a moment she moves into the foreground, and all the other stories become a context for interpreting hers.

This effect has already been described by the narrator: we choose one point in an elaborate network "as a centre of illumination, and lo! the scratches will seem to arrange themselves in a fine series of concentric circles round that little sun." The parable of the pier-glass reminds us that in a system of analogies the sense of a single center is illusory, but the capacity for many moments, characters, or stories to become temporary focal points for the entire composition is an important part of the method of *Middlemarch*. Focusing on the crisis in Mrs. Bulstrode's life allows her to emerge as an equivalent center; her decision involves a radical change in her conception of herself and of her relation to her husband, a reinterpretation which in turn becomes the subject of the reader's broader interpretation. The multiple and shifting focus of George Eliot's narrative works to undermine egocentric illusions, but at the same time her focus seeks centers of consciousness which can enact a process of interpretation like the reader's. In the more fully developed consciousnesses of the major characters, the parallel becomes more apparent. Here, for example, is a moment when we can observe Lydgate "reading" analogies, experiencing the tension of similarity and difference, generalization and exception, as he bleakly compares his wife with the two other women who have strongly impressed him:

> His mind glancing back to Laure while he looked at Rosamond, he said inwardly, "Would *she* kill me because I wearied her?" and then, "It is the way with all women." But this power of generalising which gives men so much the superiority in mistake over the dumb animals, was immediately thwarted by Lydgate's memory of

17. *The Novels of George Eliot*, pp. 102–04.

wondering impressions from the behaviour of another woman—
from Dorothea's looks and tones of emotion about her husband
when Lydgate began to attend him—from her passionate cry to be
taught what would best comfort that man for whose sake it seemed
as if she must quell every impulse in her except the yearnings of
faithfulness and compassion. [58]

The French actress who killed her husband has appeared much
earlier, in chapter 15, as an ironic anticipation of Rosamond, one
which is fulfilled in the "Finale" by Lydgate's bitter image of his
wife as "his basil plant . . . which had flourished wonderfully on
a murdered man's brains." Here Lydgate, who had originally
considered Rosamond the "very opposite" of Laure (16), recognizes their affinities, but this parallel no sooner becomes explicit
than it is checked, "thwarted" by recognition of an equally
significant contrast. Lydgate recalls Dorothea's plea, "Advise me
—think what I can do," linking this moment with their interview
in chapter 30 and fulfilling the narrator's anticipation there: "For
years after Lydgate remembered the impression produced in him
by this involuntary appeal." Moved by this memory, he appeals
to Rosamond to help him with their pressing debts, but the
hopeful analogy he tried to find in Dorothea's words is immediately checked by Rosamond's chilling inversion of them:
"What can *I* do, Tertius?"

This intersection in the novel's web of meanings engages the
character, narrator, and reader in comparable problems of
interpretation, though as in other analogies the differences between these readings are also important. Lydgate partly grasps,
partly distorts the significance of these comparisons: he senses the
common, potentially deadly egoism of Rosamond and Laure but
fails to recognize the "spots of commonness" in himself which led
him to prefer such women. Yet he can draw on the lesson of the
earlier encounter which showed the inadequacy of his preconceptions: "Women just like Dorothea had not entered into his
traditions" (30). The narrator offers both ironic criticism and
sympathetic confirmation of his thoughts, extending their significance: "That voice of deep-souled womanhood had remained
within him as the enkindling conceptions of dead and sceptered
genius had remained within him (is there not a genius for feeling
nobly which also reigns over human spirits and their con-

clusions?)." For Lydgate, however, this scene remains another groping, largely frustrated attempt to make sense of his life, while for the reader it contributes to growing understanding. It recapitulates and gives sharper definition to the opposition between the novel's two most important women and looks forward to the later scene in chapter 81 where Dorothea's "genius for feeling nobly" will succeed in influencing Rosamond. But beyond these specific parallels and discrepancies there is the larger correspondence, the bond between reader and character formed by their participation in a common process of interpretation, a process which is not aimed at any final truth but, like the lives of the characters themselves, remains open to change and development.

This correspondence is particularly close in passages such as the one we have been examining, where a character's thoughts are directed toward the same relationships the reader must construe, or where a character's general outlook, such as Lydgate's scientific method, offers an analogy for the activity of author and reader, as it does in his metaphor of systole and diastole or in the dependence of his research on a "testing vision of details and relations" (16). But in a more general sense such correspondences run through the entire novel, involving its presentation of both private and public life: throughout *Middlemarch* George Eliot presents her characters' responses to experience as varieties of interpretation. The narrator's commentary underscores this aspect in the opening chapters, which draw on the comedy of manners' traditional concern with interpreting behavior, observing of the mutual misunderstanding between Dorothea and Sir James, for example, that "manners must be very marked indeed before they cease to be interpreted by preconceptions" (2), or of the large "inferences" Dorothea draws from her brief acquaintance with Casaubon that "signs are small measurable things, but interpretations are illimitable, and in girls of sweet, ardent nature, every sign is apt to conjure up wonder, hope, belief, vast as a sky, and coloured by a diffused thimbleful of matter in the shape of knowledge" (3). Similarly, Dorothea's illusions about Casaubon are sustained through the period of their engagement by her tendency to interpret him as she would a sacred text or providential design:

Dorothea's faith supplied all that Mr Casaubon's words seemed to leave unsaid: what believer sees a disturbing omission or infelicity? The text, whether of prophet or of poet, expands for whatever we can put into it, and even his bad grammar is sublime. [5]

His efforts at exact and formal tenderness had no defect for her. She filled up all the blanks with unmanifested perfections, interpreting him as she interpreted the works of Providence, and accounting for seeming discords by her own deafness to the higher harmonies. And there are many blanks left in the weeks of courtship, which a loving faith fills with happy assurance. [9]

Against Dorothea's overinterpretation the narrator sets the depreciative versions of Celia, Mrs. Cadwallader, and Sir James, and then sets all these aside to "turn from outside estimates of a man, to wonder, with keener interest, what is the report of his own consciousness about his doings or capacity" (10). The shifts of perspective which we began by considering as consequences of a moral imperative also appear as part of a larger concern with problems of interpretation. As Quentin Anderson observes,

all novelists must somehow convey the quality of each character's self-regard and the opinions that others have of him. But George Eliot's special success in *Middlemarch* is the consequence of making the reciprocal workings of self-regard and opinion primary—in effect an extraordinary economy of means, and not simply of means, for it appears when we look closely that the matter of the book is people's opinions about one another. [18]

It is only a short step beyond this observation to say that *Middlemarch* is "about" interpretation. A brief review shows how much of the novel's action turns on such questions. Though more explicitly analyzed in Dorothea's courtship, they are equally important in the mutual misconceptions of Lydgate and Rosamond, and the account of Lydgate's career requires a detailed analysis of public opinion, both in his fluctuating medical reputation and in the way his fate becomes linked with Bulstrode's. Bulstrode's story also turns on the relation between his own interpretation of his actions and the community's, both

18. "George Eliot in *Middlemarch*," in *From Dickens to Hardy*, ed. Boris Ford (Harmondsworth: Penguin, 1958), p. 277.

their opposition and their subtler interpenetration: "Who can know how much of his most inward life is made up of the thoughts he believes others to have about him, until that fabric of opinion is threatened with ruin?" (68). This process of defining oneself in terms of another's opinion also informs the two successful love stories, in Mary Garth's influence on Fred Vincy ("Even much stronger mortals than Fred Vincy hold half their rectitude in the minds of the being they love best." [24], and, in a more idealized strain, Dorothea's on Will Ladislaw.[19] By exerting such influence, interpretation becomes an active force, not just the "matter" but the main action of the novel, which reaches its climax in parallel crises of opinion and belief about Bulstrode, Lydgate, and Ladislaw. Through this persistent emphasis George Eliot builds up a comprehensive account of the way men create their own world. Where Dickens' satiric vision exposes a system of collaborative fictions, George Eliot traces a web of intersubjectivity, a network of interpretations.

These collective and individual acts of interpretation parallel our own assessments and comparisons, but the two levels are usually separated by an ironic distance, the gap between opinion and knowledge. Exempted from the characters' limitations, guided by the narrator's analyses, we can recognize their errors, the distortions produced by ignorance, bias, or self-deception. The most important form of error, the distortion which not only the narrative conventions but the structure of the novel works to correct, is the imposition of a single center or principle of unity. Its most common form is of course the egocentrism that flaws so may characters' perceptions, but it also appears in more general terms of method and knowledge. Casaubon, for example, tends "to think that others were providentially made for him" (10), and a similar illusion lies behind his search for a "Key to All Mythologies," the assumption "that all the mythical systems or

19. To Will, Dorothea is "the crystal" he wants "to see the light through" (37, repeated in 47); he feels "delight that he could dwell and be cherished in her thought as in a pure home" (39); her nature is one of those "in which, if they love us, we are conscious of having a sort of baptism and consecration: they bind us over to rectitude and purity by their pure belief in us; and our sins become that worst kind of sacrilege which tears down the invisible altar of trust" (77). The replacement of religious sanctions by personal relations in this last passage indicates the humanistic thrust of George Eliot's focus on acts of interpretation.

erratic mythical fragments in the world were corruptions of a tradition originally revealed. Having once mastered the true position and taken a firm footing there, the vast field of mythical constructions became intelligible, nay luminous with the reflected light of correspondences" (3).

It is another version of the pier-glass effect, and its groundlessness and futility cast an ironic light on Lydgate's search for the common origin from which the tissues of all organs are derived. "What was the primitive tissue? In that way Lydgate put the question—not quite in the way required by the awaiting answer" (15), but Lydgate's experimental method permits correction of mistaken hypotheses, while Casaubon's proceeds in self-enclosed, self-confirming solipsism.[20] The more important error Lydgate makes is an unwarranted assumption of difference between the demands of science and those of practical life, between his own experience and that of others, "bringing a much more testing vision of details and relations into [his] pathological study than he had ever thought it necessary to apply to the complexities of love and marriage" (16), failing to make connections ("but—is it not rather what we expect in men, that they should have numerous strands of experience lying side by side and never compare them with each other?" [58])—errors which the novel's method will not allow us to repeat.

Similar but simpler distortions are produced by characters who project an egocentric order onto the world by an "imaginative activity which fashions events according to desire" (23). The assumption of a unique, central position and a corresponding personal providence is repeated in Rosamond ("Rosamond had a

20. A later passage indicates this difference: "Doubtless a vigorous error vigorously pursued has kept the embryos of truth a-breathing: the quest of gold being at the same time a questioning of substances, the body of chemistry is prepared for its soul, and Lavoisier is born. But Mr Casaubon's theory of the elements which made the seed of all tradition was not likely to bruise itself unawares against discoveries: it floated among flexible conjectures no more solid than etymologies which seemed strong because of likeness in sound, until it was shown that likeness in sound made them impossible: it was a method of interpretation which was not tested by the necessity of forming anything which had sharper collisions than an elaborate notion of Gog and Magog: it was as free from interruption as a plan for threading the stars together" (48). For the relation of Lydgate and Casaubon to the history of physiological and mythological research, see W.J. Harvey, "The Intellectual Background of the Novel," in *Middlemarch: Critical Approaches*, pp. 25–37.

Providence of her own" [27]), in Fred ("What can the fitness of things mean, if not their fitness to a man's expectations? Failing this, absurdity and atheism gape behind him" [14]), and finds its fullest development in Bulstrode's interpretations of events which assist or thwart his desires as providential "sanction" or "chastisement."

> This was not what Mr Bulstrode said to any man for the sake of deceiving him: it was what he said to himself—it was as genuinely his mode of explaining events as any theory of yours may be, if you happen to disagree with him. For the egoism which enters into our theories does not affect their sincerity; rather, the more our egoism is satisfield, the more robust is our belief. [53]

The irony with which the narrator exposes these illusions can range from sharp satire to amused tolerance; it appears in the wit that permits us to recognize comparable forms of misinterpretation in science, religion, and love, in scholarly research and in barroom gossip, so that Casaubon's and Bulstrode's solipsistic modes of explanation are echoed in the inventions of "Mrs Dollop, the spirited landlady of the Tankard in Slaughter Lane, who had often to resist the shallow pragmatism of customers disposed to think that their reports from the outer world were of equal force with what had 'come up' in her mind" (71).

In all these cases, we enjoy a detached, superior perspective on a world which at times seems little more than a web of misconceptions, where individual perceptions are flawed by our native "moral stupidity" of "taking the world as an udder to feed our supreme selves" (21), and the world reciprocates by taking the individual "merely as a cluster of signs for his neighbors' false suppositions" (15).[21] As the narrator repeatedly reminds us,

21. The narrator's assertion of the universality of egoism is the most prominent and sweeping of all the novel's generalizations, but we should note how its inclusiveness and positing of a common origin immediately become the basis both for differentiation and for affirming the importance of irreducible differences: "We are all of us born in moral stupidity, taking the world as an udder to feed our supreme selves: Dorothea had early begun to emerge from that stupidity, but yet it had been easier to her to imagine how she would devote herself to Mr Casaubon, and become wise and strong in his strength and wisdom, than to conceive with that distinctness which is no longer reflection but feeling—an idea wrought back to the directness of sense, like the solidity of objects—that he had an equivalent centre of self, whence the lights and shadows must always fall with a certain difference."

these are failings to which "we are all of us" liable, but, as we have already seen, the novel seeks more than "the fellowship of illusion" (34) to link its readers and characters, and in that search it turns its focus on moments like Mrs. Bulstrode's crisis, on characters who can reinterpret their experience, "emerge from that stupidity" of egocentrism in the struggle toward a larger perspective that converges with the expansive narrative movement, "the reaching forward of the whole consciousness toward the fullest truth, the least partial good" (20).

This brings us back to the problematic position of Dorothea, for it is in her story that the possibilities of a narrative centered in the growth of a character's consciousness are most fully explored, and it is there that the tension between the impulses toward multiplicity and toward unity are most strongly felt. The shift at the end of Book 1 from single to multiple narrative can be seen as another, perhaps the most important instance of exposing the illusion of centered form, one that clearly leads to an increase of narrative range and variety, of moral and aesthetic complexity; but it is also experienced as a disturbing loss. The "Prelude" prepares us to regard Dorothea as the novel's heroine by aligning her with the heroic prototype of Saint Theresa, whose "passionate, ideal nature demanded an epic life. . . . wherein there was a constant unfolding of far-resonant action." For "later-born Theresas" like Dorothea, however, there is no opportunity for such a life; their energies "are dispersed among hindrances, instead of centering in some long-recognizable deed."

Here we can find an early indication of the course the narrative will take: Dorothea cannot retain a central position because she cannot be another Saint Theresa. Instead, after Book 1, her story is dispersed among others; the focus seldom returns to her for more than one or two chapters at a time, and even in these she frequently appears as a part of other stories, so that the course of her continuing experience must be reconstructed from fragments. The terms of the "Prelude" prepare for this dispersion, but they also insist that it entails loss as well as gain, the absence of a center in both her life and the novel's form and, behind both, the absence of any sustaining cultural or metaphysical order, "for these later-born Theresas were helped by no coherent social faith and order which could perform the function of knowledge for the ardently willing soul."

These problems are brought into intense focus in chapter 20, where the fragmented narrative returns to Dorothea at the point where she herself is experiencing the "stupendous fragmentariness" of Rome. She has expected marriage to Casaubon to help her ardently willing soul with knowledge of a coherent historical order, "a binding theory which could bring her own life and doctrine into strict connection with that amazing past, and give the remotest sources of knowledge some bearing on her actions" (10). Now, in "the city of visible history," her disappointment and confusion are reflected and amplified by "the oppressive masquerade of ages, in which her own life seemed to become a masque with enigmatical costumes."

> To those who have looked at Rome with the quickening power of a knowledge which breathes a growing soul into all historic shapes, and traces out the suppressed transtions which unite all contrasts, Rome may still be the spiritual centre and interpreter of the world. But let them conceive one more historical contrast: the gigantic broken revelations of that Imperial and Papal city thrust abruptly on the notions of a girl who had been brought up in English and Swiss Puritanism, fed on meagre Protestant histories and on art chiefly of the hand-screen sort; a girl whose ardent nature turned all her small allowance of knowledge into principles, fusing her actions into their mould, and whose quick emotions gave the most abstract things the quality of a pleasure or a pain.

Here the correspondence between reader and character lies first in the experience of disorientation—for Dorothea in suffering the "weight of unintelligible Rome," for the reader in confronting the narrative's discontinuity, the gap between chapters 10 and 20 which is the novel's most important suppressed transition. But the reader doesn't actually share Dorothea's confusion; we are well ahead of her, having already been reoriented by the narrative's expansion into multiplicity. The narrator's comments later in this chapter guide us in filling in this gap, sketching the beginnings of Dorothea's disillusionment with her husband, suggesting the sexual failure of their honeymoon as well as the frustration of her spiritual aspirations. Tracing such transitions, we reconstruct the development of characters whose stories interrupt each other, just as we trace the connections between contrasting characters. Rome figures as center and interpreter not because it reveals an objective, coherent order but because it offers the materials from which meanings can be constructed. It thus corrects the notion of a fixed, preexisting meaning suggested by the structural image of the web.

The reader's experience prefigures the character's, for Dorothea is now beginning a painful process of reinterpretation, discovering the path of duty not through Casaubon's strength but through his weakness, recognizing unsuspected similarities through "the waking of a presentiment that there might be a sad consciousness in his life which made as great a need on his side as on her own" (21). In her disorientation we recognize the potential for a development that will bring her perspective closer to ours. But Dorothea's experience is not simply presented as a necessary stage of moral development; it also offers a truth of its own, correcting our tendency to read the novel's themes and patterns too abstractly. She reappears here as a focus of attention because of her capacity to give "the most abstract things the quality of a pleasure or a pain," to register problems of interpretation in terms of emotion and the limitations of ordinary experience. We anticipate her movement toward a larger perspective, but we are also urged to descend from our advanced, privileged position to realize a greater depth of feeling. In place of the earlier ironic presentation of her illusions, the narrator works to render the intensity of her bewilderment, "the dreamlike strangeness of her bridal life," and the irony now turns against the reader's superior detachment:

> Forms both pale and glowing took possession of her young sense, and fixed themselves in her memory even when she was not thinking of them, preparing strange associations which remained through her after-years. Our moods are apt to bring with them images which succeed each other like the magic-lantern pictures of a doze; and in certain states of dull forlornness Dorothea all her life continued to see the vastness of St Peter's, the huge bronze canopy, the excited intention in the attitudes and garments of the prophets and evangelists in the mosaics above, and the red drapery which was being hung for Christmas spreading itself everywhere like a disease of the retina.
>
> Not that this inward amazement of Dorothea's was anything very exceptional: many souls in their young nudity are tumbled out among incongruities and left to "find their feet" among them, while their elders go about their business. Nor can I suppose that when

Mrs Casaubon is discovered in a fit of weeping six weeks after her wedding, the situation will be regarded as tragic. Some discouragement, some faintness of heart at the new real future which replaces the imaginary, is not unusual, and we do not expect people to be deeply moved by what is not unusual. That element of tragedy which lies in the very fact of frequency, has not yet wrought itself into the coarse emotion of mankind; and perhaps our frames could hardly bear much of it. If we had a keen vision and feeling of all ordinary human life, it would be like hearing the grass grow and the squirrel's heart beat, and we should die of that roar which lies on the other side of silence. As it is, the quickest of us walk about well wadded with stupidity.[22]

Dorothea's potential for growth and her interest as a focus of feeling distinguish her as the novel's most important center of consciousness, but these qualities emerge most clearly only after the shifting focus has displaced her from the central position. Her distress registers the loss of meaning which is involved in that dislocation, and like the reader she must discover new principles of coherence, learn to give decentering a positive value. That is what happens at the climax of her story, the crisis which begins in chapter 77 when she discovers Will and Rosamond together and believes the person she loved and trusted most has betrayed her. After this scene, the focus shifts to show its impact on Will and Rosamond for two chapters before returning to Dorothea, who, after a night of anger and despair, manages to respond to this new disillusionment by a comparable shift of perspective and reinterpretation:

It was not in Dorothea's nature, for longer than the duration of a paroxysm, to sit in the narrow cell of her calamity, in the besotted misery of a consciousness that only sees another's lot as an accident of its own.

22. This insistence on the depth of feeling beneath the commonplace recalls Thackeray's concern with the pathos of hidden suffering, but where Thackeray tends to maintain a sharp opposition and unsettling alternation between ironic detachment and sympathetic participation, George Eliot seeks to preserve a balance that avoids extremes of both distance and involvement. Thus this passage gives powerful expression to the nightmarish quality of Dorothea's experience, yet the image of the diseased retina also suggests the distortion of perception which results from immersion in her own feelings; it eloquently urges us toward a more sensitive response to ordinary life but does so through an ascending series of generalizations that detach us from the particular case.

> She began now to live through that yesterday morning de-
> liberately again, forcing herself to dwell on every detail and its
> possible meaning. Was she alone in that scene? Was it her event
> only? [80]

Her earlier efforts to recognize her husband's equivalent center of
self, her recent concern with Lydgate's troubles—"all this vivid
sympathetic experience returned to her now as a power; it
asserted itself as acquired knowledge asserts itself and will not let
us see as we saw in the day of our ignorance." She forces herself
to repress her own suffering and ask what she can do for Will,
Rosamond, and Lydgate. "It had taken long for her to come to
that question, and there was light piercing into the room." It has
taken not just the whole night but all of the novel: at this point
Dorothea catches up with the reader and narrator; together we
contemplate the symbolic scene that embodies the novel's moral
vision:

> She opened her curtains, and looked out towards the bit of road
> that lay in view, with fields beyond, outside the entrance-gates. On
> the road there was a man with a bundle on his back and a woman
> carrying her baby; in the field she could see figures moving—
> perhaps the shepherd with his dog. Far off in the bending sky was
> the pearly light; and she felt the largeness of the world and the
> manifold wakings of men to labour and endurance. She was a part
> of that involuntary, palpitating life, and could neither look out on it
> from her luxurious shelter as a mere spectator, nor hide her eyes in
> selfish complaining.

Regarding this moment as the culmination of the novel, we can
see George Eliot attempting to reconstitute the dispersed center
through the history of a consciousness which converges with the
narrative perspective. Yet a gap remains here, for we already
know that, as Rosamond tells her in the next chapter, Dorothea
is "thinking what is not true," and that discrepancy between the
reader's and character's perceptions is the sign of a persisting
tension which checks the centripetal tendency of Dorothea's role
in the novel and preserves the possibility of multiple interpretations.

This tension can be felt more strongly when we consider the
novel's plotting not just as internalized action but as causal

sequences. To do so we must return once more to the pier-glass parable, and this time look more closely at its immediate context:

> These things are a parable. The scratches are events, and the candle is the egoism of any person now absent—of Miss Vincy, for example. Rosamond had a Providence of her own who had kindly made her more charming than other girls, and who seemed to have arranged Fred's illness and Mr Wrench's mistake in order to bring her and Lydgate within effective proximity. [27]

At first the application seems easy: refusing to share Rosamond's egocentric interpretation, we can see that the episode of Fred's illness has several different meanings and functions. For Fred it serves as a penitential ordeal, a consequence of his habits of dissipation and a contributing factor to his reform. For Lydgate it figures as a significant episode in his medical career: replacing and quarreling with Wrench is a step in his immediate professional advancement and ultimate isolation and ostracism. Yet Rosamond is also right: the most important function of this event will be to throw her and Lydgate together and so lead to their engagement, and it may even be that the issue of misinterpretation is raised here to disguise this minor piece of plot manipulation. Certainly the model of the pier-glass is misleading in one respect, for while actual events, like the scratches, may be "going everywhere impartially," the events of a novel are always purposeful. George Eliot becomes the "Providence" her irony attempts to dissolve.

The issue of a providential design becomes much more prominent in Bulstrode's story. The account of "his mode of explaining events" as dispensations of a personal providence comes immediately before his first encounter with Raffles, in which his general "doctrinal conviction" of unworthiness is suddenly given painfully specific content from his suppressed past. "I am not so surprised at seeing you, old fellow," Raffles explains, "because I picked up a letter—what you may call a providential thing" (53). The irony obviously works against Bulstrode's doctrine, but it also raises the question of the novel's designs by recalling the earlier episode in chapter 41 where, without reading it, Raffles picks up Bulstrode's letter to Rigg Featherstone and wedges it in his brandy flask. The narrator both stresses and obscures the significance of this event by prefatory reflections on unpredictable consequences ("Who shall tell what may be the effect of writing?") and on apparent coincidences that may seem less improbable when viewed in the cosmic perspective of "Uriel watching the progress of planetary history from the Sun."

These maneuvers may succeed in dispelling any suggestion of divine intervention, but they also indicate a comparable transgression or shift between orders of meaning. The sequence of events that results in Bulstrode's exposure cannot be regarded simply as the representation of contingency, of the trivial incidents and "low people" by which "the course of the world is very much determined." It rather displays the operation of a secularized nemesis, converting the scientific analysis of "minute causes" to the ends of a moral determinism that guarantees appropriate punishment: "the train of causes in which he had locked himself went on" (61). Here the logic of equivalent centers is suspended in favor of the centripetal force of objectified paranoia. A mode of interpretation which appears on one level as egocentric illusion reappears on another as part of the novel's argument.

The effort to convert plot into moral argument also plays an important part in Dorothea's story and her movement back toward a central position. Her private crisis, resolution, and the vision which confirms it mark the culmination of her development as a center of consciousness, but her decision to return to Rosamond is also a crucial turning point in the plot, as she herself is partially aware during their interview: "She tried to master herself with the thought that this might be a turning-point in three lives—not in her own; no, there the irrevocable had happened, but—in those three lives which were touching hers with the solemn neighborhood of danger and distress" (81). Overcoming her own grief, she succeeds in moving Rosamond, who, "taken hold of by an emotion stronger than her own," is brought for one moment out of her habitual cold self-possession. This is the "destiny," the crucial convergence of Dorothea's and Lydgate's lives for which the novel has made such long and elaborate preparation, and the narrator's commentary in the next chapter makes clear its high significance:

> But it is given to us sometimes even in our everyday life to witness
> the saving influence of a noble nature, the divine efficacy of rescue

that may lie in a self-subduing act of fellowship. If Dorothea, after her night's anguish, had not taken that walk to Rosamond—why, she perhaps would have been a woman who gained a higher character for discretion, but it would certainly not have been as well for those three. . . . [82]

Dorothea's influence leads to a muted reconciliation and accommodation between Rosamond and Lydgate and also results in freeing Will from "discontented subjection" to an entanglement he seems unable to break. But its most important consequence is prompting Rosamond to correct Dorothea's mistake about Will and to tell Will that she has done so, bringing the two lovers together at last. By demonstrating the saving influence of Dorothea's noble nature, the novel's argument recovers the possibility of realizing a Saint Theresa's spiritual heroism "even in our everyday life"; the divine efficacy of human acts replaces an absent divinity: "In this way our brother may be in the stead of God to us" (*Daniel Deronda*, 64). This resolution requires less obvious contrivance than Bulstrode's punishment, yet it involves an even more acute conflict between different interpretive and structural principles, between action as a process of interpretation and as a causal or teleological sequence. Dorothea's decision reaffirms the principle of equivalent centers, but its consequences obey a contrary logic that reinstates her at the center of the novel and rewards her self-subduing act of fellowship with the promptness and precision of fantasy, that egocentric "imaginative activity which fashions events according to desires."

We should not overlook these breaks in the fine web of *Middlemarch,* but neither should we give them too much emphasis. The novel's tensions ensure that any tendency to channel its significance in one direction will be checked by others. Dorothea may seem to regain the center from which she has been displaced, both as the agent for resolving the plot and as the exemplar of its argument. She can be, and often has been seen as the focus for all the novel's analogies, her story as the central action which all the others serve to illuminate.[23] But to impose this kind of unity, to

23. See, for example, David R. Carroll, "Unity through Analogy: An Interpretation of *Middlemarch,*" *Victorian Studies* 2 (1959): 305–16. Carroll locates the center in Dorothea's "quest" for a principle of unity: "The analogies help to define the central search and at the same time universalize its significance" (p. 306).

make Dorothea the candle held up to the novel's pier-glass threatens to suppress the expansive force of its multiple narration. Our reading of *Middlemarch* should follow its own principles of rhythmic alternation: consideration of "systolic" convergence should be balanced by recognition of the diverging possibilities which its separate plot lines explore.

The opening words of *Middlemarch* address its narrative to the reader "that cares to know the history of man, and how the mysterious mixture behaves under the varying experiments of Time," and it is perhaps through these terms that we can best expand our focus again and renew our sense of the novel's "vastness and variety." They serve initially to introduce the notion of historical relativity, the premise that the conditions of place and time, sixteenth-century Spain or nineteenth-century England, determine the possibilities of individual development. But they also point to the varying experiments the novel will perform, the various meanings time itself will assume in the course of different stories, each defining its own world, establishing its own norms. As the narrator observes, "the limits of variation are really much wider than any one would imagine." We can remind ourselves of their range by turning from the moments of crisis and concentrated significance which structure Dorothea's story to the digressive opening of chapter 12:

> The ride to Stone Court, which Fred and Rosamond took the next morning, lay through a pretty bit of midland landscape, almost all meadows and pastures, with hedgerows still allowed to grow in bushy beauty and to spread out coral fruit for the birds. Little details gave each field a particular physiognomy, dear to the eyes that have looked on them from childhood: the pool in the corner where the grasses were dank and trees leaned whisperingly; the great oak shadowing a bare place in mid-pasture; the high bank where the ash-trees grew; the sudden slope of the old marl-pit making a red background for the burdock; the huddled roofs and ricks of the homestead without a traceable way of approach; the grey gate and fences against the depths of the bordering wood; and the stray hovel, its old, old thatch full of mossy hills and valleys with wondrous modulations of light and shadow such as we travel far to see in later life, and see larger, but not more beautiful. These are the things that make the gamut of joy to midland-bred souls—the things they toddled among, or perhaps learned by heart standing between their father's knees while he drove leisurely.

The relaxed pace, the loving attention to particularizing details make this description a striking contrast to the intensity with which George Eliot renders the dreamlike strangeness of Dorothea's bridal life in Rome; the sense of a familiar world, of continuity with a personal past is precisely what Dorothea lacks. This passage, which at first may seem an unmotivated intrusion of autobiographical reminiscence,[24] in fact provides an appropriate context for the relationship of Fred Vincy and Mary Garth, which is introduced later in this chapter. Their story resembles others in the way Fred's development presents a version of moral reform and the discovery of an appropriate vocation, but it is also unique as a love story that works toward its resolution in the fulfillment of loyalties rooted in the past, the childhood "engagement" with the umbrella-ring, recalling the values (as well as the pastoral mode) of earlier novels such as *The Mill on the Floss*.[25]

Bulstrode's story intersects with Fred's through the plot nexus of Stone Court, but it also diverges widely from the sunlit world of pastoral comedy. Its "slightly artificial cast" and "melodramatic tinge" may seem, as they did to James, "unfriendly to the richly natural coloring of the whole,"[26] but they should also be recognized as features of a mode which deliberately departs from the "natural" norms of domestic realism to pursue different purposes. As they do in Dickens, the contrivances of melodrama articulate the discontinuities and reversals of a life founded on the suppression of the past. The return of Raffles shifts Bulstrode's story from the realm of public affairs to that of private nightmare, in which the respectable banker is confronted by the shabby double who parodies his rationalizing doctrines and revives his repressed guilt.[27] For Bulstrode, the past, which had been distant, "dead history," invades the present like a hallucination:

24. Gordon Haight cites it as an example of George Eliot's persisting memories of her Warwickshire childhood. See *George Eliot: A Biography* (Oxford: Oxford University Press, 1968), p. 4.

25. For a discussion of George Eliot's conservative tendency to make such early memories and affections the basis of duty and morality, see Thomas Pinney, "The Authority of the Past in George Eliot's Novels," *Nineteenth-Century Fiction* 21 (1966): 131–47.

26. *The Critical Heritage*, p. 358.

27. The motif of the waking nightmare repeatedly marks Bulstrode's relations with Raffles: "Raffles' slow wink and slight protrusion of his tongue was worse

Night and day, without interruption save a brief sleep which only wove retrospect and fear into a fantastic present, he felt the scenes of his earlier life coming between him and everything else, as obstinately as when we look through the window from a lighted room, the objects we turn our backs on are still before us, instead of the grass and the trees. The successive events inward and outward were there in one view: though each might be dwelt on in turn, the rest still kept their hold in the consciousness. [61]

The presence of the past, the landscape of memory which expresses security in the context of Fred and Mary's story expresses guilty terror in Bulstrode's. The merger of "events inward and outward," the interpenetration of mood and world also recurs in Dorothea's story: "the dream-like association of something alien and ill-understood with the deepest secrets of her experience seemed to mirror that sense of loneliness which was due to the very ardour of Dorothea's nature" (34). These moments yield persisting, painful memories: the image of St. Peter's which returns "in certain states of dull forlornness . . . all her life" (20), the scene of Featherstone's funeral, which "always afterwards came back to her at the touch of certain sensitive points in memory" (34); but for Dorothea the pain comes from the loss of connection, not the reestablished connections that threaten Bulstrode, and her development brings her at last to the clarity of her dawn vision, where the window does not give back a reflection of hidden secrets but discloses "the largeness of the world" of which she now feels herself a part.

Flanked by the stories of Fred and Mary and of Bulstrode, with their very different orientations to the past, the stories of Dorothea and Lydgate are shaped by decisions made in the present, by the effort to realize new possibilities. Lydgate's commitment to medicine and research, his desire to continue the work of Bichat and "make a link in the chain of discovery" (15) is an act of self-determination he is unable to sustain, a hopeful beginning from which we see him fall away step by step into the empty routine of "what is called a successful man" ("Finale"). Dorothea's aspirations are similarly frustrated, but her loss leads to gain, her errors to knowledge. Shaking off Casaubon's dead

than a nightmare, because it held the certainty that it was not a nightmare, but a waking misery" (53). "It was as if he had had a loathsome dream, and could not shake off its images" (68).

hand, she can give her history a new meaning: "her past was come back to her with larger interpretation" (62). Both plots are more open to the future, but Lydgate's is set in an austerely ironic mode in which the pressures of circumstance and the consequences of decisions are unrelieved, while the more romantic mode of Dorothea's, employing an elevated style that admits a religious vocabulary and such idealizing elements as mythic parallels, permits a wider range of possibilities.[28] One could develop these brief observations into a fuller account of the way the novel's plots explore different stylistic and temporal modes, but my purpose in introducing them here has simply been to stress the importance of difference itself. Each story is illuminated by comparison with the others, but each also unfolds according to its own logic and must be read in its own terms.

The conclusion of the novel preserves the balance between its impulses of expansion and contraction, offering the traditional satisfactions of a final review which brings all the characters on stage once more while reminding us that this sense of completion is deceptive: "Every limit is a beginning as well as an ending." In Fred and Mary's idyllic marriage we get the pattern of complete closure: "the two lovers who were first engaged with the umbrella-ring may be seen in white-haired placidity," but all the other major characters disperse from Middlemarch: there is an effect of opening out as well as rounding off.[29] The central position to which the stealthy convergence of human lots brought Dorothea at the moment of crisis now appears as only momentary; viewed in the longer perspective of the "Finale" her divine efficacy becomes "incalculably diffusive." "Diffusive" recalls the "dispersed" of the "Prelude" but also reinterprets it with the hope that the incalculable effects of such hidden lives contribute to "the growing good of the world." But this muted affirmation of progress is checked by the repeated note of regret for the lost possibilities of Saint Theresa's epic life, a regret Dorothea herself

28. On the use of mythic parallels, see Brian Swan, "*Middlemarch* and Myth," *Nineteenth-Century Fiction* 28 (1973): 210–14. J. Hillis Miller discusses the divergent modes of the major plot lines in "Narrative and History," *ELH* 41 (1974): 469–70.
29. The terms are E.M. Forster's: "Expansion. That is the idea the novelist must cling to. Not completion. Not rounding off but opening out." *Aspects of the Novel* (New York: Harcourt, Brace, 1927), p. 169. In *Daniel Deronda* this balance between openness and closure is replaced by a more radically open ending.

shares, "feeling that there was always something better which she might have done, if she had only been better and known better."[30] As anonymous agent of human progress or as victim of social restrictions, Dorothea is interpreted in terms of consequences and of her specific historical moment, but we have also learned to read her story as an internalized action, the emergence from the "moral stupidity" of egoism, an achievement that cannot be measured simply by its efficacy, a perpetual possibility that is not dependent on time and place. All these meanings are held in suspension: as the "Prelude" promised, "the indefiniteness remains."

This indefiniteness, the complex balance of mutually qualifying interpretations which *Middlemarch* sustains, is replaced in George Eliot's last novel by a remarkable definiteness of both form and asserted meaning: "With *Daniel Deronda*, George Eliot moves from the conditional to the categorical."[31] Instead of the shifting emphasis and relations between several plot lines developed in *Middlemarch*, *Daniel Deronda* returns to the pattern of double plot which had governed *Silas Marner*, *Romola*, and *Felix Holt*. The pattern is stressed by the developmental structure, which experiments with a more stylized narrative form, beginning in medias res with the first encounter between Deronda and Gwendolen at the German spa and then moving into a double flashback which traces the previous experiences of each character. The question of the possible impact they may have on each other is thus raised immediately and held in suspension while we observe them separately and compare them. A few common features serve to focus the comparison: the retrospect of Gwendolen's past, for example, begins by deploring her lack of established roots and affections, and we later see that Deronda,

30. That note was much stronger in the first edition, which bitterly attributed Dorothea's mistakes to the "prosaic conditions," the defective values and institutions of her society. Reviewers seized on this passage, complaining that it did not tally with the narrative in attempting to shift all blame from the character to her environment, and the passage was removed in later editions. See Harvey, "Contemporary Reception," pp. 133–34. The earlier version is reprinted in Gordon Haight's Riverside edition (Boston: Houghton Mifflin, 1956), p. 612.

31. U.C. Knoepflmacher, *Religious Humanism and the Victorian Novel: George Eliot, Walter Pater, and Samuel Butler* (Princeton: Princeton University Press, 1965), p. 121.

ignorant of his parentage, is also rootless, lacking a definite social position and role. But such similarities only heighten our awareness of their profound differences. Gwendolen's is the isolation of the spoiled child; her "potent charm" and "inborn energy of egoistic desire" (4) enable her to dominate her little world, and her self-absorption is broken only by momentary spasms of fear when faced with something beyond her limited knowledge and control. Deronda is located at the opposite end of George Eliot's moral scale. His distress at his supposed illegitimacy leads not to withdrawal but to a sense of "fellowship" with other suffering; he combines "a meditative yearning after wide knowledge" with "a subdued fervour of sympathy, an activity of imagination on behalf of others" (16).

This familiar contrast between narrowness and breadth opposes not only the moral states of the two main characters but the novel's two separate worlds as well, the English world of genteel country society, whose shallowness and complacency are exposed by sharp satiric criticism, and the Jewish world, which offers an alternative and escape from these restrictions in a living spiritual tradition and the promise of an exalted destiny. The divergence of modes in *Middlemarch* is controlled by the presence and pressures of a common world, but here the two worlds are widely separated, and the two plots are set in sharply different modes. Gwendolen's story deals with the familiar novelistic subjects of social codes, personal relations, and individual psychology; it analyzes motives, focuses on choices, and traces their consequences in a painful process of moral education. Deronda's story turns from the familiar and conventionally probable toward the idealized figures, mythic patterns, and visionary utterances of romance; it unfolds not as a sequence of choices and consequences but as a process of discovery, of prophecy and fulfillment, where meaning is determined by a remote, mysterious origin and a remote, beckoning goal.[32]

32. From the beginning, several crtitics have attempted to come to terms with *Daniel Deronda* by focusing on its elements of romance. For Edward Dowden it represented a shift from the "realistic" to the "ideal" (*Critical Heritage*, p. 441); for R.E. Francillon it was "George Eliot's First Romance" (*Critical Heritage*, pp. 382–98). Leon Gottfried has revived this approach to explain the novel's defects: "*Daniel Deronda* does not, as a whole, cohere organically" because "George Eliot has attempted . . . to join into a single work a novel and a romance." See

Opposed by these contrasts, the two plots are linked not only by implicit comparisons but by the same type of convergence which figured significantly in *Middlemarch* (and which, in fact, plays an important role in much of George Eliot's fiction from "Janet's Repentance" onward), the action of moral rescue. The opening episode, in which Deronda fixes Gwendolen with his "measuring gaze" and redeems her necklace, prefigures their later relation, in which he becomes "a part of her conscience" (35) and attempts to help her by urging her toward a broader perspective: "Try to care for what is best in thought and action—something apart from your own lot" (36). By playing this part in Gwendolen's story, moving freely between the two worlds of the novel, Deronda assumes the central position, exempted from the irony and dislocations which disperse the center of *Middlemarch*. Those pressures are exerted only on Gwendolen. Her experience, and especially her relation with Deronda, are always circumscribed by dramatic irony: we, and Deronda, are aware of complexes of events and regions of experience of which she remains ignorant until their final interview, when his announcement of his plans to marry Mirah and depart for the East bring her a new sense of the largeness of the world, not as fulfillment or release but as a humiliating shock that leaves her isolated once more: "The world seemed getting larger round poor Gwendolen, and she more solitary and helpless in the midst" (69).

The radical division of worlds and modes, the polarization of values, and the assignment of an unambiguously central position to its hero give *Daniel Deronda* a highly simplified moral scheme. Like *Wuthering Heights* and *Vanity Fair*, it develops an antithetical structure, but it seems to lack the dialogical play and tension, the possibilities of reversal and reinterpretation which give those earlier double plots their complexity. This simplification, with its idealization of Daniel, Mirah, Mordecai, and a resolution that grants the hero "the very best of human possibilities . . . the blending of a complete personal love in one current with a larger duty" (50), probably accounts for much of the resistance with which readers have so often met the argument of the novel's all

---

"Structure and Genre in *Daniel Deronda*," in *The English Novel in the Nineteenth Century*, ed. George Goodin (Urbana: University of Illinois Press, 1972), pp. 164–75.

too palpable design. But that design does not completely control the novel's meaning. The numerous analogies with which George Eliot attempts to make "everything in the book . . . related to everything else there" develop implications that exceed the requirements of her moral scheme and make its assertions problematic.

These complications arise primarily from the extreme isolation of the two main characters and the way George Eliot presents the relation between the self and the world, that is, from the extension and intensification of problems that were already present in *Middlemarch*. Gwendolen's desire to predominate, her belief that the world will conform to her desires, and her impulse to assert herself in disregard or defiance of resistant circumstances are all shown in her behavior at the roulette table; they are all expressions of the self-absorption which is enacted emblematically in the next scene when she kisses her reflection in the mirror. The movement of her story up to her marriage alternates between such acts of self-assertion and events which thwart her will and threaten her self-possession. We see her gambling, entertaining Grandcourt's suit with a pleasurable sense of "her power to refuse him" (11), breaking off to fly to the Continent, and finally accepting and marrying him with proud defiance, "much the same condition as that in which she stood at the gambling-table" (31); but each of these assertions meets a corresponding check: Deronda's disturbing disapproval, Mrs. Glasher's revelations, the loss of her family's fortune, the curse of the "poisoned gems," and finally the unshakable ascendency which Grandcourt gains after their marriage.

These episodes appear to follow a familiar pattern: egoistic illusions shattered by objective reality. But here the pattern becomes blurred, for the checks to Gwendolen's egoism are largely internalized; their significance is grounded less in an objective reality than in her idiosyncratic responses, especially the liability to fear which becomes in time a liability to guilt. This emerges first in her response to "the picture of an upturned dead face, from which an obscure figure seemed to be fleeing with outstretched arms" (3). It represents the threat not just of death but of the uncontrollable, the unacknowledged, "things which were meant to be shut up." Its apparition again interrupts her self-satisfied performance, transforming her from a revived Hermione to "a statue into which a soul of Fear had entered" (6), in a contrived symbolic tableau which clearly presents a conflict of forces within Gwendolen rather than an encounter with external reality. This is followed by exposition on her liability to "fits of spiritual dread. . . . Solitude in any wide scene inspired her with an undefined feeling of immeasurable existence aloof from her, in the midst of which she was hopelessly incapable of asserting herself." Again, the emphasis falls not on the objective existence of an alien universe but on Gwendolen's fear of whatever negates her will, a fear which is given more concrete psychological expression in her rejection of Rex's advances: "she objected, with a sort of physical repulsion, to being directly made love to" (7), and this revulsion reappears in intensified form when she learns of Grandcourt's mistress.

In Grandcourt Gwendolen encounters a distorted reflection of herself. They have "equality in the need to dominate" (27), but his is unchecked by fear or scruple. Her main attraction for him lies in her resistance: "The evident hesitation of this destitute girl to take his splendid offer stung him into a keenness of interest such as he had not known for years" (27), and his satisfaction at her acceptance lies in the sense of mastery it gives: "She had been brought to accept him in spite of everything—brought to kneel down like a horse under training for the arena, though she might have an objection to it all the while" (28). The extraordinary glimpse we get of Grandcourt's thoughts reveals "a state of the inward world, something like premature age, where the need for action lapses into a mere image of what has been, is, and may or might be; where impulse is born and dies in a phantasmal world, pausing in rejection even of a shadowy fulfillment" (28). It is an advanced stage of a condition Gwendolen shares, a solipsistic isolation in which the world is swallowed in the stagnant pool of the self.

The process by which Gwendolen's liability to fear becomes the "root of conscience" (54), a fear of her own potential for evil, offers a demonstration of the extent to which her story unfolds in an inward world. This development is linked to the pledge to Mrs. Glasher which she violates in marrying Grandcourt. Through this situation, George Eliot attempts to present Gwendolen's transgression in conventional moral terms as a question of consequences, of wrong done to another. It is revealing to compare this turn in her development with the moment in *Middlemarch* which marks the growth of moral awareness in Fred Vincy, when he announces he cannot pay the debt for which Caleb Garth has given surety. Suddenly being made aware that this will force Mrs. Garth and Mary to give up their savings makes him "feel for the first time something like the tooth of remorse."

> Curiously enough, his pain in the affair beforehand had consisted almost entirely in the sense that he must seem dishonourable, and sink in the opinion of the Garths: he had not occupied himself with the inconvenience and possible injury that his breech might occasion them, for this exercise of the imagination on other people's needs is not common with hopeful young gentlemen. Indeed we are most of us brought up in the notion that the highest motive for not doing a wrong is something irrespective of the beings who would suffer the wrong. But at this moment he suddenly saw himself as a pitiful rascal who was robbing two women of their savings. [24]

Gwendolen is prompted to a similar exercise of the imagination. She finds an analogy between the wrong of Deronda's supposed loss of inheritance because of his illegitimacy and the wrong of her standing in the way of Mrs. Glasher and her children, seeing "the position which tempted her in a new light, as a hard, unfair exclusion of others" (29); she believes she is repeating the sin she committed in gambling, which, as Deronda instructs her, lies in making one's gain of anther's loss. But this interpretation is far more dubious than Fred Vincy's: there is no reason to suppose that Grandcourt would ever have married Mrs. Glasher (and in the end the illegitmate son inherits anyway). As Calvin Bedient observes, "the only certain injury resulting from Gwendolen's marriage is to herself."[33] In the tightly woven fabric of Middlemarch society, morality is much more a question of obligation to others, but in *Daniel Deronda* the community has disappeared. Making Gwendolen's guilt a question of her effects on others seems an attempt to disguise the extremity of her

33. *Architects of the Self: George Eliot, D.H. Lawrence, and E.M. Forster* (Berkeley and Los Angeles: University of California Press, 1972), p. 64.

isolation, a condition in which actions and consequences have been completely internalized.

The sense of guilt, fear of herself, and the misery of her domination by Grandcourt which overwhelm Gwendolen after her marriage thoroughly destroy her self-satisfaction, but they also increase her isolation. As in *Middlemarch*, "the beings closest to us, whether in love or hate, are often virtually our interpreters of the world" (54), and Gwendolen desperately seeks an alternative to Grandcourt's cynical, deadening influence in Deronda's idealism. Deronda advocates the "refuge" of "the higher, the religious life," but his advice seems calculated only to intensify her inner conflict: "Turn your fear into a safeguard. Keep your dread fixed on the idea of increasing that remorse which is so bitter to you. . . . Try to take hold of your sensibility, and use it as if it were a faculty, like vision" (36). Gwendolen's sensibility does indeed become visionary, but the only refuge it can imagine depends on Grandcourt's death:

> The thought of his dying would not subsist: it turned as with a dream-change into the terror that she should die with his throttling fingers on her neck avenging that thought. Fantasies moved within her like ghosts, making no break in her more acknowledged consciousness and finding no obstruction in it: dark rays doing their work invisibly in broad light. [48]

Further isolated, cut off from Deronda when Grandcourt takes her with him on the yacht, she becomes completely possessed by these fantasies:

> her vision of what she had to dread took more decidedly than ever the form of some fiercely impulsive deed, committed as in a dream that she would instantaneously wake from to find the effects real though the images had been false: to find death under her hands, but instead of darkness, daylight; instead of satisfied hatred, the dismay of guilt; instead of freedom, the palsy of a new terror—a white dead face from which she was for ever trying to flee and for ever held back. [54]

At last the dream becomes real, the dead face becomes Grandcourt's, and Gwendolen's worst fears seem confirmed: "I am a guilty woman," she tell Deronda, who, though he believes she has not actually caused her husband's death, agrees with her insistence on the murderous intention itself: "Within ourselves our evil will is momentous, and sooner or later it works its way outside us" (57).

When we turn from the solipsistic nightmare of Gwendolen's experience to Deronda's, we are, according to the novel's scheme, turning from dark enclosure to wide, expanding horizons, from a "narrowly personal" life to one "charged with far-reaching sensibilities" (50). Deronda begins at a stage of moral development which Gwendolen is barely approaching at the end, a capacity to subordinate self-concern to the needs of others; his only "demerits" are "on the side of reflective hesitation" (16), a tendency to passivity which his eventual commitment to Zionism corrects. But along with these differences we find some surprising similarities between the novel's two worlds. One of the most surprising is the way Deronda's passivity and need for motivation link him with Grandcourt. They seem to have nothing in common: the first time we see them together the narrator observes that they "might have been a subject for those old painters who liked contrasts of temperament" (15), and the contrast between their moral natures is the most extreme of all the novel's oppositions. But both are isolated, receiving no direction from social or personal duties; both require some external stimulus to action ("what [Deronda] most longed for was either some external event, or some inward light, that would urge him into a definite line of action, and compress his wandering energy" [32]; cf. Grandcourt's "want of regulated channels for the soul to move in" [15]). Grandcourt finds his motivation in objects on which he can exercise his will to power, Deronda in those he can help: "Persons attracted him . . . in proportion to the possibility of his defending them, rescuing them, telling upon their lives with some sort of redeeming influence" (28). In rescuing Hans Meyrick, Mirah, and Mordecai, and most of all in attempting to rescue Gwendolen, he finds a purpose that is absent from his life before the discovery of his ancestry. The moral quality of these acts is antithetical to that of Grandcourt's, but in both we see the need to confirm one's sense of existence by exerting influence on another.

Other analogies between the novel's "higher" and "lower" worlds both mark contrasts and suggest affinities, especially in the important part which dreams, fantasies, and visions play in each. Some are primarily devices of formal parallelism, like the comparison of Gwendolen as a child "afraid to be alone in the night" (6), who always slept in her mother's room, and Mirah, after her father had taken her away and told her that her mother was dead:

> I never thought of its not being true; and I used to cry every night in my bed for a long while. Then when she came so often to me, in my sleep, I thought she must be living about me though I could not always see her, and that comforted me. I was never afraid in the dark, because of that; and very often in the day I used to shut my eyes and bury my face and try to see her and to hear her singing. I came to do that at last without shutting my eyes. [20]

This indicates at an early point the parallel between the two women with whom Deronda will become most closely involved; it plays off the account of Gwendolen as spoiled child to suggest that Mirah, for all her vulnerability, has greater resources of spiritual strength. Other comparisons produce larger implications, such as the passage which considers the possibility of "second-sight."

> "Second-sight" is a flag over disputed ground. But it is matter of knowledge that there are persons whose yearnings, conceptions— nay, travelled conclusions—continually take the form of images which have a foreshadowing power: the deed they would do starts up before them in complete shape, making a coercive type; the event they hunger for or dread rises into vision with a seed-like growth, feeding itself fast on unnumbered impressions. [38]

This introduces a discussion of Mordecai as visionary, but it could also describe Gwendolen's murderous fantasies. Mordecai's visions center on his need for a friend and disciple to embody his "expanded, prolonged self" and carry out his ideas: "he habitually thought of the Being answering to his need as one distantly approaching or turning his back towards him, darkly painted against a golden sky," a scene he associates with Blackfriars Bridge at sunset, as he comes to associate his Messianic hopes with Deronda. In their encounter two chapters later, these images become actual; inner and outward vision coincide, and Mordecai feels "that his inward prophecy was fulfilled. Obstacles, incongruities, all melted into the sense of completion with which his soul was flooded by this outward satisfaction of his longing. . . . The prefigured friend had come from the golden background, and had signalled to him: this actually was: the rest was to be" (40). This fulfillment works to endorse Mordecai's authority and create the expectation that the rest of his hopes will be realized. The narrator compares him to a scientific "experimenter" whose hypotheses have been confirmed, but what we see looks less like objective confirmation than the triumph of the will, of "an ideal life straining to embody itself" (38). As in the fulfillment of Gwendolen's nightmare visions, the distinction between inner and outer, dream and fact, loses its meaning, virtually disappears. The fantasy is no longer the character's but the novel's.

Deronda's is "not one of those quiveringly-poised natures that lend themselves to second-sight" (37), but his experience also leads to the identification of inward and outward worlds. Here unification takes place not by assertion but by suspension of the will, by a quality of "receptivenenss" which, we are told, "is a rare and massive power" (40). We first see it exercised in the earlier scene of fateful encounter on the river. "Deronda of late, in his solitary excursions, had been occupied chiefly with uncertainties about his own course" (17), but here he abandons these thoughts to let himself drift, becoming absorbed in the wide space of open water and evening sky as he indulges himself in "solemn passivity."

> He was forgetting everything else in a half-speculative, half-involuntary identification of himself with the objects he was looking at, thinking how far it might be possible habitually to shift his centre till his own personality would be no less outside him than the landscape.

It is from this mood that he is roused by the appearance of Mirah and, realizing her intention to drown herself, intervenes and rescues her. In one respect this is a reversal, a movement from passivity to action, and indeed a paradigm of his whole development from diffused sympathy to concentrated purpose; but it is also a realization in outward events of an inner necessity. The receptive mood, in which subject and object merge, "when thinking and desiring melt together imperceptibly, and what in other hours may have seemed argument takes the quality of passionate vision," leads by a kind of dream-logic to the fulfillment of his need for direction. As in the parallel scene of his meeting with Mordecai, the turn of the plot contrives to answer the longing for "some external event, or some inward light [the distinction no longer matters] that would urge him into a definite line of action and compress his wandering energy" (32). Deronda is too rare and noble to indulge in commonplace egoistic fantasies about beautiful maidens in distress whom he can rescue. The novel does it for him.

The novel, indeed, is bent on doing everything for him, eventually conferring what it and he conceive as "the very best of human possibilities," the perfect merging of ideal love and friendship with an elect vocation, the recovered heritage of a chosen people and the "grand and vague" historical destiny it entails.[34] Announcing his discovery of his ancestry and mission to Mirah and Mordecai, Deronda experiences the culminating union of inward and outward, imagined and actual, "enjoying one of those rare moments when our yearning and acts can be completely one, and the real we behold is our ideal good" (63). The isolation, the absence of community which leads to the internalization of Gwendolen's development is also reflected in Deronda's vocation of "restoring or perfecting [the] common life" of the Jews (60), reconstructing community from its scattered fragments. Though his story seems to move from isolation to engagement, expanding outward into the larger life of historical reality, its development follows the same principle of wish-fulfillment that governs Gwendolen's. Gwendolen, trying to tell him what "really" happened at the moment of Grandcourt's death, cannot distinguish dream from fact: "I know nothing—I only know that I saw my wish outside me" (56). Deronda might well say the same of his strange experience, except that, since his wish is not feared but wholeheartedly desired, he accepts its realization as truth.

Through the analogies of wish-fulfillment we can trace the suppressed transitions which unite the contrasts of vision and

34. "There will I know be disappointment at not hearing more of the failure of Gwendolen and the mysterious destiny of Deronda," Blackwood wrote to George Eliot, "but I am sure you are right to leave all grand and vague." *Letters*, 6: 272.

nightmare and which even suggest a reversal of the novel's polarities. Gwendolen, torn between the interpretations of Deronda and Grandcourt, can at moments sense that "there was a world outside this bad dream" (48); and at the end, forced to recognize that Deronda is not simply a figure in her private drama, she confronts that larger world, "for the first time feeling the pressure of a vast mysterious movement, for the first time being dislodged from her supremacy in her own world, and getting a sense that her horizon was but a dipping onward of an existence with which her own was revolving" (69). But Deronda can feel no such pressure, for that vast mysterious movement is perfectly aligned with his deepest needs and desires; as Gwendolen emerges from her dream world we can see him becoming completely engulfed in his. In this way the duality of the novel's structure undoes the simplifications of its argument; the masterfully controlled interplay of perspectives and interpretations in *Middlemarch* is replaced by a radical instability which makes possible a reading opposed to the novel's manifest intentions.

I have suggested that this shift involves the disappearance of community, of dramatic interaction between the individual and his social context. It also involves a change in the conception of moral development. In *Middlemarch*, as in George Eliot's earlier fiction, successful moral development is presented as self-subordination, the replacement of self-concern with a concern for others best exemplified by Dorothea's crisis. In *Daniel Deronda* George Eliot seems to be moving toward a conception of development as self-discovery, not a movement outward but a realization of one's own nature. In Gwendolen's experience it is a discovery of evil, of the destructive potential within her, a discovery that produces in her "something like a new soul, which had better, but also worse possibilities than her former poise of crude self-confidence" (29). In Deronda self-realization is presented as the formation of new relations with others and the discovery of a public role; but in the discovery of his identity it also takes the form of anamnesis, the revival of family or racial memory, "an inherited yearning—the effect of brooding, passionate thoughts in many ancestors—thoughts that seem to have been intensely present in my grandfather" (63). Whether or not we are meant to take this notion literally, its metaphorical thrust is clearly toward the discovery of a hidden potential within the self. Even the remote origin that supposedly guarantees meaning is now internalized.

This redirection, the internalization of narrative in literal psychological terms or in the symbolic terms of romance, carries *Daniel Deronda* far from the middle ground and mediated conflicts of *Middlemarch*. Instead of tracing the gradual action of ordinary causes, it explores inward extremes of demonic and visionary possibilities; external events become the register of projected wishes. The experience of nightmare and vision plays an important but restricted role in *Middlemarch;* here it expands until it becomes nearly all-inclusive. Deronda's extraordinary destiny reclaims the heroic possibilities denied to Dorothea, and, as if in compensation, this indulgence is opposed in Gwendolen's story by a punitive action far more severe than the destruction of Rosamond's dream world. But the shifting perspectives that multiple narrative requires permit us to reinterpret this antithesis: *Daniel Deronda* demonstrates, in an extreme form, what we have already observed in *Middlemarch*, the equivocal significance of equivalent centers.

⤜ FIVE ⤛

Trollope: Eccentricities

By the measure of quantity, Trollope would have to be judged the most important Victorian multiplot novelist. His forty-seven novels outnumber the combined works of Dickens, Thackeray, and George Eliot, and most of them exploit the conventions of multiple narrative. From the double plot of *The Kelleys and the O'Kellys* (1848) to the expanding subplots of *Mr. Scarborough's Family* (1882–83), in a career spanning the entire period in which the multiplot novel flourished, Trollope repeatedly multiplied narrative lines to enlarge and diversify his novels. Not only do all his major works employ the form, but the series of Barchester and Palliser novels, for which he is best known, also depend in part on an extension of the principles of multiple narrative, in which the main characters of one story reappear on the margins of another, or secondary figures later emerge as the focus of independent developments.

If, in spite of such reasons, Trollope does not seem more important than the novelists we have already examined, one reason may be his lesser artistic ambitions. His largest novels, such as *The Last Chronicle of Barset* or *The Way We Live Now*, achieve an inclusiveness like that of *Bleak House*, *Vanity Fair*, or *Middlemarch*, but they are not animated by such powerful impulses toward unity nor pulled taut by the oppositions which check or reverse those impulses. Even friendly critics have frequently deplored the typical looseness of Trollope's composition, his supposed tendency "to pad out simple narratives with multiple plots, subplots, and episodes,"[1] so that "some of his finest achievements are marred by irrelevant subplots."[2] The

1. Bradford Booth, *Anthony Trollope: Aspects of His Life and Art* (Bloomington: Indiana University Press, 1958), p. 161.
2. A.O.J. Cockshut, *Anthony Trollope: A Critical Study* (London: Collins, 1955), p. 123.

predictable response to such complaints has been the efforts of other critics to demonstrate that the typical "centerless" Trollope novel, in which "there are frequently four or five weakly related plots going at once" is in fact unified by a central theme.[3] Such readings only tend to obscure Trollope's greatest interest and importance for the study of multiple narrative, which is to be found precisely in his looseness, in the absence of a strong controlling center and the "weak" relations of both plot and theme which open up the structure of his novels and permit more play of differences than we find in his contemporaries.

This openness is most apparent in the largest and loosest of Trollope's multiplot novels, but the same factors that work to disperse the narrative lines of *The Last Chronicle* or *He Knew He Was Right* can also be observed in his more tightly organized works. *Can You Forgive Her?* is a good example, since it develops from the traditional dramatic pattern, which Trollope took from his unsuccessful play *The Noble Jilt*, of a serious action paralleled by a comic subplot. Alice Vavasor's prolonged hesitation between "the worthy man" John Grey and "the wild man" George Vavasor is echoed by Mrs. Greenow's indecision whether to favor Mr. Cheeseacre or Captain Bellfield, and is doubled again by Glencora Palliser's temptation to leave her husband for Burgo Fitzgerald. This close parallelism appears to be organized by a sharp thematic opposition between prudent conformity to social conventions or worldly interests and the attractions of "romance" (a recurrent motif) or rebellion.[4]

Yet as the narrator relates these themes to particular cases their categorical outlines become blurred, their terms take on different values. Thus "prudence" appears as a source of salvation for women like Glencora who have "doubts" and yet resolve them "on the right side" through "that half-prudential, half-

3. Jerome Thale, "The Problem of Structure in Trollope," *Nineteenth-Century Fiction* 15 (1960): 147–57. For a more recent example of this approach, see Juliet McMaster, " 'The Unfortunate Moth': Unifying Theme in *The Small House at Allington*," *Nineteenth-Century Fiction* 26 (1971): 127–44.

4. David S. Chamberlain, "Unity and Irony in Trollope's *Can You Forgive Her?*," *Studies in English Literature* 8 (1968): 669–80, argues that each of the three women must compromise between "romance and prudence." John Christopher Kleis, "Passion vs. Prudence: Theme and Technique in Trollope's Palliser Novels," *Texas Studies in Language and Literature* 11 (1970): 1405–14, applies the scheme to the whole series.

unconscious knowledge of what is fitting, useful, and best under the circumstances" (50), but the term becomes strongly ironic at the point it receives its most explicit abstract formulation, in chapter 35, "Passion versus Prudence," where it refers to George's scheme to appropriate Alice's money by renewing their engagement, while his "passion" is the anger he feels at her refusal of any expression of love. George's angry impulse to repudiate the engagement is, the narrator observes, "the better part of his nature," and its subordination to prudential considerations marks his moral deterioration. Under still different circumstances this irony can soften again, as it does when the narrator approves the "prudence" of Mrs. Greenow's choice of her "romantic" alternative Captain Bellfield, an indulgence she can reasonably afford herself (65).

Trollope's contextual modification of his thematic terms involves a less radical irony than Thackeray's deconstruction of thematic antitheses, but it does play effectively on the gap between general terms and particular situations. In each of these cases characters confront significant alternatives in which the narrator can indicate "the right side," but his judgments are quite limited, based on individual circumstances rather than a consistent general principle, and indeed seem to be presented in such a way as to resist the formulation of an inclusive moral scheme.[5] The narrator's comments are usually presented as opinions about particular situations (for example, "I think that Mr. Grey was right in answering Alice's letter as he did; but I think that Lady Macleod was also right in saying that Alice

5. Trollope's emphasis on the intricacies of particular cases which cannot be assimilated to general rules is well demonstrated in Ruth apRoberts' discussion of his moral "casuistry." See *The Moral Trollope* (Athens: Ohio University Press, 1971), esp. pp. 34–54. James R. Kincaid, *The Novels of Anthony Trollope* (Oxford: Oxford University Press, 1977), pp. 12–16, argues that while Trollope often complicates traditional norms, he never advocates complete relativism and "never gave up trying" to reestablish "the simple and beautiful values basic to the comedy of manners" (p. 260). Although apRoberts' interpretation might seem more compatible with my concept of dialogical form, it is actually more restrictive, since she attempts to identify Trollope with a single, consistent ideological position. Kincaid's readings of the novels are more conservative than mine, but his stress on form and the effects of openness produced by Trollope's use of the dramatized narrator and subplots that run counter to the main action leads to several parallels between our analyses.

should not have gone to Switzerland in company with George Vavasor"[5]), and when they engage more general issues it is usually to take exception to conventional wisdom ("People often say that marriage is an important thing, and should be much thought of in advance, and marrying people are cautioned that there are many who marry in haste and repent in leisure. I am not sure, however, that marriage may not be pondered over too much"[11]).[6] The narrator's tone of personal opinion rather than omniscient assertion, the emphasis on particular cases rather than general principles restrict not only the range but also the authority of his commentary. Trollope's narrator is as prominent an authorial persona as George Eliot's, but he "knows" less. He cannot maintain her continual modulation "between the whole human horizon and the horizon of an object glass" (*Middlemarch*, 63), and his observations articulate much less of the novel's larger implications.

Even when stated with firm conviction, the narrator's interpretations and evaluations offer only provisional formulations which are open to dispute and revision. His general remarks on the possibility of thinking too much about marriage, for example, lead to the assertion "That Alice Vavasor had thought too much about it, I feel quite sure. . . . she had gone on thinking of the matter till her mind had become filled with some undefined idea of the importance to her of her own life." Infected by feminist notions, mistakenly believing she should do more with her life than "fall in love, marry the man, have two children, and live happy ever afterwards," Alice is criticized for being both overly romantic in her vague dreams of involvement in a political "cause" and "over prudent in calculating the chances of her happiness" in marriage with Grey. Several hundred pages later, as Alice's story is approaching its conclusion, the narrator reviews her troubled career and attempts once more to define her qualities, this time by summarizing the comparison between her and Glencora. Again, she is considered "too thoughtful"; her love lacks "romance" and involves an excessive amount of "self-devotion":

6. Cf. the comments quoted earlier on women who "doubt" yet are saved, which are offered as exceptions to the "proverb" that "she who doubts is lost" (50).

> In all the troubles of her love, of her engagements, and her broken promises, she had thought more of others than of herself,—and, indeed, those troubles had chiefly come from that self-devotion. She had left John Grey because she feared that she would do him no good as his wife,—that she would not make him happy; and she had afterwards betrothed herself for a second time to her cousin, because she believed that she could serve him by marrying him. [69]

In the earlier passage the narrator attributes Alice's troubles to her thinking too much of herself, here to her thinking too much of others. Both interpretations have some basis in her thoughts and actions, but neither is adequate, and we are left free to make as much use of either as we choose.

The problematic relation between Trollope's narrative commentary and the more concrete level of the characters' thoughts, speech, and behavior can produce the sense that one understands some of the characters better than the "author" does. The three pages of free indirect discourse which present Alice's reactions to Grey's letter in chapter 3, for example, offer a subtle and detailed dramatization of her state of mind, her conflicting feelings of love and resentment toward her fiancé, her attempts at self-justification which reveal unconscious guilt for the break with him she does not yet know she intends to make. The complexity of such concrete presentation far exceeds the narrator's powers of summary generalization and clearly reveals the inadequacy of his comments about Alice's excessive thoughtfulness. "How am I to analyze her mind," the narrator exclaims at a later point, "and make her thoughts and feelings intelligible?" (37). The very inadequacy of the narrator's analyses serves to strengthen the sense of the character's complex individuality, the element of fiction to which Trollope gives the greatest importance. His *Autobiography* insists that the successful novelist must "live with" his characters, directing his imagination toward particularizing details:

> It is so that I have lived with my characters, and thence has come whatever success I have attained. There is a gallery of them, and of all in that gallery I may say that I know the tone of the voice, and the colour of the hair, every flame of the eye, and the very clothes they wear. Of each man I could assert whether he would have said

these or the other words; of every woman, whether she would then have smiled or so have frowned.[7]

Behind this practice is the assumption that the significance of fictional characters lies more in their differences from each other than in their similarities, in the ways they resist analysis and classification, deviate from general rules.

Trollope's use of multiple narration also works toward differentiation: the parallels of *Can You Forgive Her?* become a means of giving greater emphasis to discrepancies of character, situation, and tone. This is most apparent in his skillful, though rather conventional development of contrasts, the use of Mrs. Greenow's comic subplot as a foil to the more painful dilemmas of Alice and Glencora, and the running contrast between the two heroines themselves, "between [Glencora's] candour and Alice's reticence, between her volatile spontaneity and Alice's enclosed self-consciousness, between her provocations and Alice's correctness."[8] Less obvious, and less conventional, is the way these contrasts are never moralized, never made to illustrate a consistent opposition of values. As the shifting sense of general thematic terms indicates, both parallels and contrasts are used to define situations which must be regarded independently. The crucial issue of marriage without love is a clear instance of this incommensurability: for Alice to consent to marry George without loving him is presented as her greatest transgression, while for Mrs. Greenow to have married a wealthy old man to escape spinsterhood is apparently no such disgrace, and Glencora's marriage of convenience to Palliser is not so much a fault as a grievance, not so much a grievance as a problem to be explored and developed. Comparisons play an important part, but because their main effect is to heighten the sense of differences, they contribute to the centrifugal tendency which allows separate narrative lines to develop their independent interest.

Yet this tendency toward dispersion, toward realizing the individuality of each character, never completely dominates

7. *An Autobiography*, World's Classics ed. (London: Oxford University Press, 1953), p. 200.

8. Stephen Wall, "Introduction," Penguin ed. (Harmondsworth: Penguin, 1972), p. 18.

Trollope's fiction. The significance of his characters may lie in their differences, but that significance is often quite problematic, and the traits which mark their individuality are often suspect. Alice, for example, is distinguished by her inwardness, her troubled efforts to understand her situation and choose her own course. When the narrator criticizes her for being "too thoughtful," he indicts the quality with which she attempts to defend her individuality against the conventional asumptions and judgments of others. When Grey attempts to dissuade her from breaking their engagement, he elaborates the criticism by attributing her decision to "that irrational spirit of sadness, which, when over-indulged, drives men to madness and self-destruction" (11). The extreme form of his warning indicates the larger implications of Alice's nonconformity. She is one of a number of Trollope's protagonists who define themselves by their eccentricity, their deviation from social convention or morality, common sense or rationality.[9] These figures lead us beyond the usual sense of eccentricity as purely comic idiosyncrasy, and some are indeed driven to such extremes as Grey invokes, to the madness of Louis Trevelyan in *He Knew He Was Right* or the self-destruction of Ferdinand Lopez in *The Prime Minister*. Most, like Alice, are spared such drastic consequences, but all are used to explore the possibilities and dangers of individualism.

Alice's "sadness" is "irrational" because it proceeds from a restless discontent with all the possibilities her world offers. She resents the assumption that she must surrender her individuality in marriage and adopt her husband's "manner of life," but she can find no terms to express her dissent: "She was silent, having things to say but not knowing in what words to put them" (3). Turning toward the "wild" alternative represented by George briefly enables her to articulate her discontent as "ambition," but this attempted self-assertion becomes another form of self-negation, subordinating herself to another's "cause," and her support

---

9. "Trollope's specialty is for perversely obstinate characters, clergymen who jib and fume over a question of conscience, girls who, from pride or a spirit of sacrifice, reject the men they love, married couples who, out of stubbornness, allow their relationship to become poisoned, friends who, having become enemies, are relentless in their bitterness." Mario Praz, *The Hero in Eclipse in Victorian Fiction*, trans. Angus Davidson (London: Oxford University Press, 1956), p. 302.

of George's political ambitions soon becomes a defensive tactic, substituting her money for the physical commitment he demands. With both men she can define her individuality only in the negative terms of resistance, refusing the expected response. The terms in which her case is presented for judgment are similarly restrictive, beginning with the title, which presumes her guilt, and continuing in the narrator's rhetoric, which asks for our understanding only that we may forgive, not approve her actions. And Alice herself accepts those terms, especially the conventional censure of the "jilt." She has hardly withdrawn from her engagement with Grey when, "in an agony of despair she told herself that she had been an idiot and a fool, as well as a traitor" (14); she has hardly renewed her engagement with George when she repents again: "She knew that she had done wrong . . . and knew that she could not forgive herself" (37).

Alice's harsh self-accusations make it clear that she is quite unlikely to carry her dissent to such extremes as those of which Grey warns her. Such active resistance to social restrictions is represented instead by George's and Burgo's "laughing to scorn all the rules which regulate the lives of other men" (18), the one increasingly "driven" by a "Fury" (56), the other pursuing a less desperate rake's progress, until they both simply disappear from the novel. Alice recoils from such possibilities and comes to believe that "all her misery had been brought about by this scornful superiority to the ordinary pursuits of the world,—this looking down upon humanity" (63). Her self-condemnation internalizes and intensifies the "world's" judgment, but it also serves as a last line of defense for her independence, since she can now consider herself unworthy of conventional happiness. The function of guilt as her final refuge becomes clear at the moment when her long resistance to Grey is at last overcome:

> Of course she had no choice but to yield. He, possessed of power and force infinitely greater than hers, had left her no alternative but to be happy. But there still clung to her what I fear we must call a perverseness of obstinacy, a desire to maintain the resolution she had made,—a wish that she might be allowed to undergo the punishment she had deserved. She was as a prisoner who would fain cling to his prison after pardon has reached him, because he is conscious that the pardon is undeserved. And it may be that there was still left within her bosom some remnant of that feeling of

rebellion which his masterful spirit had ever produced in her. He was so imperious in his tranquillity, he argued his question of love with such a manifest preponderance of right on his side, that she had always felt that to yield to him would be to confess the omnipotence of his power. [74]

Just as Grey triumphs by insistently forgiving her, the novel also puts Alice in her place by imposing "happiness as an enforced necessity" (75), but her potential for evading this conventional resolution has been dissipated much earlier, not only by her own limitations but by the multiplication of narrative lines. The only theoretical consideration of multiple narration in Trollope's *Autobiography* treats it as an answer to the novelist's problem of achieving "the required length" of three volumes while preserving unity.

> Though his story should be all one, yet it may have many parts. Though the plot itself may require but few characters, it may be so enlarged as to find its full development in many. There may be subsidiary plots, which shall all tend to the elucidation of the main story, and which will take their places as part of one and the same work,—as there may be many figures on a canvas which shall not to the spectator seem to form themselves into separate pictures.[10]

In this spatial analogy the "main story" figures as the center of composition and focus of relevance, but few of Trollope's multi-plot novels actually follow this pattern. In *Can You Forgive Her?* Alice's is clearly the main story for the first quarter of the novel, but the introduction of Glencora's does not so much elucidate as displace it. The effect is clearly registered in the *Autobiography*, where Alice is dismissed in one sentence, "The character of the girl is carried through with considerable strength, but is not attractive," in order to allow Trollope to expand on the more congenial subject of the Pallisers.[11] The lively, outspoken Glencora is certainly more attractive than her sad, withdrawn cousin, and from the moment they are brought together in chapter 22, Alice is demoted to the role of a secondary figure, a cautious adviser, confidante, and sober foil to Glencora's more brilliant eccentricities, becoming the voice of convention and prudence in opposition to Glencora's irreverence and rebelliousness. In her

10. *Autobiography*, p. 205.
11. Ibid., p. 155.

own dilemma she can find no terms with which to give her discontent a positive meaning, and here she is completely assimilated by the conventional codes.

The relative attractions of the two heroines are only part of the reason for this shift of emphasis; more important is the fact that Glencora's problem is actually less difficult. She can articulate her own "sadness," her resentment and longings, much more fully in the terms of romantic love; but for all her desperate talk and thoughts, she accepts the established meaning of "adultery," and it is never a real possibility for her, as she realizes once Burgo directly offers her the opportunity. Once the vertigo of their romantic waltz has ebbed, the conventional terms regain their authority: "She was no longer in a dream, but words and things bore to her again their proper meaning" (50)—"proper," not "true": determined by the canons of propriety. After this the possibility of mutual accommodation with her husband develops quickly. Palliser's sacrifice of his political ambitions for the sake of his marriage is a much more meaningful act of compromise than Grey's corresponding gesture of agreeing to enter Parliament, yet Trollope makes it clear that the growth of understanding between Palliser and Glencora does not fully resolve their many differences, so that their relationship remains open to further development. Glencora's deviations from conventional opinion and behavior will continue to disturb and enliven the later Palliser novels, but her eccentricity will never again threaten to spin out of control. The stable resolution of Mrs. Greenow's story in a comfortable mixture of "worldliness and sentimentality . . . like brandy-and-water" (78), is similarly appropriate, but to give Alice's story an equally closed form is incongruous. What George Levine calls its "pretense to finality" constitutes not a resolution but an evasion of the problems she has raised.[12]

Thrust aside by the introduction of a more engrossing, more manageable double, Alice becomes less a challenging deviation, more a displaced focal point—another meaning of eccentricity. The term designates both the individualizing idiosyncrasies with which Trollope is so much concerned and his refusal to allow his more unconventional protagonists to dominate the center of his

12. "Can You Forgive Him? Trollope's *Can You Forgive Her?* and the Myth of Realism," *Victorian Studies* 18 (1974): 26.

composition. In a rare attempt at the sort of philosophical generalization more common in George Eliot, the narrator of *Can You Forgive Her?* asserts that "Every man to himself is the centre of the whole world;—the axle on which it all turns. All knowledge is but his own perception of the things around him. All love, and care for others, and solicitude for the world's welfare, are but his own feelings as to the world's wants and the world's merits" (29). In George Eliot such a condition of subjectivity is presented as a state of egoistic "moral stupidity" which can be outgrown, and her narrator's comprehensive vision represents the possibility of that transcendence. In Trollope this condition is in itself morally neutral, but it is also inescapable, and his narrator represents only the corrective of pluralism, setting one limited perspective against another, attempting to represent each side of a situation fairly. The inevitably self-centered individual is thus displaced, shown to be not the center of the world but eccentric; yet the norm from which he deviates is only the collective opinion and standards of "the world," for which the narrator can also speak.

Trollope's structural dialogue relativizes both individual and general perspectives: the authority by which eccentricity is determined, by which errors and aberrations are evaluated, is not a consistent or transcendent truth but only the pragmatic sense of "what is fitting, useful, and best under the circumstances" (50). In *Can You Forgive Her?* circumstances allow only limited scope for individual deviations. The compromises struck by Glencora and Mrs. Greenow permit them to preserve considerable independence, but Alice is forced not just to compromise but to surrender to her lover's "omnipotence." The more subversive potential of her resistance to her world's conditions is forced off center into increasing error; it can be sustained only by "perverseness of obstinacy" and must at last be entirely repressed. Others among Trollope's novels disclose a wider range of possibilities between conventionality and madness.

Of all his novels, none offers more of such scope, more diversity of subject matter or multiplicity of perspective than *The Last Chronicle of Barset*; none produces more successfully the representational effect described by Hawthorne's well-known image: "as if some giant had hewn a great lump out of the earth and put it under a glass case, with all its inhabitants going about their daily business, and not suspecting that they were being made a show of."[13] This sense of confident possession of a familiar world owes much to the novel's function as conclusion to the Barchester series. Most of its major characters and many of its minor ones are carried over from previous works, as are some of its themes and situations. Like *Middlemarch*, which it may have influenced, it offers a panoramic view of provincial life, more extensive in some respects because of the ways it draws on and draws together so many aspects of its predecessors.[14] Of particular interest is the way Trollope's use of reappearing characters not only adds depth to the novel's secondary figures but augments the presentation of those in the foreground. It is not just that, having read *The Warden* and *Framley Parsonage* for example, we know more about characters like Mr. Harding and Mark Robarts, but recalling the way each has been a previous focus of public controversy provides additional perspectives on Mr. Crawley's ordeal and helps to generalize the recurrent conflict of worldly and unworldly values.

By making use of such comparisons Trollope enlarges the possibilities of multiple narrative. To some extent *The Last Chronicle* transforms the whole series into a continuing multiplot novel; reviewed here, its many stories can be considered concurrently as well as in sequence.[15] But the novel also reinterprets the series by shifts of emphasis and the introduction of new elements. The prominence given to Crawley and his ugly, impoverished parrish of Hogglestock, the sordid and farcical scenes of London life disclosed by Johnny Eames's adventures make its world less comfortable and securely enclosed than those of the previous novels. Placing the coherence and self-sufficiency of the Barsetshire microcosm in question, it uses Crawley's story to

13. *Trollope: The Critical Heritage*, ed. Donald Smalley (London: Routledge, 1969), p. 110. Trollope quotes Hawthorne's letter of 1860 in the *Autobiography* and adds that it "describes with wonderful accuracy the purport that I have ever had in view in my writing" (p. 125).

14. T.H.S. Escott claims that George Eliot acknowledged an important debt to Trollope in *Middlemarch*. See *Anthony Trollope: His Work, Associates and Literary Originals* (London: John Lane, 1913), p. 185.

15. Cf. Trollope's comments in his *Autobiobraphy* on the detailed cross-references with which he builds up the characters of Plantagenet and Glencora through the Palliser series, pp. 309–10.

develop a much deeper division between the individual and the community, while the large number and diversity of figures and situations it presents open up both structural gaps and possibilities of comparison.

The multiplication of perspectives both within *The Last Chronicle* and in its relation to the whole series can be observed in chapter 21, "Mr. Robarts on his Embassy," where the younger, more prosperous clergyman tries unsuccessfully to persuade Crawley to retain a lawyer in his defense. One perspective on the scene is produced by comparison with the dramatic confrontation between Crawley and the Proudies in chapter 18, to which Robarts explicitly refers. There, in spite of the extreme disadvantage of his position, Crawley's proud intransigence enabled him to defend his rights; here the same qualities with which he "crushed" his adversaries are turned against his friend: "Mr. Robarts . . . knew that behind the humility there was a crushing pride—a pride which, in all probability, would rise up and crush him before he could get himself out of the room." The earlier interview presented the poor, embattled Crawley as a victim of social injustice; here his estrangement indicates his flaws: "There was something radically wrong with him, which had put him into antagonism with all the world, and which produced these never-dying grievances." His refusal to compromise now seems not heroic but perverse, "so far removed from the dominion of sound sense" as to be considered "mad."

This, at least, is the way Crawley appears to Robarts, whose point of view the narrator adopts and apparently endorses throughout the scene. But we are also given a different perspective by another comparison which is introduced through Robarts' thoughts at the beginning of the chapter:

> He was a little afraid of Mr. Crawley, acknowledging tacitly to himself that the man had a power of ascendancy with which he would hardly be able to cope successfully. In old days he had once been rebuked by Mr. Crawley, and had been cowed by the rebuke; and though there was no touch of rancour in his heart on this account, no slightest remaining venom—but rather increased respect and friendship—still he was unable to overcome the remembrance of the scene in which the perpetual curate of Hogglestock had undoubtedly had the mastery of him.

The scene recalled here takes place in chapter 15 of *Framley Parsonage*, where the positions of the two men are reversed. Robarts has gone astray among "worldly pleasure-seekers" and Crawley comes as a stern spiritual ambassador, recalling him to his clerical duties. In the second scene, Robarts' more worldly outlook appears in a more favorable light, but this comparison reminds us that Crawley's "power of ascendancy" involves not just the force of his crushing pride but an appeal to a higher authority than the "sound sense" of collective social judgment. The issue between the two men comes to a focus in the different meanings they assign to the word *character* when Robarts tries to invoke the authority of Archdeacon Grantly.

> "We had the archdeacon over at Framley the other day," he said. "Of course you know the archdeacon?"
> "I never had the advantage of any acquaintance with Dr. Grantly. Of course I know him well by name, and also personally —that is, by sight."
> "And by character?"
> "Nay; I can hardly say so much as that. But I am aware that his name stands high with many of his order."
> "Exactly; that is what I mean."

For Robarts "character" is the same as "name," or reputation; for Crawley there is an important difference. He stands for the sense of character as intrinsic moral quality, independent of others' opinions. Sure of his own innocence, he refuses to hire an advocate to persuade others: "What the world says of me I have learned to disregard very much, Mr. Robarts."

What the world says of Crawley and his response are major concerns of the novel, and as he does in this scene, Trollope allows us to entertain different interpretations of their relationship. The device of having him accused of stealing a check for twenty pounds serves to shift this "very poor . . . unhappy, moody, disappointed man" from the obscurity of his precarious existence on the margins of Barsetshire to the center of public attention: "The whole county was astir in this matter of this alleged guilt of the Reverend Josiah Crawley" (1). Tracing the repercussions of this disturbance contributes to the novel's broad social survey and helps to place Crawley in perspective by correcting for his own limited, often distorted point of view; but at the same time the comfortable, reasonable attitudes of men like Mark Robarts are challenged and measured by Crawley's formidable integrity and fierce unworldliness.

Perhaps the most remarkable, certainly the most fully developed of Trollope's eccentric protagonists, Crawley displays a rare ability to maintain his individuality. His obstinacy in deciding his own course, despite the efforts of both friends and enemies to influence him, often seems excessive, but his situation partially justifies the extreme terms in which he regards all moral questions. Unlike Alice Vavasor, who can find no terms in which to express herself but those of oppressive conventionality, Crawley speaks his own distinctive language, a formal, old-fashioned idiom flavored by biblical and scholastic phrases, which continually marks his difference from those around him. It can be an expression of his "power of ascendancy," as when he rebukes Mrs. Proudie: "Peace, woman. . . . The distaff were more fitting for you" (18); but it can also mark him with the taint of pedantry and affectation, as when he speaks to his wife of his plans to consult Mr. Toogood: "*In formâ pauperis* I must go to him, and must tell him so. . . . I will tell your cousin that I am sore straitened, and brought down into the very dust by misfortune" (32), and especially once his troubles are over, its incongruity becomes a source of humor, as when he pleads to have his new frock coat made unfashionably long: "Surely the price of the cloth wanted to perfect the comeliness of the garment cannot be much" (83). The range of effects produced by his distinctive idiom reflects the mixture of respect, disapproval, and amusement with which Crawley's eccentricity is regarded, its potential for both elevated dignity and absurd inflexibility.

Whether his idiosyncrasies are admired or disparaged, Crawley repeatedly appears as a unique figure: "Such a queer fish—so unlike anybody else in the world!" (40). Those who defend him base their position on this unlikeness: "You must not judge him as you do other men." What would be considered theft by anyone else can be considered innocent confusion in him, a result of his "madness." This view of his case, which for most of the novel seems the most plausible interpretation, allows others both to recognize Crawley's extraordinary individuality and to insulate themselves from its subversive force. He becomes an exception but not a challenge to their rules.

Crawley's eccentricity is set apart from the rest of the novel's world, yet it also displays a strong tendency to become the novel's compositional center, determining the meaning of its other elements by centripetal reference. Its force is already at work in the opening chapters, even before Crawley has appeared, not just because we see others discussing his case but because they are also defined by implicit comparison with him. Thus, in the first scene, the prosperous lawyer Mr. Walker is introduced: "He was a man between fifty and sixty years of age, with grey hair, rather short, and somewhat corpulent, but still gifted with that amount of personal comeliness which comfortable position and the respect of others will generally seem to give. A man rarely carries himself meanly, whom the world holds high in esteem" (1). Again, when the focus shifts in the next two chapters to parallel domestic scenes among the Grantlys, the familiar figure of the archdeacon is set in a similar ironic alignment: "He was a generous man in money matters—having a dislike for poverty which was not generous" (3).

Crawley's story exerts its power of attraction across a wider distance on the novel's other narrative lines. Unlike the introduction of parallels to Alice's story in *Can You Forgive Her?*, the multiple narrative of *The Last Chronicle* sets Crawley's lonely ordeal against three other plots which bear no immediate resemblance to it. The stories of Henry Grantly and Grace Crawley, Johnny Eames and Lily Dale, and Conway Dalrymple and Clara Van Siever are all versions of the romantic love story, the staple pattern on which Trollope worked so many variations throughout his career. As such, they are often and easily drawn into comparison with each other, as in chapter 27 when Henry and Johnny take the same train to Allington, both to make declarations of love, or when Mrs. Dale compares "the good fortune which was awaiting Grace, with the evil fortune which had fallen on her own child" (28).

But much more interesting and difficult is the relation between these narrative lines and Crawley's. There are, of course, some causal connections, of which the most important is the way Crawley's plight complicates the relationship between Grace and

Henry, leading to her refusal to marry him and the archdeacon's threat of disinheritance. Through these links, Trollope appears to achieve a tight economy of means, whereby the long-delayed solution to the mystery of the check also removes the obstacle between the lovers and leads to Henry's reconciliation with his father. (An additional link is formed when Johnny undertakes the search for Mrs. Arabin, not just to help Crawley but to help himself win Lily: "He hoped that by this chivalrous journey he might even yet achieve the thing necessary" [70].) But these gestures toward integration are deceptive, for the causal connections produce no decisive effects. By the time Crawley is freed from disgrace, Henry has become thoroughly committed to the marriage, and his father is quite ready to yield; Johnny's quest turns out to have been unnecessary, and Lily persists in refusing him. The most active relations between the other narrative lines and Crawley's are not causal but thematic.

The most obvious effects produced by the gap between Crawley's story and the others are those of contrast. The sense of ironic discrepancy between his world and those of Mr. Walker and the archdeacon is intensified by the ludicrous charades of the London scenes. Dobbs Broughton puts on an ostentatious but unconvincing display of wealth ("They stink of money," Johnny observes, "but I'm not sure they've got any all the same" [24]), while his wife fills her empty life by playing "the game of love-making," which provides "the charms of a fevered existence" without the inconvenience of any actual emotional disturbance (26). Conway Dalrymple, her able partner in this game, also pursues a professional career of flattering make-believe, gathering a rich harvest of "gilt sugar-plums" with his fashionable portraits: "This countess was drawn as a fairy with wings, that countess as a goddess with a helmet"—and Mrs. Dobbs Broughton as all three Graces (24). Her friend Madalina Desmoulines prefers the game of melodramatic intrigue, in which she manages to involve Johnny despite his disbelief: " 'It's as good as a play,' he said to himself" (25). Similar games are played in the government office, where Johnny is regarded as a romantic "hero" by the junior clerks while he fights a running battle with his superior, Sir Raffle Buffle, refusing "to pretend to believe" in his lies and bluster, and at one point winning a leave of absence "by the affectation of a costume" (48).

The seriousness of Crawley's situation and character stands out in sharp relief against all this trivial pretense and self-dramatization, but the questions of role-playing and collaboration also arise at several points in his story, as when he tells his wife how humbly he will approach Mr. Toogood: "she could not quite believe that her husband's humility was true humility. She strove to believe it but knew that she failed" (32). Even Crawley's genuine virtues are, according to the narrator, flawed by an element of self-regarding performance:

> It was the fault of the man that he was imbued too strongly with self-consciousness. He could do a great thing or two. He could keep up his courage in positions which would wash all the courage out of most men. He could tell the truth though truth should ruin him. He could sacrifice all that he had to duty. He could do justice though the heaven should fall. But he could not forget to pay tribute to himself for the greatness of his own actions; nor, when accepting with an effort of meekness the small payment made by the world to him, in return for his great works, could he forget the great payments made to others for small work. It was not sufficient for him to remember that he knew Hebrew, but he must remember also that the dean did not. [61]

The criticism of Crawley's excessive self-consciousness, which recalls the criticism of Alice Vavasor for being "too thoughtful," expresses mistrust of the estranging inwardness that produces eccentricity, but it is misleading to imply that Crawley's strengths and weaknesses can be so clearly separated. His self-consciousness is pervasive, as much a part of his stubborn integrity as of his self-pity. Even when he tries to escape it by adopting Giles Hoggett's stoical maxim, "It's dogged as does it. It ain't thinking about it," he can only be self-consciously dogged, resigning his curacy in order to show his capacity for bearing the worst "with a greater show of fortitude than had been within his power when the extent of his calamity was more doubtful. . . . It certainly seemed as though the very extremity of ill-fortune was good for him" (68).

Invoking the tragic prototypes of fallen strength, "Polyphemus and Belisarius and Samson" (62), Crawley's role-playing is both self-destructive, a perverse courting of disaster, and a form of self-realization, a search for the extreme conditions that will justify and reinforce his individuality. Even when Trollope most emphasizes the discrepancy between self and role, the effect is to increase, not diminish, Crawley's stature, an effect realized most powerfully in the scene where Crawley attempts to refuse Henry permission to marry Grace.

> "There is unfortunately a stain, which is vicarial," began Mr. Crawley, sustaining up to that point his voice with Roman fortitude —with a fortitude which would have been Roman had it not at that moment broken down under the pressure of human feeling. He could keep it up no longer, but continued his speech with broken sobs, and with a voice altogether changed in its tone—rapid now, whereas it had before been slow—natural, whereas it had hitherto been affected—human, whereas it had hitherto been Roman. "Major Grantly," he said, "I am sore beset; but what can I say to you? My darling is as pure as the light of day—only that she is soiled with my impurity." [63]

This is followed directly in the next chapter by a parallel breakdown of affectation in the scene where Dalrymple tells Mrs. Broughton her husband has killed himself:

> she gazed at him with fixed eyes, and rigid mouth, while the quick coming breath just moved the curl of her nostrils. It occurred to him at the moment that he had never before seen her so wholly unaffected, and had never before observed that she was so totally deficient in all the elements of real beauty. . . .
> Then she dropped his hands and walked away from him to the window—and stood there looking out upon the stuccoed turret of a huge house that stood opposite. As she did so she was employing herself in counting the windows. [64]

Mrs. Broughton's "natural" self is numb and empty, and Crawley gains by the close comparison all the more intensity and depth. We should observe, however, that despite the narrator's antithesis of "affected" and "natural" tones, Crawley's movingly "human" speech still depends on his distinctive language ("sore beset," "soiled with my impurity"), not the common idiom of others. Rather than establishing a clear separation between his true self and false role-playing, the scene confirms their in-

terdependence.[16] The following scene also permits comparison of
Crawley's compromised self-realization and Dalrymple's own
story, which attempts to sketch a purely positive movement from
affectation to truth, from the meretricious games of love-making
with Mrs. Broughton to his genuine love for Clara, declared in a
gesture of awkward sincerity as he takes off his Turkish cap and
painter's apron to propose (60). But this simplifying resolution
remains a peripheral alternative, not an effective counterweight to
the more complex interpenetration of self and role in Crawley.[17]
Whether they are presented under their "false" or "true" aspects,
these characters appear relatively pale and conventional beside
his singularity.

Less marked oppositions sometimes tend to make other characters appear not as distinct alternatives but as lesser versions of
Crawley. Henry, increasingly attracted by the prospect of doing
"the magnificent thing" (7), sacrificing his wordly interests to
marry Grace, eventually becomes so taken with the role that he
resists being reconciled with his father: "The cross-grainedness of
men is so great that things will often be forced to go wrong, even
when they have the strongest possible natural tendency of their
own to go right" (63). This comment is directly concerned with
"these affairs between the archdeacon and his son," but it
immediately follows the chapter in which Crawley resigns his
curacy and thus invites us to regard their quarrel as a comic
variation on his more drastic act. He may be equally "cross-
grained" but in circumstances which show no natural tendency
to go right. Johnny presents another comic echo of Crawley's
doggedness in his efforts to act like "a hero of romance" (70),
taking boyish pride in traveling from London to Venice to
Florence without sleeping in a bed. Later, trying to give his life a

16. Cf. the discussion above of collaborative fictions in Dickens, pp. 80–83,
where the opposition of "true" and "false" undergoes a similar complication. The
structural tension between Dickens' subdued protagonists and the more vivid
eccentric figures that surround them can be seen as an inverse form of the
problematic of eccentricity in Trollope.
17. Dalrymple's development is also recomplicated: the momentarily clear
opposition between false role-playing and true simplicity is somewhat blurred
when, soon after his proposal, he performs the theatrical gesture of slashing the
painting of Jael and Sisera (followed later by the comical practicality of repairing
and exhibiting it).

new direction after Lily has refused him again, he thinks he will "go deep into Greek and do a translation" (80) but gives it up after one day, recalling Crawley's tenacity as well as his mastery of the classics. Such moments make these characters seem to be unsuccessfully emulating Crawley, recognizing his preeminence, as Henry explicitly does after he and Mr. Toogood have announced the solution of the mystery: "I call that man a hero" (74).

To trace such connections, to recogize Crawley's claims as hero or organizing center, is to read *The Last Chronicle* according to Trollope's general prescription, regarding the other narrative lines as "subsidiary plots, which . . . all tend to the elucidation of the main story"; but there is much in both the form and logic of the novel which resists this kind of reading. One source of resistance is Trollope's relativism: Crawley figures as a common point of comparison, but his eccentric individuality does not become a consistent standard of judgment. As the narrator observes, in considering whether Johnny is "worthy" of Lily, "there is no standard for such measurement" (76). We can locate moments in which characters like Johnny or Henry are subordinated as foils to Crawley's singularity, but they also clearly develop independent interest, and there are other parallels whose significance is more problematic, of which Lily's story is the best example.

As a continuation from *The Small House at Allington*, the account of her troubled love life stands as an independent narrative line, yet in the context of *The Last Chronicle* we can also recognize important similarities between her and Crawley. Her resentment at becoming the subject of wide-spread gossip, her resistance to the well-meaning interference of all those who want her to marry Johnny, clearly recall Crawley's irritable pride and intransigence.[18] Not only her "obstinacy" (76) but her self-con-

18. "How had it come to pass that matters which with others are so private, should with her have become the public property of so large a circle? Any other girl would receive advice on such a subject from her mother alone, and there the secret would rest. But her secret had been published, as it were, by the town-crier in the High Street! Everybody knew that she had been jilted by Adolphus Crosbie, and that it was intended that she should be consoled by Johnny Eames. And people seemed to think that they had a right to rebuke her if she expressed an unwillingness to carry out this intention which the public had so kindly arranged for her" (59).

sciousness about marriage ("The shipwreck to which she had come, and the fierce regrets which had thence arisen, had forced her to think too much of these things" [77]) and her attempt at unconventional self-definition in her choice of the role or "title" of Old Maid (35) all invite comparison with Crawley. The interpretation of these parallels, however, remains open. We may regard them as indications of equivalent perversity, or integrity, or as the basis of a comparison which favors either one or the other, but neither becomes subordinated, and the eventual effect of these undecidable possibilities is to make us view each case independently. Here there is no centripetal convergence, and the parallel thus tends to qualify Crawley's singularity.

Even when its parallels and oppositions are less evenly balanced, the novel's multiple narration works to question Crawley's preeminence as well as affirm it. His power to focus the entire composition is shown at several points, but it is also resisted as a powerful delusion, for it projects the centripetal pattern of his own paranoia and self-pity, his conviction that the whole world has conspired against him, "that of all God's creatures he was the most heavily afflicted" (12).[19] In Crawley's brooding inwardness Trollope shows, more clearly than in Alice Vavasor's, the potential development of eccentricity to the extremes of "madness and self-destruction." Crawley himself senses such possibilities and views them with both horror and fascination: "What if the idea should come to him in his madness that it would be well for him to slay his wife and his children? Only that was wanting to make him of all men the most unfortunate" (41). The novel recoils from such possibilities and rejects the paranoid logic that projects them, displacing Crawley's story much as *Can You Forgive Her?* displaces Alice's. In both cases the eccentric protagonist dominates the first quarter of the novel and then recedes as other narrative lines are introduced and developed. Crawley is never subordinated to another character, as Alice is to Glencora, but once his situation has been fully presented at the beginning it receives relatively little development. The affairs of the Grantlys, of Johnny and Lily, and of all the London characters receive

19. Cf. Helen Storm Corsa, " 'The Cross-Grainedness of Men': The Rev. Josiah Crawley—Trollope's Study of a Paranoid Personality," *Hartford Studies in Literature* 5 (1973): 160–72.

expansive development throughout the central portion of the novel, which, between chapters 21 and 61, returns to Crawley in only two (32 and 41). Other chapters deal with aspects of his story but only as it concerns others, as in Mr. Toogood's investigations or the formation of the clerical commission, staying at a distance from Crawley himself; and when he regains a more prominent position toward the end, the main emphasis is still on the efforts of others to solve the mystery of the check.

Trollope professed dissatisfaction with this aspect of the novel: "I have never been capable of constructing with complete success the intricacies of a plot that required to be unravelled."[20] But despite the rather awkward contrivances on which it depends, the mystery plot serves as an extremely effective device for both establishing and undermining Crawley's unique position in the novel. It not only gives him public prominence but reinforces his claim to singularity, since it appears that he can be acquitted only on the grounds of his unlikeness from others, the probability that he found the check, forgot where it came from, and used it without any deliberate dishonesty. But when the long-delayed solution is at last produced and we learn that he came by the check legitimately, he is exonerated on the same grounds as anyone else would be. The unraveling of the plot's intricacies, such as they are, thus produces a logical assimilation and also opens the way to social assimilation as Crawley is brought by the archdeacon's favor into secure prosperity. As in *Can You Forgive Her?* Trollope deflects the eccentric protagonist from tragedy by imposing happiness as an enforced necessity: "Mr. Crawley is Conquered" (83), but the force is much less violent here: "Mr. and Mrs. Crawley became quiet at St. Ewold's, and, as I think, contented" (84).

The Last Chronicle manages to contain the disquieting and potentially destructive power of eccentricity without entirely repressing it, bringing the man who conceives of himself as a fallen tragic hero into the company of comic eccentrics like the archdeacon and Mr. Toogood. The movement involves a reduction of scale and intensity but not the complete assimilation of individual differences. Rather than imposing conformity, it affirms the possibility of community, as in the mutual under-

20. *Autobiography*, pp. 236–37.

standing and appreciation which develop between such dissimilar men as Crawley and Toogood, the possibility of release from self-preoccupation, as in the moment when Crawley, in the midst of his confrontation with the bishop, sees how Mrs. Proudie embarrasses her husband: "The bishop . . . looked so unutterably miserable that a smile came across Mr. Crawley's face. After all, others beside himself had their troubles and trials" (18). The tolerance which animates this modulation into comedy can be extended more fully to the characters' various forms of role-playing in a novel which itself concludes with an affirmation of self-conscious make-believe: "to me Barset has been a real county, and its city a real city, and the spires and towers have been before my eyes, and the voices of the people are known to my ears, and the pavement of the city ways are familiar to my footsteps."

In *Can You Forgive Her?* and *The Last Chronicle of Barset*, Trollope's eccentric protagonists are eventually assimilated; their erratic careers end in enclosure within the more or less confining limits of conventional happiness. In *He Knew He Was Right*, begun only a year after he had finished *The Last Chronicle*, Trollope for once allows his protagonist to realize the possibilities of madness and self-destruction which the earlier novels had invoked but avoided. The extremity to which Louis Trevelyan is brought is all the more remarkable for its commonplace origin in a domestic quarrel; it requires no unusual or contrived circumstances such as those to which Crawley is subjected, but only the obstinacy of both Louis and Emily in believing themselves entirely right. This, and the paranoid imagination of disaster which they share with Crawley, soon serve to make themselves and each other miserable and to point the way to the most drastic consequences. "As for standing this kind of life, it is out of the question," Emily declares at quite an early stage of their troubles. "I should either destroy myself or go mad" (9).

"Here," James wrote in admiration, "Trollope has dared to be thoroughly logical; he has not sacrificed to conventional optimism; he has not been afraid of a misery which should be too much like life,"[21] but in order to pursue the logic of eccentricity

21. Henry James, "Anthony Trollope," in *The Critical Heritage*, p. 543.

to its bitter end, Trollope must maintain very strict rhetorical control over Trevelyan's story. In his *Autobiography,* Trollope considers *He Knew He Was Right* a singular failure: "I do not know that in any literary effort I ever fell more completely short of my own intention than in this story," the unrealized intention being his "purpose to create sympathy for the unfortunate man."[22] But the novel's presentation of Trevelyan clearly works in several ways to restrict sympathy. There is nothing attractive about him, nothing exceptional but his inflexibility, and the narrator offers little in his defense. There are several passages of acute and persuasive psychological analysis which enable us to understand Trevelyan's state of mind at each stage of his deterioration, but they all rest on the assumption that his ruin is the result of his own weakness and deficiencies ("he was jealous of authority, fearful of slights, self-conscious, afraid of the world, and utterly ignorant of the nature of a woman's mind" [27]).

When Trollope's narrative commentary stresses the flaws and errors of Alice Vavasor or Mr. Crawley, the reader is free to adopt a different perspective and to consider their individualizing traits as positive values, but no such perspective is available here. Trevelyan's self-conscious inwardness offers no countertruth to the norms of his world; his estrangement can be understood only as loss. Unlike Alice and Crawley, he is always and only eccentric, never a possible center of value and judgment. Sympathy, therefore, can operate only in the narrow form of pity. We may well pity his prolonged and extreme misery, but we can never consider him in any sense "right." These differences between *He Knew He Was Right* and the earlier novels do not represent a radical change but only a different form of the same problematic. In all three cases we can observe Trollope's acute ambivalence toward the eccentric protagonist, whose subversive potential must be contained either by assimilation at the end or by rigorous control of distance from the beginning.

This control can also be observed in the novel's use of multiple narrative. Trollope introduces additional plot lines and divides the narrative focus much sooner here, so that Trevelyan is not allowed to dominate even the early stages of the novel as much as Alice and Crawley are. The opening account of the quarrel is

22. *Autobiography,* p. 276.

interrupted after three chapters in order to introduce the story of Nora Rowley and Hugh Stanbury, and again after another two chapters to introduce Miss Stanbury. From this point the narrative proceeds by regular shifts between London, Exeter, and Nuncombe Putney, and after the separation of Emily and Trevelyan in chapter 11, producing another division of focus, there are more scenes dealing with her and Nora than with him. As Trollope introduces additional, parallel love stories (Dorothy Stanbury and Brooke Burgess, Caroline Spalding and Charles Glascock, the two French sisters and Mr. Gibson), the main story is once again not just elucidated but displaced by the cumulative mass of secondary plot lines, yet this effect comes not as a shift of emphasis but as part of a consistent defensive strategy. Simply to complain that the "fascinating abnormal psychology" of Trevelyan's story is "smothered . . . by tedious subplots and hundreds of unnecessary pages"[23] is to miss the point of that strategy and the structural tensions it produces.

Trevelyan's story is in tension with the others because it traces a process of estrangement that leads to death while they are negotiating ordinary social and personal difficulties of courtship on the way to their various comic resolutions; but along with this discrepancy of mode Trollope also develops a close thematic interplay. Here too, the clearest effect is that of control, the use of analogies and oppositions to define Trevelyan's deficiencies. The running counterpoint between him and Miss Stanbury is the most important of these comparisons. She first appears as a comic eccentric with a set of rigid, conservative opinions on everything from politics to diet ("All change was to her hateful and unnecessary" [7]); her willfulness is plainly presented as a parallel: "a most excellent woman . . . with no fault but this, that she likes her own way" (8; cf. chapter 1, where the same trait is attributed to both Trevelyan and Emily). But while Trevelyan and Emily are ruining their lives by their inflexibility, we are offered several incidents in which Miss Stanbury first asserts herself and then apologizes or admits her error (for example, when she mistakenly believes Colonel Osborne has visited Nuncombe Putney [18]). She tries to match Dorothy with Gibson and

23. Robert M. Polhemus, *The Changing World of Anthony Trollope* (Berkeley and Los Angeles: University of California Press, 1968), p. 164.

opposes her marriage to Brooke, yet on these and several other points she eventually yields. At the end she feels "her life had been a failure" (89), "very vain" (97), because she has so often reversed herself and has been brought to doubt the truth of her cherished opinions, yet her inconsistencies and uncertainties are clearly preferable to Trevelyan's fatal rigidity.

Comparisons such as this reinforce the novel's opposition of modes, but there are others which cut across it. In Trevelyan's story, Trollope does not avoid tragedy by imposing a comic resolution, but he does refuse to allow his eccentric protagonist tragic stature or dignity, and in the process the notion of "tragedy" itself becomes as much a thematic focus as the notion of the "hero" does in *The Last Chronicle*. For Trevelyan the term represents the extremity which obsesses him when he has "almost come to have but one desire,—namely, that he should find her out, that the evidence should be conclusive, that it should be proved, and so brought to an end. Then he would destroy her, and destroy that man,—and afterwards destroy himself, so bitter to him would be his ignominy. He almost reveled in the idea of the tragedy he would make" (45). Later, when he is broken by his sufferings, it serves to dignify his self-pity: "Emily," he says near the end, "it has all been a terrible tragedy, has it not?" (98).

The claim to tragic stature consistently works to reinforce Trevelyan's sense of being right, attributing his ruin to others ("He considered himself . . . the victim of so cruel a conspiracy among those who ought to have been his friends") or to "the terrible hand of irresistible Fate" (84). It appears most explicitly in the moments when he appropriates the language of Shakespearean tragic heroes, of Othello ("He would speak of dear Emily, and poor Emily, and shake his head slowly, and talk of the pity of it. 'The pity of it, Iago; oh, the pity of it' " [95]), of Hamlet ("Do you think you would do more for her than I would do," he asks Sir Marmaduke, "drink more of Esill?" [78]), and especially of Lear, who provides the model for the self-righteous diatribe of chapter 92, "Trevelyan Discourses on Life." Here, as Trevelyan's estrangement touches its furthest limit, he claims the authority to indict the whole world from which he has withdrawn, the power of eccentricity to expose the hollowness of conventional values and beliefs:

It has been my study to untie all the ties; and, by Jove, I have succeeded. Look at me here. I have got rid of the trammels pretty well,—haven't I?—have unshackled myself, and thrown off the paddings, and the wrappings, and the swaddling clothes. I have got rid of the conventionalities, and can look Nature straight in the face.

It is not that "Trollope gives Louis the quality of a mad, possessed seer, and lets loose some of his own fierce resentment against Victorian society."[24] It is rather Trevelyan who affects such a role, while Trollope musters his rhetorical devices to undercut it, most obviously in the narrator's comments on his "attempt at satire, so fatuous, so plain, so false," but more subtly in the ways characters in other stories parody Trevelyan's histrionic bent. Two chapters before Trevelyan discourses on life, Lady Rowley stresses the absurdity of such Learish posturing in response to her husband's threats to disown Nora for refusing to give up Hugh:

As for disinheriting her, casting her off, cursing her, and the rest,— she had no belief in such doings at all. "On the stage they do such things as that," she said; "and, perhaps, they used to do it once in reality. But you know that it's out of the question now. Fancy your standing up and cursing at the dear girl, just as we are all starting from Southampton!" [90]

This parodic function provides the main thematic relevance of Gibson's farcical misadventures. Shuttling erratically between Camilla and Arabella French, he echoes Trevelyan's "irresistible Fate":

"I fancy sometimes that some mysterious agency interferes with the affairs of a man and drives him on,—and on,—and on,—almost,— till he doesn't know where it drives him." As he said this in a voice that was quite sepulchral in its tone, he felt some consolation in the conviction that this mysterious agency could not affect a man without imbuing him with a certain amount of grandeur. [65]

Similarly, when he has jilted Camilla, she warns that if her sister replaces her, "there shall be such a tragedy that nobody every heard the like" (74). As Camilla's "low nature" becomes "nearly poetic under the wrong inflicted upon her" (82), her hysterical

24. Polhemus, *The Changing World*, p. 166.

"sublimity of indignation" helps to diminish the sense of Trevelyan's tragic elevation.

It seems clear that to allow his eccentric protagonist to spin out of control, Trollope must impose unusually narrow restrictions on interpretation, but while so much of the novel's organization works to determine the meaning of Trevelyan's story with comparisons which define his errors and undercut his pretensions, the interplay between it and the others also produces occasional reversals of the dominant perspective. Not that he ever seems right, but his madness can elucidate more common, less extreme irrationality in others. A clear example arises from the narrator's comments on how Trevelyan "almost came to hope" his wife would be proved unfaithful:

> —not, indeed, with the hope of the sane man, who desires that which he tells himself to be for his advantage; but with the hope of the insane man, who loves to feed his grievance, even though the grief should be his death. They who do not understand that a man may be brought to hope that which of all things is the most grievous to him, have not observed with sufficient closeness the perversity of the human mind. [38]

Here Trevelyan's insanity appears not as a singular aberration but as an instance of a common quality, an interpretation which is immediately confirmed in the next chapter, where Hugh declares his love to Nora. Although she has "confessed to herself frankly that nothing but this,—this one thing which was now happening . . . could make her happy," she nevertheless refuses to admit her own love and flees from him. The perversity of rejecting what is most desired is clearly comparable to that of desiring what is most grievous, though the two cases are not equivalent. Nora acts in part out of conventional propriety, in part out of obedience to an education which has taught her "that it is a crime to marry a man without an assured income," and when the narrative returns to her two chapters later, we see that in spite of her efforts to be angry, she cannot suppress her actual happiness at what has happened, but for a moment her resistance has aligned her with Trevelyan's more extreme perversity.

In addition to such analogies, there are points at which Trevelyan's madness brings out comparable qualities in others through direct influence, as when Mr. Outhouse receives the letter filled with hysterical accusations and threats which Trevelyan writes after learning of Colonel Osborne's visit to the clergyman's house.

> If Trevelyan was mad when he wrote this letter, Mr. Outhouse was very nearly as mad when he read it. . . . Such a letter as he had received should have been treated by him as the production of a madman. But he was not sane enough himself to see the matter in that light. He gnashed his teeth, and clenched his fist, and was almost beside himself. [45]

Trevelyan exerts a similar maddening influence on Sir Marmaduke, whose efforts to maintain a rigid, righteous posture toward Nora also, as we have seen, invite comparison with Trevelyan's behavior toward Emily. Through such metaphoric or metonymic connections we see insanity and self-destructive perversity as more common possibilities than the opposition between Trevelyan's story and the others seems to imply, yet the occasions on which he becomes not only mad in himself but a cause or measure of madness in others are relatively few, and they do not represent the most important way he can serve to focus the novel's significance. (The point rather tends to get dispersed in inconsequential thematic echoes, such as the weak jokes about Glascock being a "lunatic" [40, 80].)

A more productive way of relating the novel's narrative lines can be developed by recognizing how Trevelyan's story redefines the problem of eccentricity. In his *Autobiography*, Trollope describes Trevelyan as being "led constantly astray by his unwillingness to submit his own judgment to the opinion of others,"[25] which seems to define him and his errors in terms of an opposition between the individual and the group. This is indeed the way eccentricity is usually conceived, the way Crawley, for instance, is presented in *The Last Chronicle;* but Trevelyan is not presented in relation to any actual community. This is not simply the result of the shift from Barsetshire to London, since even in the Exeter scenes, where Miss Stanbury's story is firmly placed in the context of provincial society, her eccentricities are not defined by opposition to public opinion, nor does the flexibility she eventually demonstrates involve submitting her judgment to the

25. *Autobiography*, p. 276.

opinion of others. In *He Knew He Was Right* the emphasis has shifted from the relation of the individual and the group to the private relations of several more or less isolated individuals, and it is here that Trevelyan's extreme withdrawal reveals most about the general conditions of his world.[26]

The virtual disappearance of institutional public life, such as the ecclesiastical or parliamentary politics of the Barsetshire or Palliser novels, gives unusual prominence to personal relationships, especially marriage and courtship, and places an unusually heavy burden on them. They offer the only significant roles, the only avenues to self-realization, and thus they often tend to become contests in which each character's self-conception is at stake. This stress accounts for the importance of being "right," which reappears in the various quarrels and conflicts that constitute so many of the novel's episodes. "What is it that we all live upon but self-esteem?" Priscilla asks Emily. "Every one to himself is the centre and pivot of all the world" (16).

In Trevelyan this egocentricity is not complacent but anxious; his desperate need to be right arises from insecurity: "jealous of authority, fearful of slights, self-conscious, afraid of the world" (27), he must constantly defend his precarious self-esteem. The effort drives him to increasingly violent and irrational self-assertion in the struggle not only against his wife's resistance and his friends' opinions, but against his own anxious, inadmissable self-doubt: "He told himself from hour to hour that he knew he was right;—but in very truth he was ever doubting his own conduct" (60). Other characters display a similar tendency to believe themselves right, but in them self-esteem is presented as a sign of strength, as in the narrator's comments on the Stanburys, who are all "filled with the same eager readiness to believe themselves to be right,—and to own themselves to others to be wrong, when they had been constrained to make such confession to themselves. . . . in all was to be found the same belief in self,—which amounted almost to conceit,—the same warmth of affection, and the same love of justice" (22).

26. Cf. Cockshut's discussion of "The Drama of Loneliness" in the novel, in *Anthony Trollope*, pp. 169–79. See also the discussion, above, of the disappearance of community in *Daniel Deronda*, which also leads to the exploration of extremity in the modes of vision and nightmare, pp. 170–79.

The opposition between belief and doubt in self is the basis of the novel's moral psychology, which in turn determines the possible forms of relationship. Doubt defines all relationships in terms of power, of dominance and submission, as in the struggle of wills between Trevelyan and Emily; belief gives the strength to admit error, to recognize another's point of view, and to love. Miss Stanbury, for instance, takes in Dorothy because of her "desire to have some one near to her to whom she might not only do her duty as guardian, but whom she might also love" (8), and that desire, which implies not only a lack but a positive strength, repeatedly overcomes her highly developed urge to dominate. Hugh, as he is falling in love with Nora, also feels "that he had within his breast a double identity," divided between his conception of himself as a "Bohemian," requiring "absolute freedom . . . freedom from unnecessary ties, freedom from unnecessary burdens," and his increasing attraction to the "idea of self-abnegation . . . of caring more for other human beings than for himself" (25). The stories of Nora and Dorothy present the growth of belief in self that enables them both to commit themselves in love and to resist pressures to accept different suitors or withdraw their commitments, both acquiring great firmness ("With all her girlish ways," Emily says of Nora, "she is like a rock;—nothing can move her" [92]), a firmness which is quite unlike the rigidity that arises from Trevelyan's inner weakness.

Through such comparisons, Trevelyan's eccentricity is primarily defined not as deviation from collective norms but as eccentricity to his own self, which lacks any center of belief. He and most of the other characters are presented in relation not so much to any actual community as to the possibility of community which is manifested in the success or failure of individual relationships. In the failure of Trevelyan's marriage and his retreat into isolation and madness, Trollope dramatizes the forces of human weakness and perversity which destroy the possibility of community, forces which pose a far more serious threat than the nonconformity of eccentrics like Alice and Crawley. This explains both the extremity to which Trevelyan is brought and the tight control of perspective which requires us to see that development as purely negative.

The difference is registered quite precisely in terms of language and communication. In *Can You Forgive Her?* the possibilities of dissent are limited by the absence of adequate terms to articulate them and closed off by the reassertion of conventional "proper meaning." In *The Last Chronicle*, Crawley's eccentric individuality finds fuller expression through his distinctive idiom, which not only marks his difference but allows him to appropriate the terms of conventional discourse, such as "character," to articulate his own values. Trevelyan also develops his own private language, based on the moral and religious vocabulary of "sin," "transgression," and "repentance," which he uses to justify himself and condemn his wife. Their struggle comes to a focus in a drama of contested meaning, where language and interpretation become instruments of power rather than of communication. He repeatedly accuses her of having sinned against him and insists that she must confess and repent before they can be reconciled, always leaving his meaning ambiguous: does he accuse her of disobedience or of adultery, the transgression which cannot be directly named? Their exchanges pivot on this conventional taboo; the prohibited term becomes an absent center, making discourse erratic, as they approach explicitness and then veer off into euphemism and evasion:

> "Say that you have sinned;—and that you will sin no more."
> "Sinned, Louis;—as the woman did,—in the Scripture? Would you have me say that?" [67]

The narrator observes that Trevelyan does not actually believe Emily guilty of adultery, "but in his desire to achieve empire, and in the sorrows which had come upon him in his unsuccessful struggle, his mind had wavered so frequently, that his spoken words were no true indicators of his thoughts; and in all his arguments he failed to express either his convictions or his desires" (79).[27] It is his insecurity, his fear that any concession or

27. Cf. the American Minister Mr. Spalding, who feels no contradiction between his anti-English speech "on the platform of the Temperance Hall at Nubbly Creek, State of Illinois" and his warm speech of welcome to Mr. Glascock in Florence. "On both occasions he half thought as he spoke,—or thought that he thought so. Unless it be on subjects especially endeared to us the thoughts of but few of us go much beyond this" (46). The parallel marks another way in which Trevelyan's madness appears as only a heightened form of common disorders.

clarification "might weaken the ground upon which he stood," that produces this gap between thought and speech. His private language expresses no values of his own but only destroys communication.

In the last stage of Trevelyan's story, this drama of meaning becomes the main action. Once Emily and Hugh have succeeded in getting Trevelyan back to England, she feels she has gained a sufficiently strong position to make some concession to him: "There is nothing that a woman will not forgive a man, when he is weaker than she is herself. . . . They had the carriage to themselves, and she was down on her knees before him instantly. 'Oh, Louis! Oh, Louis! say that you forgive me!' What could a woman do more than that in her mercy to a man?" (94). But this act of mercy, or assumption of superior strength, proves to be a tactical error, as Trevelyan seizes on it and interprets it as the confession he has long demanded, now laden more than ever with sexual innuendoes: "You know that she has confessed?" he asks Nora. "I think you ought to know" (95). Emily, unable to repudiate this interpretation, now regards her words as the product not of generosity but of torture: "My nails have been dragged out, and I have been willing to confess anything," and in the last days of Trevelyan's life she becomes increasingly obsessed by the need to gain an "acquittal" from him before it is too late.

The struggle continues to the very moment of death, producing a deathbed scene which is as remarkable in its own way as the more histrionic deathbed scenes of Dickens or that of Thackeray's Colonel Newcome. In Dickens and Thackeray death is presented as the threshold between this world and the next, but here the stress falls on finality. Nora tries to persuade Emily that if Trevelyan is permitted retrospective knowledge after death he will know the truth, but Emily cares only "to be acquitted in this world," and her need to be right at last becomes so urgent that in the final words between them she overcomes her reticence, only to be evaded once more:

> "Can you say one word for your wife, dear, dear, dearest husband?"
> "What word?"
> "I have not been a harlot to you;—have I?"
> "What name is that?" [98]

Beyond words and names, she presses for a sign: " 'Kiss my hand, Louis, if you believe me.' And very gently she laid the tips of her fingers on his lips." The tension here involves not only her agonized suspense but the suspended meaning of the novel, the possibility that at the last moment Trevelyan will be at least symbolically reassimilated, redeemed by a gesture of belief, and brought back into the order of proper meaning on which both communication and community depend.

> For a moment or two the bitterness of her despair was almost unendurable. She had time to think that were she ever to withdraw her hand, she would be condemned for ever;—and that it must be withdrawn. But at length the lips moved, and with struggling ear she could hear the sound of the tongue within, and the verdict of the dying man had been given in her favour. He never spoke a word more either to annul it or to enforce it.

The presentation is highly equivocal, since it is confined to Emily's point of view, and we cannot know whether Trevelyan means to acquit her or whether his final movements and sounds are only the involuntary effects of death. What we do see quite clearly is how Emily interprets this slender, ambiguous evidence as the acquittal she desires: she goes at once to Nora and tells her "the tale of her tardy triumph. 'He declared to me at last that he trusted me,' she said,—almost believing that real words had come from his lips to the effect." Once more, the need of the lonely, insecure individual to be right predominates.

The juxtaposition of this uncompromisingly bleak ending with the comic resolutions of the other narrative lines restates the complex relationship between Trevelyan's story and the others. On the one hand, it reinforces the moral contrast between the waste and destruction produced by the perverse insistence on being right and the reconciliation of differences and renewal of community traditionally represented in marrying and giving in marriage. But it also asserts the possibilities of isolation, suffering, and death which conventional happy endings try to repress, the sense of a terrible absence at the center of the self or behind the shared meanings of language, an alternate vision of life that cannot be circumscribed by the calculus of rewards and punishments. The issue of conventional resolutions and their limitations is explicitly raised by the narrator in a passage of playful self-consciousness as the focus shifts from the completed marriage of Caroline and Charles Glascock to the coming marriage of Dorothy and Brooke Burgess:

> It is rather hard upon readers that they should be thus hurried from the completion of hymeneals in Florence to the preparations for other hymeneals in Devonshire; but it is the nature of a complex story to be entangled with many weddings towards its close. In this little history there are, we fear, three or four more to come. We will not anticipate by alluding prematurely to Hugh Stanbury's treachery, or death,—or the possibility that he after all may turn out to be the real descendent of the true Lord Peterborough and the actual inheritor of the title and estate of Monkhams, nor will we speak of Nora's certain fortitude under either of these emergencies. But the instructed reader must be aware that Camilla French ought to have a husband found for her; that Colonel Osborne should be caught in some matrimonial trap,—as, how otherwise should he be fitly punished?—and that something should be at least attempted for Priscilla Stanbury, who from the first has been intended to be the real heroine of these pages.[88]

The last point is the most suggestive: Priscilla becomes a minor double of the eccentric protagonist, displaced from her "intended" central position. The notion is recalled more seriously in the later interview between Priscilla and Dorothy, which stresses the contrary fates of the two sisters: "I wonder why it is that you two [Dorothy and Nora] should be married, and so grandly married, and that I shall never, never have any one to love" (97). Priscilla's isolation and deprivation are partly an appropriate choice for her ascetic nature, partly a self-inflicted suffering which she herself calls "morbid," but they are also the product of arbitrary narrative convention. "Romance is a very pretty thing in novels," Miss Stanbury says, "but the romance of a life is always a melancholy matter. They are most happy who have no tale to tell" (35). Yet in novels those who, like Priscilla, have no tale are the more melancholy because they are necessarily excluded. Trevelyan is not so thoroughly shunted aside, but like Priscilla he creates a discord among all the "hymeneals" of the conclusion, interfering with their comic satisfactions, and the tension this produces is revealed and released in a moment of violent revulsion as the narrator begins the last chapter: "At last the maniac was dead" (99). Once he is dead, all efforts toward understanding can cease; he can be relegated to the subhuman category of "maniac" and be forcefully dismissed, expelled as the scapegoat of perversity.

These three novels present only some of the possible developments of eccentricity, a problematic of theme and structure that appears in many forms in Trollope's fiction, in many more novels that can be examined in equally close detail. Not every instance displays the sort of dynamic instability and tension I have been emphasizing. In *Phineas Redux* for example, Robert Kennedy follows a development quite similar to Trevelyan's, in which increasingly obsessive jealousy leads to insanity and death; but because Kennedy is always a secondary figure rather than the focus of an independent plot line, his erratic course never exerts a strong tension against the other lines. (There is, however, an interesting parallel movement of estrangement in the main line which develops through the ordeal of Phineas' trial for murder. He is soon reassimilated after his vindication, but for a while he loses all his former belief in public institutions and values, having "somehow learned to dislike and distrust all those things that used to be so fine and lively to [him]" [70].)

The next novel in the Palliser series, *The Prime Minister*, extends this type of parallel into a full doubling of the eccentric protagonist which produces greater complexity of structure and meaning. The novel is organized by an antithesis of Palliser and Lopez, the man of honor and extreme scrupulousness living at the center of political power and social status set against the amoral, marginal adventurer. The development of the plot both entangles their lives and complicates their categorical opposition as, through the episode of the Silverbridge election, Trollope establishes surprisingly detailed parallels between them. Each is drawn into a conflict with his wife which involves their relation to another man, Arthur Fletcher coming between Lopez and Emily as Lopez comes between Palliser and Glencora. In each marriage love is compromised by the desire for power, by Lopez' attempt to use Emily to get money from her father and by Glencora's attempt to use Palliser's political influence to support her protégé.[28] Trollope does not, as Thackeray does, collapse his antitheses into complete equivalence, but such parallels contribute to the presentation of both Lopez and Palliser as eccentric figures, both trying to achieve or hold positions for which they are unfit (the one above, the other below society's standards), and both eventually failing. Without blurring the distinction between Lopez' faults and Palliser's virtues, Trollope uses both to present an ironic portrait of a world whose social and political conventions enforce a complacent mediocrity that excludes them.

The Way We Live Now presents a much harsher criticism of contemporary society. This enormous work makes heavy use of multiple narrative, but because the purpose of multiplication here is satiric, it places more stress on the repetition of similarities, much less on the play of differences than is usual in Trollope. Exposing similar moral corruption in Lady Carbury's literary politics, the fortune-hunting of her son and Lord Nidderdale, the dissipations of the Beargarden, and Melmotte's grandiose swindles, the novel tends to sacrifice variety and subtlety of comparison for the sake of polemical emphasis. A certain degree of structural tension does develop, however, out of the problem of the center. In Trollope's advance layout, he described Lady Carbury as "the chief character" and Roger Carbury as the "hero of the book." Melmotte appears late in the list of characters and only as Marie's father.[29] As he develops in the novel, Melmotte becomes the most important figure, the one most capable of organizing the entire composition, but as in the cases of the other eccentric protagonists, he is not allowed to dominate it. Since he comes into greater prominence in the later stages of the novel, however, he is not so much a displaced as a deferred center, and since the novel is strongly satiric, the relation between deviation and norm is ironically inverted. Melmotte is always an outsider, excluded and destroyed at the end, but he is also, at the

28. Several parallels between Palliser and Lopez are discussed in Helmut Klingler, "Varieties of Failure: The Significance of Trollope's *The Prime Minister*," *English Miscellany* 23 (1972): 168–83.

29. Trollope's notes are printed as an appendix to Michael Sadleir, *Trollope: A Commentary* (London: Constable, 1927), pp. 422–24.

height of his success, the object of widespread adulation, accepted as the embodiment of Napoleonic "greatness" which transcends ordinary moral standards. Set against him, Roger Carbury appears as an exponent of those traditional values who lives on the periphery of a world that has lost respect for them. In this way, *The Way We Live Now* employs a reversal of the pattern of double focus established in *The Prime Minister*, though it is not developed so symmetrically. The satiric mode thus draws more fully on the potential, glimpsed through Trevelyan, for the eccentric figure to serve as an extreme embodiment of the general tendencies of his world.

These additional examples not only illustrate more of the possibilities of form and meaning which Trollope developed from the problematic of eccentricity but also help to confirm its crucial importance in his work. The "complete appreciation of the usual," which was, for James, Trollope's "great, his inestimable merit,"[30] acquires its full value only when subjected to the challenge, the threat or attraction of the unusual, the eccentric. The resistance of the eccentric individual to social or logical assimilation produces both the dramatic and the structural tensions which energize many of Trollope's novels, tensions which can be understood both as expressions of his particular vision and as expressions of the larger problematic of Victorian dialogical form. As an individual artistic theme, Trollope's concern with eccentricity can be attributed to the early experience of isolation and exclusion at school still vividly recalled in his *Autobiography:* "how well I remember all the agonies of my young heart; how I considered whether I should be always alone. . . . I could appreciate at its full the misery of expulsion from all social intercourse."[31] From the disparity between this early loneliness and Trollope's later success and acceptance as a popular novelist, one can derive the problem of eccentricity, the conflict between his imaginative concern with individualizing differences and the high value he grants to social norms and the security of an established position in a community.

Beyond such a personal psychological interpretation, however, there are the more general structural implications of the double

30. *The Critical Heritage,* p. 527.
31. *Autobiography,* pp. 8–10.

logic that reappears in all the major Victorian multiplot novels. J. Hillis Miller has described the development of the typical Victorian novelist as a movement from social isolation to a position in which, by adopting the role of an omniscient narrator, he embodies the "general consciousness" of his world.[32] Of all Victorian multiplot novelists, Trollope best fits this model, and yet in his novels, as in the others we have examined, the movement between individual and general perspectives is not a completed progression but a continual alternation, producing a dialogical tension that is never fully resolved. Trollope's narration places much more emphasis on the norms of common sense and collective values, but the significance of his fiction depends on the possibility of alternative perspectives represented by the eccentric protagonist, even when, as in *He Knew He Was Right,* that possibility is most strenuously denied. This tension between perspectives is as much an expression of a common form as of a common theme, arising from a narrative process given over to a play of differences that resists closure and subverts univocal meaning.

It is in nearly his last novel, *Mr. Scarborough's Family,* that Trollope allows fullest scope to the claims of eccentricity. In old Mr. Scarborough he presents the most aggressively unconventional of all his eccentric protagonists, who "sets God and man at absolute defiance, and always does it with the most profound courtesy" (8). Instead of being either assimilated or destroyed, defeated or punished for his opposition to convention and law, he is permitted a series of "deathbed triumphs," exercising through the double text of his two marriage certificates a power like that of a controlling author: "Like a romantic plot maker, he creates alternate versions of the truth in order to mystify and fool the world."[33] In this portrait of the artist as an old eccentric, Trollope releases the impulses of extreme individualism which his earlier novels had held under such taut control. This indulgence is justified by freeing Mr. Scarborough's willfulness from any taint

32. *The Form of Victorian Fiction* (Notre Dame, Ind.: University of Notre Dame Press, 1968), pp. 53–90.

33. Donald D. Stone, "Trollope, Byron, and the Conventionalities," in *The Worlds of Victorian Fiction,* ed. Jerome H. Buckley (Cambridge, Mass.: Harvard University Press, 1975), p. 202. Stone discusses a number of Trollope's eccentric figures as examples of Byronic individualism.

of perversity or selfishness and by placing all his manipulations and deceptions in the service of a higher, private code of values:

> In every phase of his life he had been actuated by love for others. He had never been selfish, thinking always of others rather than of himself. Supremely indifferent he had been to the opinion of the world around him, but he had never run counter to his own conscience. For the conventionalities of the law he entertained a supreme contempt, but he did wish so to arrange matters with which he was himself concerned as to do what justice demanded. [58]

The result is to open up the imaginative possibility of a complete reversal in the relation between social norms and the deviant individual: "One cannot make any apology for him without being ready to throw all truth and all morality to the dogs. But if you can imagine for yourself a state of things in which neither truth nor morality should be thought essential, then old Mr. Scarborough would be your hero."

Like Dickens in *Our Mutual Friend* and George Eliot in *Daniel Deronda,* Trollope in this late romance submits the shows of things to the desires of the mind, projecting forms of individual existence freed from actual social constraints; yet even here the multiplication and division of the narrative work to check the claims of Mr. Scarborough as the triumphantly eccentric hero. As in the earlier, more conservative versions, his story must share our attention with several others in which individuals cannot so easily have their own way. In Mr. Prosper, for example, the effort to control an inheritance reappears in the form of ludicrous farce. Mr. Scarborough can afford to be supremely indifferent to public opinion, but Harry Annesley cannot, and he is made to suffer considerable hardship by the effects of deceptive appearances which Augustus Scarborough manipulates by a suppression of the truth quite similar to his father's. Beyond the qualifying effect of such parallels, the proliferating complications of the various subplots also produce the familiar effect of displacement: Mr. Scarborough's story, extraordinary as it is, becomes only part of a larger social scene. In these ways, even as he revises his image of eccentricity, Trollope preserves the tension between his perspectives. His multiplot novels, like those of Dickens, Thackeray, and George Eliot, continue to the end to exploit and explore the possibilities of dialogical form.

Conclusion

Each of the preceding studies has ended by raising the question of closure, briefly considering a novel written late in each author's career in which the structural dialogue appears to be resolved. In *Our Mutual Friend, The Newcomes, Daniel Deronda,* and *Mr. Scarborough's Family,* one of the opposed perspectives seems to become dominant, but in each case my interpretation has insisted on the factors that block, subvert, or reverse that resolution, preserving the tension and perpetuating the play of dialogical oppositions. A conclusion to these studies might do well to reopen the question of closure for their own interpretations, considering whether they can be left within the boundaries marked off by their chosen terms or whether they require us to draw further conclusions. George Eliot, in beginning the "Finale" of *Middlemarch,* reminds us that "every limit is a beginning as well as an ending," a principle that holds true for interpretation as well as narrative. Introductions and conclusions to critical studies set their limits not only by indicating what they include but also by implicitly or explicitly indicating what they exclude, erecting defensive outworks against the threat of invasion or engulfment by other modes of interpretation. But by considering the way those limits might also serve as new beginnings, we can try to identify some possibilities of additional interpretation that might be developed from the readings of Victorian multiplot novels I have presented.

To carry interpretation beyond the unresolved tensions of dialogical oppositions we would have to move from description to explanation and from the enclosures of texts to larger interpretive contexts, to account for the qualities we have discovered in these novels by relating them to tensions that might be located in the minds of their authors, in their common historical situation, or perhaps in the forms of narrative themselves. We have already touched on some of these possibilities in briefly considering J. Hillis Miller's model for the development of Victorian novelists from a sense of isolation to the personification of a general consciousness. This opposition does indeed appear in the formative experience of each novelist, in Dickens' sense of being abandoned and degraded when he was sent to work in the blacking factory as well as in Trollope's misery at school, in George Eliot's estrangement from her family, religious faith, and provincial origins as well as in Thackeray's lonely and unhappy childhood. In their fiction they return to the experience of estrangement and attempt to overcome it, not just by adopting the role of an omniscient narrator, but also by elaborating multiple narratives that propose a confident and inclusive grasp of their large, diverse fictional worlds. But since in each case we find not a successful completion of the movement from individual to general consciousness but a persistent, unstable tension between them, a psychological interpretation would have to postulate deep, unresolved conflicts.

Such conflicts can be found in different forms in each of the novelists we have studied. Dickens' plots repeatedly find surrogate families and happy endings for his isolated protagonists, and the intricate networks of connections between plot lines that he reveals can be seen as enlarged projections of the same desire to reestablish relations that define identity. But those inclusive systems are the object of fear as well as desire, perceived as deterministic mechanisms that threaten individual autonomy instead of offering security or fulfillment. And when the later novels attempt to oppose that threat by granting their characters greater autonomy, the threat reappears in the form of inner divisions and compulsions that once again subvert the self. Thackeray takes up the stance of detached, demystified, retrospective wisdom, from which apparent differences between characters and narrative lines can be assimilated into a vision of inclusive vanity. Yet because that development is also experienced as loss, he attempts to reverse it and regain an immediacy of experience that always eludes him. (The regressive aspect of this impulse may also be observed in the careers of protagonists like Pendennis and Esmond, who end up marrying maternal figures.) George Eliot's inclusive, general vision is more regularly checked and balanced by a scrupulous regard for individual qualities, just as her multiple narratives play off similarities against differences. But in the development of her protagonists there is often a loss of equilibrium between detachment and involvement, a pressure of wish-fulfillment that covertly seeks to reinstate the self at the center of the world or regain the security of a religiously based community. Trollope also stresses the importance of individualizing differences, yet the eccentric figures who most strongly represent such individuality in his novels are repeatedly assimilated, suppressed, expelled, or destroyed. To maintain his identification with collective values requires a continual repression of the alienation he claims he has escaped.

In all these forms of ambivalence and contradiction, a deeper psychological interpretation might trace the working of defensive mechanisms of identification and dissociation; in the tensions produced by the attempt to embody a collective consciousness, it might ultimately find disguised forms of the guilty aggression and desire involved in the effort to replace and repossess parental figures.

The recurrent tensions between individual and general perspectives in Victorian multiplot novels might also be related to their historical situation, interpreted not just as expressions of each author's inner conflicts but as expressions of conflicts within their culture. Writing in a time when accelerating, disruptive change had produced "widespread doubt about the nature of man, society, and the universe,"[1] Victorian novelists, like other writers of the period, both express and attempt to resolve those doubts. The loss of old collective conceptions of social and moral order and the need to develop new ones are recurrent themes of the period. "Call ye that a Society," cries Carlyle's Professor Teufelsdröckh, "where there is no longer any Social Idea extant; not so much as the Idea of a common House, but only of a common over-crowded Lodging-house?" (*Sartor Resartus*, III, 5). Forty years later, the "Prelude" to *Middlemarch* strikes a similar note in observing that nineteenth-century England offers "no

1. Walter E. Houghton, *The Victorian Frame of Mind, 1830–1870* (New Haven: Yale University Press, 1957), p. 22. For Houghton, the sense of living in a state of transition produced by the emergence of bourgeois industrial society and the loss of traditional certainties is the leading characteristic of the age.

coherent social faith and order" for "later-born Theresas" like
Dorothea Brooke. These writers may attempt to formulate a new
social idea or faith, such as Carlyle's assertion that all individuals
and all generations are bound together by "organic filaments," or
the assurance offered in the closing lines of *Middlemarch* that even
those who live obscure lives of "unhistoric acts" nevertheless
contribute to "the growing good of the world."

But more effective than such general pronouncements are the
responses developed in the multiple narrative form of the major
novels, which enact different possibilities of collective vision. As
popular art, these novels offered widely shared imaginative
experiences in which readers could transcend the limitations of
their individual points of view and comprehend their world as an
inclusive system of interrelationships. In this way, the novelist's
dramatization of a general consciousness becomes a creative act
which supplies something lacking in the culture, not just the
expression of a previously existing consensus.

Yet the persisting tensions we have found in these novels would
again require further interpretation. We might postulate a cultural function for the Victorian multiplot novel like the one Lévi-
Strauss assigns to myth, which is "a working out in formal terms
of what a culture is unable to resolve concretely. . . . a means of
resolving a real contradiction in the imaginary mode."[2] The
development of a narrative form that permits extended treatment
of the private lives and personal relations of several individuals
yet also shows through plot connections and analogies how they
are all part of a single, coherent pattern would offer such an
imaginary resolution to the cultural contradiction between indi-
vidualist and collectivist values. But instead of resolving this
tension, the novels can only reproduce it in the imaginary mode.
Each perspective attempts to reinterpret the other and reverse its
values: the movement toward social integration that offers an
escape from alienation also appears as a suppression of individ-

2. Fredric Jameson, *The Prison-House of Language: A Critical Account of Structuralism and Russian Formalism* (Princeton: Princeton University Press, 1972), pp.
162, 197. Jameson's account of Lévi-Strauss is based primarily on his analysis of
the Oedipus myth in "The Structural Study of Myth," *Journal of American Folklore*
78 (1955): 428–44, where the binary oppositions of affirmation and denial of
man's autochthonous origin reveal a fundamental conflict of beliefs about the
relation of nature and culture.

uality; the defense of personal integrity also appears as a perverse destruction of community. A more radical analysis might see in this reproduction of tensions not just a reflection but a reinforcement of the prevailing ideological system, a generalized opposition of the individual and society that serves to preserve the values of bourgeois individualism and prevent any recognition of the revolutionary possibilities of genuine collectivity.

I hope these brief sketches of psychological and historical interpretive possibilities will not seem mere caricatures, because I do believe it could be useful to pursue them. But at the same time my suspicion of such interpretations is implicit in the disparity between these simplified programmatic outlines and the complexity I have tried to demonstrate in my readings of the novels. I suspect that the attempt to move from description to explanation, even if developed in much greater detail, will always be reductive, that every such advance will also be a retreat from engagement in the text's interplay of perspectives, an attempt to control and enclose it by considering its structural tensions as symptoms. Even to describe those tensions as an opposition of individual and general perspectives is already a considerable simplification of the manifold, shifting relationships we encounter in the novels themselves, and to assume that opposition as a stable point of departure for further interpretations is to risk losing touch with the qualities which give these novels their greatest interest.

The question here is not simply one of an aesthetic preference for complexity as opposed to explanatory simplifications. The question is rather, as Humpty Dumpty tells Alice, of which is to be master. Interpretations that withdraw from the play of the text in order to gain explanatory power are likely to end up grasping nothing but a shadow. Returning to the complexity of that play, we are likely to find that it retains the power to reinterpret its interpretations. Instead of granting any privilege to the terms of psychological or historical explanation, we can see that they too depend on narrative models, telling stories of an individual's development or of a culture's response to the stresses of change. And we can also see that, together, their models reenact on a more abstract level the same dialogical opposition of individual and collective perspectives they claim to explain. Are the stories told in these two modes mutually compatible, or does each follow its own logic, attempt to impose its own exclusive vision? If we assume they can be integrated, that they only address different aspects of a single reality, the novels stand ready to remind us how different narrative perspectives construct different realities, to show how a sustained exploration of their double logic leads to a repeatedly renewed awareness of their incongruity. A certain degree of tension between individual and general perspectives may be implicit in all narrative, but by articulating them separately and playing them off against each other, these novels not only heighten that tension but anticipate the paths which our interpretations of it might try to follow, indicating the ways they will continue to diverge and intersect as they do within the labyrinth of the text.

To recognize the power these novels have to anticipate and reinterpret our interpretations does not show that the effort to develop further implications from these readings must be futile. Rather, it confirms the relevance of extending both individual and collective perspectives; but it should also dispel any illusions of interpretive mastery by showing that such readings can only continue the play of perspectives in which the novels themselves are already engaged. An appropriate conclusion for these studies of the great Victorian multiplot novels cannot take the form of a typical closing chapter, with the whole cast called back for a final review and the distribution of rewards and punishments. It must instead be more like the end of a serial installment, a portion of the continuing reading and rereading of those texts, "to be continued in our next."

Index